Praise for *Visual Basic Developer's Guide to COM and COM+*

Wayne Freeze does a great job of introducing you to COM and COM+. This book explains COM and COM+ from a Visual Basic perspective and capitalizes on your existing knowledge of Visual Basic. The essential knowledge you need is right here in this book.

Every Visual Basic developer interested in staying a Visual Basic developer for years to come should invest in learning all there is to know about COM, COM+, and the operating system services offered. If you are serious about expanding your knowledge and mastering application development with COM, you should read this book in its entirety, from cover to cover.

—From the foreword by Ash Rofail, a regular contributor to the *Visual Basic Programmer's Journal* and coauthor of *Mastering COM and COM+ and Building N-Tier Applications With COM and Visual Basic 6.0*

Visual Basic Developer's Guide to COM and COM+

Visual Basic® Developer's Guide to COM and COM+

Wayne S. Freeze

SYBEX®

San Francisco • Paris • Düsseldorf • Soest • London

Associate Publisher: Richard Mills
Contracts & Licensing Manager: Kristine O'Callaghan
Acquisitions & Developmental Editor: Denise Santoro
Editor: Marilyn Smith
Project Editor: Elizabeth Hurley-Clevenger
Technical Editor: Dominic Selly
Book Designer: Kris Warrenburg
Graphic Illustrator: Tony Jonick
Electronic Publishing Specialist: Maureen Forys, Happenstance Type-O-Rama
Project Team Leader: Jennifer Durning
Proofreaders: Camera Obscura, Carrie Bradley, Nancy Riddiough
Indexer: Ted Laux
Cover Designer: Design Site
Cover Illustrator/Photographer: Design Site

SYBEX is a registered trademark of SYBEX Inc.

Screen reproductions produced with Collage Complete.
Collage Complete is a trademark of Inner Media Inc.

TRADEMARKS: SYBEX has attempted throughout this book to distinguish proprietary trademarks from descriptive terms by following the capitalization style used by the manufacturer.

The author and publisher have made their best efforts to prepare this book, and the content is based upon final release software whenever possible. Portions of the manuscript may be based upon pre-release versions supplied by software manufacturer(s). The author and the publisher make no representation or warranties of any kind with regard to the completeness or accuracy of the contents herein and accept no liability of any kind including but not limited to performance, merchantability, fitness for any particular purpose, or any losses or damages of any kind caused or alleged to be caused directly or indirectly from this book.

Library of Congress Card Number: 99-65756
ISBN: 0-7821-2558-1

Manufactured in the United States of America

10 9 8 7 6 5 4 3

To Jill, Christopher, and Samantha,
I love you.

ACKNOWLEDGMENTS

Nearly everyone thinks being an author is a wonderful job. You get to work at home, set your own hours, and have the freedom to do what you please. The only ones who don't believe this are the authors, their families, and the people who take the manuscripts and make them magically appear in books. They know that writing is hard work, and the few minutes of joy don't always make up for the months of 16-hour days.

I want to thank Laura Belt for all her hard work. Maybe some day we'll be able to make a real living from writing! I also appreciate Ash Rofail taking time from his busy schedule to write the foreword to this book.

I also want to say thanks to my friends at Sybex: Denise Santoro, Developmental Editor, for letting me have my pick of books for this series (when will you let me do that DirectX book?); Elizabeth Hurley-Clevenger, Project Editor; Jennifer Durning, Production Team Leader; Maureen Forys, Electronic Publishing Specialist; and Tony Jonick, Graphic Artist. And thanks to Marilyn Smith for improving my writing and pointing out all of my mistakes—I couldn't do it without you. Without your efforts and patience, this book wouldn't be worth reading. Now, when can I start on the next one?

One other aspect of writing is that it occupies so much time, I don't always find time to visit or even talk to my friends. Shaun, Elwyn, Rick, Bob W., Veronica, Scott, Bob K., and Ian, I'll be in touch soon. I promise. Thanks for your support.

Bucky and Goose are two of the best in-laws you could ask for. (Feel free to invite the kids out for three weeks next summer.)

As always, I don't get to visit my Mom and Dad as much as I'd like, but I will make the "everything party," even if I have to spend most of my time there working.

If you read this book carefully, you may find references to Christopher, Samantha, and Jill. Chris is six years old now and knows more about computers than some well-paid people I used to work with! Samantha is only five, but she's not that far behind Chris in her ability to crash Windows on demand. I love both of you a whole lot. Now who wants to take a ride in the Porsche?

My lovely wife Jill is a respected writer in her own right, having written books on Microsoft Office, Internet Explorer, and WebTV. I just want to say that if you believe in yourself, anything is possible, and that I love you.

CONTENTS AT A GLANCE

TABLE OF CONTENTS

FOREWORD

It has been six years since the introduction of COM, and longer than that since Visual Basic provided the capabilities to develop large-scale applications. But some Visual Basic developers are still working in the same comfort zone, using Visual Basic to develop user interfaces and minor business logic. After all these years of COM and Visual Basic, some developers still can't understand the relationship between the COM technology and the Visual Basic tool.

Visual Basic has matured over the past few years and embraced COM as a foundation for developing distributed applications. COM is here to stay and will continue to grow. Being the most popular development language, Visual Basic will continue to take advantage of COM. If you are a Visual Basic developer and have not yet started programming the COM way, you need to quickly get up to speed.

Visual Basic developers are no longer programming in isolation and just performing the minimum tasks that are essential to get an application up and running. With the increased complexities of application requirements, the popularity of web-based applications, and the embedded services of the operating systems, intimate knowledge of COM and COM+ is crucial to the success of enterprise distributed applications.

To understand and master COM from a Visual Basic perspective, you need to understand what Visual Basic objects are and how they work. You also need to understand how Visual Basic views COM and uses its services. Additionally, you need to learn how to structure a COM-based distributed application to take advantage of COM+ transactions and the new COM+ services. Since COM+ is an integral part of Windows 2000, you must understand how this integration impacts your application development.

In this book, Wayne Freeze does a great job of introducing you to COM and COM+. This book explains COM and COM+ from a Visual Basic perspective and capitalizes on your existing knowledge of Visual Basic. The essential knowledge you need is right here in this book. Your road to understanding COM starts from Chapter 1, where Wayne discusses the evolution of COM, and builds on that premise throughout the chapters, discussing components, queues, transactions, and new COM+ features.

Every Visual Basic developer interested in staying a Visual Basic developer for years to come should invest in learning all there is to know about COM, COM+, and the operating system services offered. If you are serious about expanding your knowledge and mastering application development with COM, you should read this book in its entirety, from cover to cover.

—Ash Rofail

INTRODUCTION

Visual Basic is my favorite programming language. BASIC was the first programming language I learned to use. I wrote programs on paper tape, which I then loaded to a mainframe many miles away. Though I've used many programming languages since then, I always keep coming back to BASIC.

Today, the dominant dialect of BASIC is Microsoft's Visual Basic. It's a very flexible, easy-to-use programming environment, and it is the best way to build programs to run under Windows. While Visual C++ may be a bit more efficient and has a few more capabilities, it is also much more time-consuming to use. In these days when computers run at speeds of 650 MHz and faster, the speed of your application isn't nearly as important as how quickly you can build and maintain it.

These days, marketing people often change the name of a product or technology to make it sound newer and more exciting. For instance Windows 2000 Server sounds more interesting than Windows NT 5.0 Server does. Upgrading to Office 2000 before the year 2000 sounds more important than upgrading to Office 9.

Even the world of the application developer isn't immune to marketing-speak. The technology originally introduced as Object Linking and Embedding (OLE) has had a new name for nearly every version of the product. No matter what its name, the core product is still the same. OLE has evolved into the Component Object Model (COM), which is Microsoft's way for Windows programmers to build reusable objects.

Microsoft has continued to introduce some new COM tools, such as the Microsoft Transaction Server (MTS) and the Microsoft Message Queues (MSMQ). Just to prove that marketing-speak isn't dead, Microsoft chose to include them as part of a new service called COM+. However, this gave the developers the excuse to change these functions and make sure that they worked better than they did in the previous generation of products.

Visual Basic and COM

Visual Basic is Microsoft's strategic language for Rapid Application Development (RAD). It is targeted at programmers who need to build enterprise applications quickly and without a lot of fuss. Thus, Visual Basic takes care of most of the grungy details of programming in Windows, leaving you free to concentrate on your application.

You can build a meaningful program in Visual Basic without a single line of code. If you don't believe me, try this: Start a new program and put a Data control on it. Specify the name of the database, and specify the name of the table you wish to access in the Data control's properties. Then put some text box and label controls on the form. Set the DataSource property to the Data control and the DataField property to the name of a column in your database. When you're finished, click Run. You have a program without a single line of code that can scroll through a database table.

To create this type of program in Visual C++ would take a lot of code and a lot more time to put all of the pieces together. While the C++ program might be faster, the average user wouldn't notice the difference in speed between the two programs. So why write in Visual C++?

There will always be a need for a programming language like C++. Visual Basic is a little too far removed from the hardware to build efficient operating systems and compilers. But when was the last time you wrote an operating system or compiler?

Unfortunately, Visual Basic isn't the language of choice for building COM and COM+ components. COM and COM+ were designed for a C++ world. This doesn't mean you can't create these components in Visual Basic, but it does mean that sometimes you need to wait for the next release to take full advantage of the capabilities.

Right now, there is very little in COM that you can't do in Visual Basic—once you understand how to do it. Unfortunately, this isn't true for COM+. Several features of COM+ remain unusable from Visual Basic at the time this book was written. Fortunately, COM+ is robust enough that you can work around these limitations. I fully expect these problems will be fixed in the next release of Visual Basic, but for now, we'll have to live with them.

Who Should Read This Book?

This book is aimed at intermediate to advanced Visual Basic programmers who want to learn more about how they can incorporate COM and COM+ into their applications. This means that you should know how to build Visual Basic programs, be comfortable with the development environment, and know how to use most of the common controls, such as TextBox, Label, and CommandButton. I also assume that you know how to use Windows and understand concepts such as files, directories, and overlapping windows. If you don't know this material, then I suggest that you read *Mastering Visual Basic 6*, by Evangelos Petroutsos (Sybex, 1998). After you finish that book, take a look at my book, *Expert Guide to Visual Basic 6* (Sybex, 1998). It covers a lot of topics that aren't covered anywhere else and will give you a lot of insight into how Visual Basic works.

What Does This Book Cover?

This book covers using both COM and COM+. Most applications can benefit from COM components. COM represents a fundamental programming technique that helps you build object-oriented, reusable components.

COM+, on the other hand, is targeted more at multiple-tier applications. COM+ allows you to create a layer of application logic that is independent of the client program and the database server. This helps you build more scalable applications.

The Book's Organization

This book is organized into four parts. The first part, "Understanding COM," is designed to give you the nuts and bolts about how the Component Object Model (COM) works under Windows. First, you'll learn what COM is, how it evolved, and why you want to use it. The next topic is how COM components are implemented in Windows, followed by an overview of how COM objects work. The final chapter in this part explains how to build class modules in Visual Basic.

The second part of the book, "Programming COM with Visual Basic," discusses how to create the three main types of COM components: ActiveX DLLs, ActiveX controls, and ActiveX EXEs. These chapters discuss the coding details that form the basis of all COM components used in the rest of this book. You'll also learn how to convert your existing ActiveX EXE programs to use DCOM. In the last chapter in this part, I cover how to create your own data-bound objects and controls. This means you can build controls that will automatically display and update database fields, without requiring any code from the application programmer using your component.

In Part 3, "Programming COM+ with Visual Basic," I discuss the key features of COM+ from a Visual Basic perspective. You'll learn how to use the COM+ Transaction Server, message queues, and the In-Memory Database system. The last chapter in this part covers the essential topic of including additional security in your COM+ applications.

The final part of this book, "Developing COM+ Transactions," is designed to show you how to use COM+ transactions in three different scenarios: a traditional client/server-based program, a web browser–based application, and a client/server application where you can't assume that the computers will always be connected.

The Programs

Nearly as important as the book are the programs. Every program discussed in this book is available for download from the Internet. You can obtain them from the Sybex web site at www.Sybex.com or from my web site at www.JustPC.com. Just follow the links to this book, and from there, follow the instructions to download the files.

You'll find parts of the code used in the examples throughout this book. However, I strongly recommend that you take the time to read the complete source code. If possible, you should also try to run the programs. If you wish, you can copy parts of these programs into your own programs.

While all of the programs I wrote for this book will run, most would need additional work to be used by a nonprogrammer. This is intentional. My goal is to communicate how to use specific features of Visual Basic, not necessarily how to build polished applications. If I can accomplish that by leaving out such nice features as an Exit button, then so be it.

What This Book Doesn't Cover

This book doesn't cover the fundamentals of Visual Basic. Some chapters will assume that you already know how to use SQL Server and database programming in general. Also, it doesn't address how to write IIS Applications and how the Internet Information Server works.

If you don't know the difference between an event and a text box, come back after you've read *Mastering Visual Basic 6* and have worked with Visual Basic for a few months. If you already know how to write Visual Basic programs, you may want to look at some of the other books in this series. *VB Developer's Guide to ADO*, by Mike Gunderloy (Sybex, 1999), covers all of the issues related to developing database applications. If you want to learn about IIS and IIS Applications, see *VB Developer's Guide to ASP and IIS*, by A. Russell Jones (Sybex, 1999). *VB Developer's Guide to the Win32 API*, by Steve Brown (Sybex, 2000), has a lot of useful material about using the Win32 APIs.

About the Author

In case you're wondering, I'm a full-time computer book author and computer technology consultant, and this is my seventh computer book. My previous books discussed programming in Visual Basic, SQL, and the Internet. I'm also the author of a popular shareware program called Car Collector, which is written in Visual Basic.

My experience with personal computers began in 1977, when I built one of the original personal computer systems, the Altair 8800, from a kit. With 4KB BASIC in ROM and 1KB of RAM, it wasn't very practical, but it was a lot of fun. Since then, I have used nearly every major type of personal computer made and many different medium- and large-scale computers. I have six or seven computers scattered around my house, but my Gateway 9100 laptop is currently my computer of choice.

Since I started writing, I don't seem to have much time for my hobbies. When I do have some free time, you might see me at an air show photographing World War II fighters (I hope to learn to fly a P-51 someday). I also collect cars, ranging in size from a 1:144 Dodge Viper to a 1:1 Porsche Turbo (driven only when there is no rain in sight). I also have a house full of pets. Currently, I have one dog (Lady Kokomo), three cats (Pixel, Terry, and Cali), and a stingray I call Raymond (named after my father-in-law), who loves to eat worms, guppies, and shrimp.

I currently reside in Beltsville, Maryland, with my lovely wife, Jill, who helps me with my writing by deleting all those unnecessary commas and making sure that everything I say makes sense. Jill is also a full-time author, with more than a half dozen books written on subjects ranging from Microsoft Office 2000 to WebTV. My son Christopher is six and was the youngest unofficial beta tester for Microsoft Windows 98, using it for over four months before it was officially released. My five-year-old daughter Samantha specializes in being cute and practicing her cart-wheels at the least convenient times.

I maintain a web site at `http://www.JustPC.com` with additional information about the books that my wife and I have written. I try to answer frequently asked questions about the books and point to other resources readers may find interesting.

You're also welcome to send me e-mail at `WFreeze@JustPC.com`. I'll try to respond to your questions and comments as best as I can. However, please understand that I make my living from writing, so you may not necessarily get as prompt or as com-plete an answer as you may desire. If you find a bug or have an idea to improve any of the sample projects, please let me know. With your permission, I'll add any good information to my web site so others can benefit from it.

PART I

Understanding COM

CHAPTER
ONE

Introducing COM

- COM elements

- The importance of COM

- A brief history of COM development

- Transactions and message queues

- COM+ features

For years, everyone has been telling you to build your applications with reusable objects. Since Visual Basic 5, you've had the ability to build your own reusable objects. But how many programmers really take advantage of this capability? Yes, building applications with objects requires more thought than building applications without them. However, the results are usually worth the effort.

COM is Microsoft's standard for building reusable objects. These objects are independent of any particular programming language. That means that Visual Basic programs can easily access COM objects written in Visual C++ or Visual J++. It also means that you can write your own objects in Visual Basic, which can be used by Visual C++ programs. Of course, if you're like me, you'll forget about those other languages and simply use Visual Basic to create COM objects that can be used by other Visual Basic programs.

In this chapter, I'm going to review some background material about object-oriented programming in general and how it relates to COM. I'm also going to discuss how COM evolved from its early days into what Microsoft's marketing team refers to as COM and COM+.

What Is COM?

COM stands for Component Object Model. It is a Microsoft specification that describes how to create reusable objects for programmers working in a Win32 programming environment. COM is a binary standard, which means that any programming language (with the proper facilities, of course) can create COM objects.

Because COM objects are binary, they can be contained in their own executable files. This makes it easy to develop objects that can be distributed independently of an application program file. In order to understand what COM is all about, you need to understand the meanings of the words *component* and *object*.

What Is a Component?

A *component* is an independent piece of code that may be shared with several different programs. When designing an application, you have the option to develop one large complex program or to break it up into several smaller pieces. If you think this sounds like structured programming, you're right.

By breaking a hard-to-solve problem into multiple smaller problems, you've reduced the complexity of the problem considerably. You've also made it practical for different people to work on the program at the same time, because each person can be responsible for one or more components.

As an example, Figure 1.1 shows the components of a typical word processor. The Document Storage component is separate from the Spelling Checker, Document Display, and Document Printer components.

FIGURE 1.1:

Components of a typical word processor

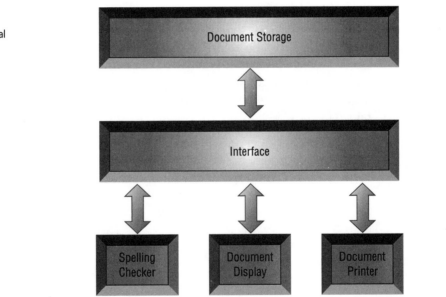

Because each component is isolated from the other components, it is important that you clearly define the boundaries of each component. At a minimum, this means that you describe how other programmers will access the component from their components. This is known as the component's *interface*. In the example shown in Figure 1.1, each of the components interacts with the Document Storage component through a well-defined interface. This interface lets programmers work independently while building their part of the application, and it also tells them how to access the information and perform functions in the other components.

What Is an Object?

An *object* is a set of code that is designed to be reusable with a well-defined interface. Aside from the interface, there is no way to access any of the information in the object. This has the advantage of isolating the details of how the object stores information from the program that uses the object. You can change how the object stores its data without affecting how the calling program works.

NOTE   A clever enough programmer can usually get around any limitations, even if it means accessing the real memory owned by an object. However, this isn't a good idea, since bypassing the object's interface could possibly corrupt the data managed by the object.

An object is actually more than just a set of code. It also represents something. It can represent a piece of information, a file, a set of data from the database, or a paragraph in a Word document—anything you choose. The interface defines a series of subroutines and functions that perform operations against the data contained by the object.

Figure 1.2 illustrates a simplified example of an object used to access a dictionary. This component has one interface—the Spelling Checker. The interface contains four functions:

- `Initialize` is called when the object is created.

- `Terminate` is called when the object is deleted.

- `WordIsSpelledOK` returns true when the word is found in the dictionary.

- `AddWordToDictionary` is used to add a word to the User Dictionary.

Internally, the component maintains three internal resources, which are used only inside the object:

- The Word Cache tracks frequently used words.

- The Master Dictionary contains all of the words supplied with the word processor.

- The User Dictionary is used to hold any words added to the dictionary by the user.

FIGURE 1.2:

A simple object

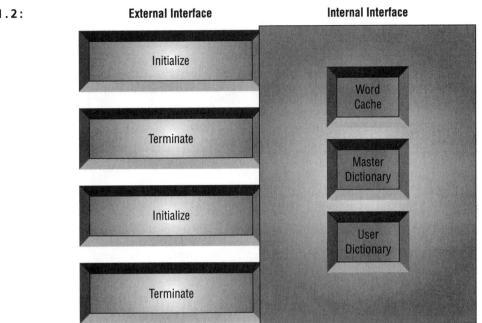

What Is the Component Object Model?

The Component Object Model, or COM, combines the ability to create individual components with the ability to create reusable objects. This gives you a powerful tool under Microsoft Windows. COM allows you to produce binary object modules that are independent of any programming language and contain well-defined, object-oriented interfaces.

COM is based on a client/server model. Each COM object operates as a server that receives and processes requests from a client program, and generates responses. Figure 1.3 illustrates this concept. Notice that I don't describe how the requests and responses are handled. That handling is up to the COM object designer.

FIGURE 1.3:

A COM object and its client

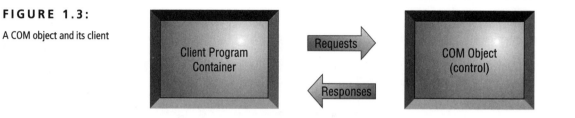

As you know from using Visual Basic, a control can communicate with your program in three ways: through properties, methods, and events.

- A *property* represents a variable in your object, although it's often implemented as a pair of routines: one to retrieve the value from the property and another to assign a value to the property.

- A *method* is merely a function or subroutine that can be called from a Visual Basic program.

- An *event* is a subroutine whose parameters are defined in the control and that exists in your program. It is called by the control to inform your program of various situations. Its response will dictate the action the control will take.

These same three elements form the basis of how your program will interact with a COM object.

> **NOTE**   A COM client is sometimes called a *container.* A COM object is sometimes called a *control.*

Why Is COM Important to You?

By now, you have a good idea why you should be using components and objects in your application. But since many languages, including Visual Basic, have the ability to include objects in source code, why should you use COM?

COM is the foundation of most things that Microsoft does. Without COM, Visual Basic wouldn't work, nor would Windows, SQL Server, or any number of

Microsoft products. The true test of Microsoft's confidence in COM is that its applications are based on COM technology. Word 2000 and Excel 2000 are based heavily on COM, as are many other Microsoft applications. So, as the saying goes, if it's good enough for Microsoft, it's good enough for me.

When you build your program using source-code-based objects, the objects are compiled into the object code. This has a couple of disadvantages:

- If you have multiple programs, each executable program has its own copy of the objects. This means that any time you change the objects, you must recompile all of the programs that use them.

- You must use the same programming language that the objects were written in to create your application programs. This restricts your choice of programming languages. Even though you may prefer to program in Visual Basic, sometimes you may find that using another programming language may help you.

Since COM objects are stored in their own independent object file, you can change the object without recompiling the applications that use it. You can also add new interfaces to the COM object to offer new features and capabilities. (Of course, if you modify the existing interfaces to the object, you may need to update the applications that use it.)

From DDE to COM+

Many of the features you see in today's COM technology go back many years. COM draws its roots from a number of different technologies, including Dynamic Data Exchange (DDE), Visual Basic Extensions (VBX), and Object Linking and Embedding (OLE). An understanding of how COM has evolved over time will give you some insight into the way that COM works and why it works that way. This will prepare you for Chapter 3, where I dissect how COM works.

DDE

In the early days of Windows, people used a clipboard much like they do today. Users could copy parts of a document in one program onto the clipboard and paste them into a document in another program. However, when dealing with complex graphical documents, users found that a simple clipboard didn't work very well.

In the late 1980s, Microsoft developed a technology called Dynamic Data Exchange (DDE) to allow programs to simplify the process of sharing data using a clipboard. This technology was available only for Microsoft applications, so it wasn't a universal solution.

OLE 1

In 1991, Microsoft created a more general solution to this problem called Object Linking and Embedding (OLE). This technology allowed users to combine documents from multiple applications into a single compound document. Developers could build the best possible word processor without worrying about adding a limited-function spreadsheet. All they had to do was link the word processing program to the spreadsheet program to handle the spreadsheet functions.

In Figure 1.4, you can see a Word document that includes an embedded Excel worksheet. I created the worksheet in Excel and then inserted it into the Word document by using the Object command on the Insert menu. Anytime I want to update the file, I can simply double-click the embedded worksheet and edit the worksheet using Excel.

Essentially, the Word application turns over the part of the screen that contains the worksheet to the Excel application. The Excel application provides any updates necessary within this area. Also, if the user clicks anywhere in this area, the click is passed through the Word application to the Excel application for proper execution. The Word document is acting as a container for the Excel worksheet. This is really the foundation of OLE.

Microsoft's first implementation of OLE, now called OLE version 1 or simply OLE 1, left a lot to be desired. The linkages were very slow, and the implementation was somewhat buggy. The people responsible for OLE recognized these problems and set out to resolve them in the next version of OLE. At the same time, other developers at Microsoft were busy reshaping the original programming language.

FIGURE 1.4:

A Word document with an embedded Excel worksheet

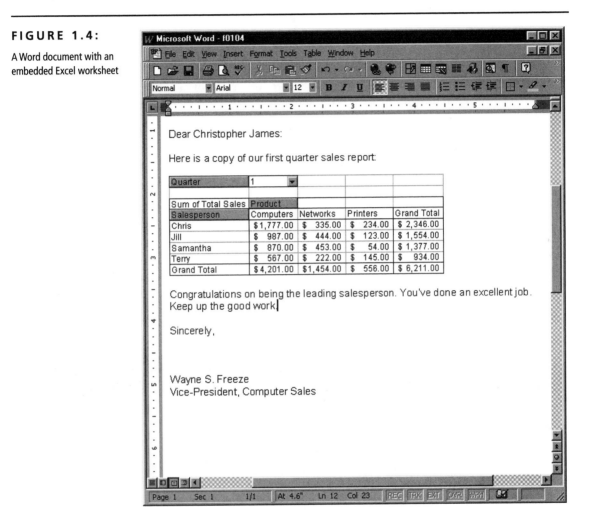

Basic Becomes Visual

The very first product written by Microsoft was a BASIC interpreter, which was written back in the days when if you wanted a computer, you had to build it yourself. In those days, BASIC occupied less than 4KB of memory (yes, I really mean 4,096 bytes of memory). It even had enough room for a simple program.

Ever since that time, Microsoft has always had a product that allows you to create and run BASIC programs. When Microsoft started selling MS-DOS, you got a free BASIC interpreter whether you wanted it or not. As time passed, however, Microsoft added other programming languages, such as FORTRAN and COBOL. Microsoft even had a number of different assemblers for those folks who needed to squeeze out every last bit of performance from their applications.

As new programming languages like C and Pascal became available and Windows was beginning to become more important, it looked like BASIC's days were numbered. Not many programmers wanted to work with a "toy" programming language like BASIC.

At this same time, most organizations were facing the problem of trying to do more with less. The economy was tight, but the end users were asking their data-processing organizations for more applications. The choice was either to hire more programmers or to make the programmers already on staff more efficient. Many companies sprung into business building programming tools that would make it easier to build and maintain programs.

Microsoft's response to this demand was to rebuild Visual Basic into a Rapid Application Development (RAD) tool. One of the key aspects of a RAD tool is that it provides high-level building blocks that perform commonly used functions. By using these building blocks, programmers reduce the amount of code required to build an application, while at the same time providing more capabilities than they would have included if they had written the code themselves. Visual Basic 3 was the first step toward making BASIC a true RAD tool.

VBX

Visual Basic includes high-level building blocks called *controls*. You simply drag a control onto the form you're working on, and instantly you have a rather complex function.

Consider for a minute the simple TextBox control. You probably don't give it much thought, but this control is surprisingly complex. It can display one line of text or multiple lines. It is smart enough to automatically break words when it needs to wrap from one line to the next. The TextBox control will automatically display scroll bars when necessary in a multiline text box, and it will scroll the displayed text with the cursor when there are too many characters to be displayed in a single-line text box. You can change the colors and fonts it uses to display its text. It will even work with the clipboard to perform the basic copy, cut, and paste functions. It can be bound to a field in a database, so that each time the current record in the database is changed, the information in the text box is automatically updated. In short, the TextBox control is one very powerful control.

Earlier versions of Visual Basic came with a handful of controls like the TextBox control. However, having several such controls wasn't sufficient, so Microsoft developed a framework called Visual Basic Extensions (VBX), which allowed programmers to create add-on controls. The VBX controls interacted with a Visual Basic program in three basic ways:

- Properties were available to read or set values inside the control. Common properties determine whether the control is active (Enabled), whether it can be seen on the form (Visible), its relative position on the form (Left and Top), and its size (Height and Width).

- Methods were used to call subroutines and functions inside the control. Common methods allow the programmer to reposition the control on the form (Move) or adjust the order in which the control is drawn (ZOrder).

- Events allowed the control to call a routine supplied by the application developer whenever the control encountered a specific condition. Common events happen when the user presses and releases a mouse button while the mouse pointer is over the control (Click) or when the user presses a key on the keyboard (KeyPress).

Microsoft supplied a number of these controls with Visual Basic 3. For example, that version included the Data control to provide easy access to a database, MAPI controls to provide access to Microsoft's Mail API, and controls that let you access common Windows functions, such as the CommonDialog control.

But more important, a number of other companies sprang up to create other useful controls. Companies developed controls that made it easier to create paper reports, simplified networking connections, and added the capability to create basic business charts. This was practical because the VBX architecture allowed the control builder to ship only a binary load module. Thus, developers could develop a really nifty control and keep the source code they used to create it private. The concept of extending the function of a programming language with only a binary module would show up again when Microsoft engineers decided to incorporate this concept when they overhauled OLE 1.

OLE 2 and COM

While working on OLE 2, the Microsoft engineers recognized that the issue of creating compound documents was really a special case of determining how two or more system or application components communicate with each other. In the past, a number of different techniques were employed. Sometimes, simple subroutine calls were used. Other times, more complex messaging systems were used. Programmers often were required to use several different techniques for communication among components.

This caused significant problems because each application would use its own techniques to request and provide services, thus making it difficult to integrate a group of applications to provide support for compound documents. While implementing OLE 2, Microsoft employed a number of new technologies; foremost among them was COM.

COM creates a layer of abstraction between software components. Each COM object is designed to operate as a server to a client application or another software module. The COM object is an instance of a specific class that defines one or more interfaces to the functions it provides. Each interface contains one or more methods to perform specific functions. An *interface* is similar in concept to the VBX framework.

With COM, it doesn't matter if the component is implemented as a simple set of subroutines or as an independent process that communicates with the application using a complex synchronization technique. You can even move the actual COM object to a different computer without changing the programming interface.

Although COM determines how two components communicate with one another, OLE 2 requires a number of other standard methods in addition to those required by COM. These include the capability for the object to present its own user interface, send events to the control's container, and let a container set the properties of the control.

OLE 2 was first supported in Visual Basic 4. Visual Basic 4 was also the first version to support 32-bit programming. In fact, two complete copies of Visual Basic were supplied on the installation disks—a 16-bit version and a 32-bit version.

Aside from the documentation and some utilities, not much was common between the two. While the 16-bit version continued to support VBX files, the 32-bit version didn't. However, both the 16-bit and 32-bit versions supported OLE-2 based controls, which were also known as OCXs after the file type used to contain the OLE 2 controls.

The same programming model used for VBXs was carried over to OLE 2. Each object accessible from Visual Basic contains one or more properties, methods, and events. This meant that Visual Basic programmers saw little or no change in how they wrote their programs.

ActiveX

When Microsoft realized that the Internet was not just a passing fad, they wanted to exploit the OLE 2 technology by allowing users to download OLE controls as part of their web document. The controls would work just like Java applets, but they would have the advantages of needing to be downloaded only once and running in native mode on the computer, rather than under the control of an interpreter.

While these goals were good, OLE 2 components had a major drawback: They tended to be fairly large because of the required interfaces, causing the user to download a lot of code, much of which was not needed. To get around this problem, Microsoft decided to make many of the required interfaces optional. This shrunk the amount of code required to build the control, thus making it easier to download. At the same time, Microsoft decided a name change was in order, so these new controls become known as ActiveX controls.

It is important to understand that the underlying model didn't change (at least not significantly) when Microsoft announced ActiveX technology. All the controls in Visual Basic continued to be based on COM objects.

Of course, to go along with the new name, Microsoft also released a new version of Visual Basic. Visual Basic 5 was notable for three things:

- The 16-bit version was dropped. Only the 32-bit version was included on the CD-ROM. If you wanted to develop 16-bit applications, you needed to use the 16-bit version found in version 4.

- This version came with a true compiler. Previously, compiling Visual Basic programs simply saved a copy of the program into an EXE file, which was run under control of a special runtime interpreter. The new compiler allowed Visual Basic applications to run significantly faster than they did before.

- The compiler also gave Visual Basic developers the ability to create their own controls in Visual Basic. Before Visual Basic 5, you needed to create OLE 2 or VBX controls in Visual C. While this was great for the third-party control market, it wasn't good for the average developer. With Visual Basic 5, developers could create their own controls and take advantage of reusable binary COM objects.

As a side effect of including the capability to build ActiveX control in Visual Basic, the Microsoft developers also included the ability to create COM objects that don't have a visible interface. This capability wasn't widely touted at the time, but it is proving to be important because it allows developers to remove the business logic from their collection of application programs and place it in a single common module.

COM and DCOM

Microsoft's attempt to convince web developers to switch to ActiveX controls from Java didn't work. Very few web sites outside Microsoft used ActiveX controls in their web pages. However, this doesn't mean that ActiveX was a failure. The same companies that developed VBXs switched to developing ActiveX controls. In addition, many other companies began developing ActiveX controls.

To help combat the negative image associated with ActiveX controls, Microsoft began using COM to refer to the controls created with the COM technology. If you believed the marketing folks, COM was a brand-new solution to your problems. But really, it was still the same COM programmers had been using for years. In addition, Microsoft began to push the idea of using COM objects to isolate your business logic into an independent component.

Distributed COM (DCOM) is the combination of COM plus the network protocols that allow you to run a COM object on a remote computer. The trick here is that a small part of the COM runtime environment inside Windows recognizes that the component you want is on another computer. The COM runtime environment locates the other computer and ensures that you have permission to access the object. Figure 1.5 illustrates how DCOM works.

FIGURE 1.5:

A COM object and its client using DCOM

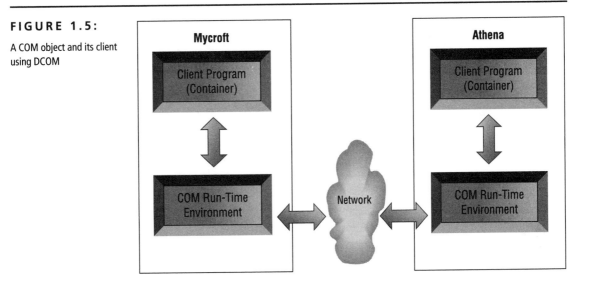

The key to making DCOM work is that your application never realizes that the COM object is not located on your local system. Information is kept in the Windows Registry to help the COM runtime environment locate the component and establish a connection with it. Once the connection is established, the COM object works as if it were in your local computer, except for any delays caused by communicating over a network.

NOTE You don't need to use DCOM to access a COM object across a network. Using normal COM capabilities, you can create a new instance of a COM object on a different computer. The main difference is that you need to specify the name of the remote computer in COM, while DCOM can automatically locate the COM object.

Transactions and Queues

While not strictly part of COM, two tools for the Windows environment are tightly coupled with COM. These tools are called the Microsoft Transaction Server (MTS) and the Microsoft Message Queues (MSMQ).

MTS

MTS simplifies programmers' lives by allowing them to create and use transactions. A *transaction* must meet four main criteria, which are also known as the ACID test:

- *Atomic* means that all of the work done by the transaction is either completed or not completed. This guarantees that a transaction can't leave the system in a half-completed state.

- *Consistent* means that a transaction will always leave the system in the consistent state.

- *Isolation* means that other transactions can't see partially completed results of another transaction.

- *Durability* means that database updates and changes to other managed resources can be properly recovered after a software or hardware failure.

MSMQ

MSMQ is a set of objects that allows you to perform asynchronous processing. In other words, you can use this technology to collect a series of messages, send them to a server for processing, and receive the results when they are finished.

Consider the case of a salesperson that travels from site to site to visit with customers. During each visit, the salesperson enters the customer's order into a laptop computer. At the end of the day, the salesperson links to the corporate network to process the orders. As each order is processed, a confirmation is returned, so the salesperson knows the current status of each order. If a customer needs the order immediately, the salesperson can dial up the corporate network to place the order and enter the order normally.

Using MSMQ, the orders are placed in a local queue that will be processed the next time the laptop is connected to the corporate network. When the laptop is connected, the orders are transmitted for processing on the remote computer. Any results generated by the remote computer are queued for return and will be transmitted the next time the laptop is connected.

When an order needs to be processed in real-time, the same process is used. However, since the laptop is connected, the order is placed immediately. And if the laptop stays connected, the results will be received as they become available. The same code works either way.

Although this may seem to have only marginal value, consider the situation where your transaction server must process requests at irregular intervals. Occasionally, it won't be able to process the request in a timely manner. MSMQ will allow the information to be processed on a first-come-first-served basis, and the application can wait for a second or two for the processing to complete. If the results aren't available that quickly, the application can issue a message saying that the request has been received and to check back for the results. When the results are available quickly, you can simply display the results as you receive them.

COM+

Windows 2000 is based on COM+. COM+ is a combination of COM, MTS, and MSMQ, with improvements to both MTS and MSMQ. It also includes some new features, such as an In-Memory Database (IMDB) and queued components.

> **NOTE**   Most of the COM+ facilities will work with Visual Basic 6. However, the queued components will require version 7.

The tighter integration between COM+ and the transaction server means less work for the application programmer. A significant feature is a more integrated tool to manage the components, offering a simpler programming interface. Another advantage is derived from the link with Windows 2000's Active Directory, which makes it easier to locate COM+ resources.

MSMQ remains basically unchanged from version 2, but a new feature called queued components is built on top of it. Queued components allow you to access your COM objects via MSMQ. Thus, it becomes a trivial matter to incorporate message queues into your application.

The IMDB is another fascinating tool. Unlike traditional databases, tables in the IMDB reside totally in memory (hence the name In-Memory Database). The primary advantage of the IMDB is speed. After all, it's much faster to access something in memory than from disk.

Final Thoughts

COM is a powerful technology that is underutilized by Visual Basic programmers. It's easier in the short run to just to keep building large programs. But sooner or later, your programs are going to need changes. These changes may be fixes to problems found by your users or enhancements that offer new features or improve performance. COM objects make it easier to implement changes. As long as you maintain the existing interface to a COM object, you can change the internals of the object as much as you want.

I'm known as the lazy programmer. I hate to do things more than once. The idea of using COM appeals to my lazy side. Not only does COM help me build more modular programs, but it also allows me to create objects that I can use in other projects. This is especially true when I'm building an application that has several different programs accessing a common set of data. By isolating the data-access logic into a set of COM objects, I not only avoid writing the data-access code multiple times, but I'm also free to change the database structures (as long as I don't change the meaning of the current properties, methods, and events). I can do this without rewriting or recompiling my application. It even means that I don't need to distribute the entire application each time I update it; I just send out the modules that have changed.

CHAPTER

TWO

Understanding Windows Architecture

- Executable code files

- A program's life cycle

- Virtual memory

- Memory allocation in Windows

- Processes and threads

- Marshaling

You can use Windows commands and write programs to a particular API without knowing what is happening at the bits-and-bytes level of the operating system. However, in order to understand how COM works, you really need to fully understand how Windows works.

Running multiple concurrent programs under Windows is not a trivial matter. In order to do this, you need special facilities to ensure that the programs don't interfere with each other. You also need mechanisms that provide standard libraries of routines that can be shared among the different programs in your computer; otherwise, the amount of memory you need to run everything increases exponentially.

In addition to providing the ability to run multiple programs at the same time, Windows also allows multiple execution streams to run in the same program. This means that you can perform two or more different tasks within the program as the same time.

Types of Program Files

There are three basic types of files that contain executable code: COM, EXE, and DLL. Other file types, like OCX and SCR, can contain executable code, but they are basically just DLLs or EXEs used for specific purposes.

COM Files

COM files were originally designed to hold programs that ran under DOS. These programs were originally intended to expand the small set of commands available in DOS.

The COM file contains an exact memory image of the program that you want to run, so it doesn't take much to load the program into memory and run it. The Windows operating system contains some COM programs, but they work only in a DOS session. Because these programs aren't true Windows programs, I'm not going to discuss them further.

EXE Files

EXE (executable) files contain object code that is run under control of Windows. EXE files use the Portable Executable format, which is common across all Windows systems, including those that run on different processors. The actual instructions in an EXE file depend on the physical CPU type. It's just the format of the file that is common.

The information that is in the EXE file is very close to what is actually loaded into memory for execution. The object code is stored in the file with a default base address. If the program can be loaded at this base address, very little work is required to load the program. If the program can't be loaded at the default address, additional information is included that identifies the memory addresses that need to be adjusted according to the new base address.

NOTE   ActiveX EXE programs are formatted identically to regular EXE files. However, there is additional information in the Windows Registry that is used to locate and identify the components in the EXE file.

DLL Files

DLL (dynamic link library) files contain collections of functions and subroutines that can be shared among multiple programs, including EXE programs and other DLLs. There isn't much difference between the structure of an EXE and a DLL. Both assume a default base address but can be loaded anywhere in the address space with a little more work.

The routines in a DLL are known as *in-process routines*, because they (and their associated data) can be accessed only from within the address space. It is also possible under the proper circumstances to access routines in a different address space, such as in an ActiveX EXE. This is known as an *out-of-process call*, because you must cross the address space boundary to get to the routine.

NOTE   ActiveX DLL files are formatted according to the same rules as normal DLLs. Components in the DLL are located using the same techniques that are used for an ActiveX EXE file.

Other Types of Files

There are a few other file types that contain executable code, but for the most part, they are merely specialized forms of an EXE or DLL file. An SCR file, for instance, is designed to hold a screen-saver program. It is expected to respond to a set of parameters that are passed as command-line arguments.

An OCX file is just a DLL file that holds one or more ActiveX controls. The same mechanisms and limitations that apply to a DLL file also apply to an OCX file. A difference is that an OCX file also contains some additional information that isn't required in a normal DLL file.

Program Execution

When you specify the name of a program to execute, the operating system performs several steps before the program actually begins to run:

- Find the program and load it into memory.

- Find the runtime libraries and load them into memory.

- Resolve any conflicts between these files.

- Perform all of the required initialization.

These steps are described in the following sections.

Locating and Loading the Program

When the user tells Windows to run a program, Windows must find where the program is located on disk. If the user specifies the exact filename including path information, this isn't a problem. However, if the user specifies only the name of the file, Windows must search for the file in the current directory and then in each of the directories specified in the Path environment variable until the file is found.

Once the program file is found, Windows loads it into memory. Because the code in the file can be placed anywhere in the address space, some work may need to be done to adjust the parts of the code that reference absolute memory locations. These changes are known as *fix-ups*.

Locating and Loading Runtime Libraries

After the code in the main program is loaded, then the calls to the external runtime libraries need to be resolved. This means that the appropriate DLL files need to be located on disk and loaded into memory.

Windows checks the directories in this order:

1. The directory where the EXE file was loaded

2. The current directory

3. The system directory

In the case of Windows 2000/NT, the \WinNt\System32 directory is checked first, and then the \WinNt\System directory is checked. The Windows directory and each of the directories in the Path environment variable are checked if the DLL can't be located anywhere else. If Windows can't locate the DLL, it terminates the process and displays a dialog box with an error message.

Given the large number of places where Windows needs to check for DLLs, two things are obvious:

- You should place any application-specific DLLs with the application program, because this is the first place Windows will check for DLLs.

- You should minimize the number of application-specific DLLs, because the time to locate and load two small DLLs is much greater than the time to locate and load one larger DLL.

NOTE   Every piece of code (including EXEs, DLLs, and OCXs) that calls routines in an OCX includes the OCX's GUID (Globally Unique Identifier). This value is used as a key in the Registry to return the complete path to the OCX file. This also applies to ActiveX EXEs and ActiveX DLLs.

Resolving Conflicts

After the DLL is located, Windows can determine if the library is already loaded. If so, then it may be possible to just point to the appropriate memory locations rather than physically loading the library a second time.

Of course, if another library is already loaded in that spot in the address space, you can't reuse the common library; you must load it again using a different base address. The same fix-up process that is used for EXE files is used here to resolve absolute addresses.

NOTE   You can set the base address of a Visual Basic DLL or OCX file by choosing Project ➢ Project Properties and selecting the Compile tab. By default, the DLL base address is set to &H11000000. Setting the DLL base address to a different value for each library will help to avoid conflicts between libraries.

Initializing Files

After each library is made available to the program, a call is made to the DLL entry point if it is present in the DLL. This routine will perform any initialization necessary to support the use of the DLL by the application.

If Windows was able to find all of the libraries, the program will be started. But that doesn't mean that all of the libraries will be loaded. Windows also allows you to load a DLL on the fly by calling various Win32 API functions. You can also use the `CreateObject` function in Visual Basic to dynamically load an ActiveX DLL. This technique has the advantage of letting your program run even if all of the libraries aren't present. Your program can issue its own error message and keep on running.

Ending the Program

When the user ends the program, Windows needs to reclaim the resources allocated to the program. In the case of shared runtime libraries, Windows needs to determine if any other programs are using the runtime libraries before releasing those resources.

Virtual Memory

Your address space can be as large as 4GB (gigabytes) in an Intel Pentium-based system. However, most computers don't have 4GB of memory. In fact, Windows itself has a limit of 2GB of real memory. This is where virtual memory comes into play.

NOTE   The actual memory limit of Windows depends on the operating system and the hardware it runs on. Certain versions of Windows 2000/NT can use 3GB of real memory. Versions of Windows 2000/NT that run on processors like the DEC Alpha can address more than 4GB of real memory.

Virtual memory is a special hardware trick that allows the operating system to break your address space into small chunks called *pages* and make them available on an as-needed basis. Unneeded pages are stored in a special disk file called `Win386.SWP` on Windows 98/95 and `Pagefile.SYS` on Windows 2000/NT.

Pages are moved from real memory to the swap file by a process called *page swapping*. Unneeded pages are swapped out from real memory; needed pages are swapped into real memory. A hardware technique called *address translation* converts address references in your virtual address space into real memory addresses at execution time. This allows the page from your virtual address space to be located anywhere in real memory. This process is controlled by the Windows virtual memory manager (VMM).

Using Virtual Memory

Let's look at a simple example of how virtual memory is used. The virtual address space containing your application contains a bunch of pages that are in sequence as far as your program is concerned. However, in real memory, only two of the pages are present—pages 1 and 2. Page 0 and the rest of the pages in the address space are stored in the swap file.

While your program is running, it references a memory location on page 3. Since page 3 isn't present in real memory, a hardware interrupt occurs and instructs Window's virtual memory manager to load page 3 into real memory. This is known as a *page fault*. The interrupt saves the complete state of your program, so that when

Windows returns from the interrupt, your program will resume without realizing that the memory wasn't there in the first place. Figure 2.1 illustrates this example.

FIGURE 2.1:

Accessing page 3 causes a page fault.

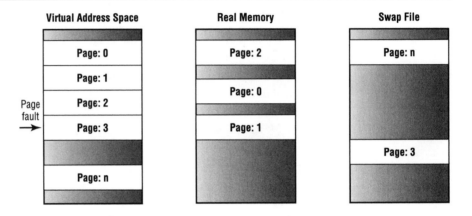

Next, Windows decides that it needs to move page 0 to the swap file in order to make room for page 3. It writes page 0 to the swap file. Then Windows loads page 3 from the swap file to real memory in the same place that held page 0. Figure 2.2 illustrates these steps. After page 3 is in real memory, Windows returns control to your program, and your program continues along, never knowing that the page-in operation occurred.

This example oversimplifies many issues. The performance of an operating system depends on the effectiveness of the virtual memory manager. A good virtual memory manager will often write pages to the swap file before a page fault occurs, so that it can move pages into memory as they are needed without waiting for a page-out operation to finish. Often, the operating system will read and write multiple pages at one time, since that is more efficient than writing them out one page at a time.

Because page-in and page-out operations generally take a lot of time to complete, Windows will sometimes let another program run while these operations finish. Choosing the right algorithms for the virtual memory manager is critical for the performance of an operating system like Windows.

FIGURE 2.2:

Moving page 0 and page 3 for a page-in operation

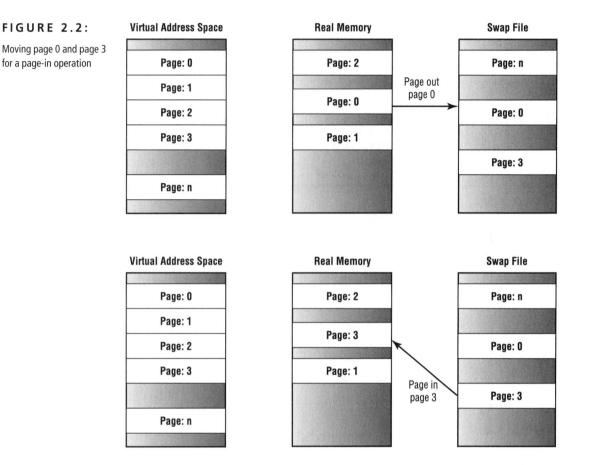

Another complicating factor is the page file itself. The size of the page file must be large enough to handle the overflow of memory from real memory. In other words, if you're running a dozen programs that each use 10MB of memory on a machine with only 32MB of main memory, you can expect to see a page file of nearly 100MB.

However, a large page file doesn't necessarily imply that you are having a problem. It simply identifies how much virtual memory you have available. Although the size of the file will change based on the amount of virtual memory in use, freeing memory doesn't always reduce the size of the file. Likewise, the size of the file will grow only if additional space is necessary. A small page file with a lot of paging activity will have a much larger impact on system performance than a large page file with minimal activity.

NOTE   In Windows 98/95, the page file is found in `C:\Windows\Win386.SWP`. In Windows 2000/NT, you should look for the `Pagefile.SYS` file in the root directory of each drive.

Allocating Memory

Your program can address 4GB of memory, but that doesn't mean that you get to use all of it. The address space is broken into a series of partitions that are reserved for various functions in your program and in the operating system.

Because of architectural differences between Windows 2000/NT and Windows 98/95, the actual partitions between the two operating systems differ slightly. The differences aren't really all that much, and they don't have a significant impact on the developer.

Memory Allocation in Windows 2000/NT

In Windows 2000/NT, the address space is broken into four partitions:

- The first partition (from 0x00000000 to 0x0000FFFF) is used to catch bad pointer assignments. Any attempt to read or write to these addresses will trigger an access violation. This is designed to help catch problems when the programmer attempts to access data based on an uninitialized pointer.

NOTE   Pointer problems are very common when programming in C or C++. Basically, the pointer is just a 32-bit value that references a memory location. Associated with the pointer is a data type that describes the data the pointer points to. If you forget to initialize a pointer to a particular memory location, it typically defaults to zero, which means the pointer is pointing at memory location 0x0000000. Without the protection, it's quite easy to store and retrieve values from this block of memory. You would never realize that the pointer was bad.

- The second partition (from 0x00010000 to 0x7FFEFFFF) represents nearly 2GB of memory for your application to use. This is where your EXE, DLL, and OCX files will be loaded and run.

- The third partition (from 0x7FFF0000 to 0x7FFFFFFF) is also used to catch bad pointers. If your program accesses any memory location in this range, your program will die with an access violation.

- The last partition (from 0x80000000 to 0xFFFFFFFF) is used to hold the operating system. It is not available to your program. Any attempt to address memory in this area will cause an access violation.

Table 2.1 summarizes these partitions and their purposes.

TABLE 2.1: Memory Partitions in Windows 2000/NT

Beginning Address	Ending Address	Size	Purpose
0x00000000	0x0000FFFF	64KB	Used to catch Null pointer assignments
0x00010000	0x7FFEFFFF	~2GB	Used by normal Win32 programs
0x7FFF0000	0x7FFFFFFF	64KB	Used to catch bad pointer assignments
0x80000000	0xFFFFFFFF	2GB	Used by the operating system

Memory Allocation in Windows 98/95

Windows 95 and 98 trace their heritage back to the old DOS days. Therefore, many compromises were made to ensure that Windows 98/95 could run as many old DOS programs as possible. The address space partitioning is designed to meet that requirement.

- The first partition is protected, much like the first partition (from 0x00000000 to 0x00000FFF) of a Windows 2000/NT address space. Any attempt to read or write these memory locations will trigger an access violation.

- The second partition (from 0x00001000 to 0x003FFFFF) is also reserved like the first partition. However, unlike the first partition, accessing this memory will not trigger an access violation.

- The third partition (from 0x00001000 to 0x7FFEFFFF) represents nearly 2GB of memory for your application to use. This is where your EXE, DLL, and OCX files will be loaded and run.

- The fourth partition (from 0x80000000 to 0xBFFFFFFF) is where the system DLLs are loaded. Libraries such as KERNEL32.DLL, USER32.DLL, and GDI32.DLL are available, plus any other libraries that are shared among all of the currently running Win32 programs. Unlike Windows 2000/NT, there is nothing to prevent a program running in the third partition from corrupting anything in this partition.

- The last partition (from 0xB0000000 to 0xFFFFFFFF) is reserved for Windows itself. The system's device drivers, memory managers, and the code for the file system are located here. Like the previous partition, there is no hardware arrangement to protect the operating system from normal user programs.

Table 2.2 summarizes these partitions and their purposes.

TABLE 2.2:   Memory Partitions in Windows 98/95

Beginning Address	Ending Address	Size	Purpose
0x00000000	0x00000FFF	4KB	Used to catch Null pointer assignments
0x00001000	0x003FFFFF	~4MB	Used by old DOS programs
0x00400000	0x7FFFFFFF	~2GB	Used by normal Win32 programs
0x80000000	0xBFFFFFFF	1GB	Shared by all Win32 programs
0xC0000000	0xFFFFFFFF	1GB	Used by the operating system; also shared by all Win32 programs

Part of the reason Windows 98/95 is not nearly as stable as Windows 2000/NT is that is it much easier to corrupt the operating system's memory. Any program can write into the memory reserved for Windows itself. If you're lucky, Windows will crash. If you're unlucky, all kinds of possible errors could creep into your machine, and you won't know about them until it's too late.

Program Execution Control

Another important aspect of how Windows works is how it controls a program's execution. Windows manages running programs as processes and threads.

An instance of a running program is known as a *process*. This corresponds to the address space I talked about in the previous section. A *thread* is defined to be an execution stream through a process. Typically, a process will have only one thread, in which case, your program will run as you would expect. However, there are times (especially when building COM objects), you might want to use multiple threads.

Processes and Threads

A process lives in its own address space, which is separate from all other processes. In the process's address space, you'll find the program's object code plus the data on which it operates. Also associated with the process are things like open files, semaphores, dynamically allocated memory, and other system resources.

Inside a process, one or more threads are used to execute the instructions loaded into the address space. The main thread in a process is known as the *primary thread*. Each thread also has complete access to all of the resources available to the process and has its own stack and its own set of CPU register values.

Threads operate independently of each other within a process. When you have one thread per process, your program operates in a linear fashion. In other words, only one piece of code can be executed at a time. This is known as *single threading*.

Multithreading

It is possible to have multiple threads active in a single process. This is known as *multithreading*. On a multiprocessor computer, all of these threads actually may be running at the exact same instant. On a single-processor computer, Windows switches between threads so quickly that the user never really knows that only one thread is active at any point in time.

While each thread has complete access to the address space, in practice, a thread has access to only the global variables in the program. As a thread calls a subroutine or function, the local variables are created using the thread's local stack and aren't directly available to the other threads.

Using multiple threads in a single process can cause problems if you don't take the appropriate precautions. Consider the situation where you have a global variable that is used as a counter, and you have two threads that are about to increment it. It is possible for one thread to retrieve the value and increment the counter, but before it has a chance to finish, the second thread has incremented the counter and saved the new value. When the first thread saves its value, the new value is wrong. The value is only one tick higher than the original, rather than the two ticks higher it should have been.

While the odds of this happening aren't very high, it's still possible. If you replace the in-memory counter with a counter that lives in a database, the odds of this happening become very significant.

To prevent this problem, facilities are available that will allow a thread to lock a resource so that any other thread can't access the resource until it has been unlocked. To avoid the counter problem I just described, the first thread would lock the counter's resource before attempting to update the counter. Then the second thread would be forced to wait for the first thread to unlock the resource before it could start. Thus, the counter would always be properly incremented.

> **WARNING** Use caution when locking resources. A deadlock can occur when one thread has a lock on resource A and is waiting on resource B, while a second thread has locked resource B and is waiting on resource A. Because each thread has locked a resource the other thread needs, both threads will wait forever, or at least until the process is killed.

Marshaling

Passing requests from one process to another or from one thread to another can be somewhat complex. Because of this, a technique called *marshaling* is used.

The basic concept of marshaling is that the request from the first thread or process is saved and then passed as a request to the main thread in the destination process. Then the main thread performs the request, packages the results, and sends them to the requesting thread. The requesting thread returns the information to the client. As well as marshaling data between threads within an address space, you can also marshal data between any two address spaces, even if those address spaces are on different computers.

Marshaling is required for a number of reasons:

- Data being passed to another process must be copied from one address space to another.

- Data stored in memory that is allocated to a particular thread in a process must be moved to a different storage area so that it can be accessed by the object's main thread.

- Data may need to be reformatted to ensure compatibility when accessing objects on another computer.

If you think that marshaling is a dumb idea, consider this: COM is designed to work on several different types of computers. Some computers expect integers to be stored in memory as <high byte> <low byte>, while others expect them to be stored as <low byte> <high byte>. Marshaling ensures that these incompatibility issues are taken care of for you automatically. A useful side effect to the marshaling process is that it prevents two or more threads from accessing a single instance of an object, thus avoiding the corrupted data problem that happens when multiple threads access the same data. Of course, marshaling does not guarantee that deadlocks will not occur. You still need to deal with the deadlock issue.

Final Thoughts

Many years ago, you always needed to worry about how much memory you used and where you placed your programs in memory. You always had less memory than you needed, so you were frugal with every byte—after all, 4KB of memory isn't much. Even when you graduated to computer with virtual memory, these issues were just as important. Although 16MB of memory seemed like a lot, if the important parts of your program couldn't stay in real memory, its performance was horrible.

In today's world, hardly anyone outside Microsoft's development labs pays attention to how much memory their programs use (and I'm not even sure that the Microsoft developers pay that much attention). However, being frugal with memory is still a good idea. You don't want your users complaining about the time that it takes to load your application.

CHAPTER

THREE

Running COM Objects

- Object creation, use, and deletion

- Standard and custom interfaces

- In-process objects

- Out-of-process objects

- DCOM objects

- COM+ objects

Using a COM object really boils down to calling a subroutine or function once the handshaking has been done to establish the object. However, that handshaking is very important to how COM operates, especially in the way that it will affect the performance.

This chapter provides an overview of how COM objects work. It begins with the life of an object, from creation to deletion. Next, it discusses standard and custom interfaces. Then you'll learn about the differences between in-process and out-of-process servers and how to use COM objects on different machines.

NOTE   This chapter is written from the perspective of a Visual Basic programmer. For a more complete discussion of how COM works, see *Mastering COM and COM+*, by Ash Rofail and Yasser Shohoud (Sybex, 1999).

The Life of an Object

Before we delve into how a COM object works, let's spend a few minutes reviewing how objects are created, used, and deleted. This discussion applies to COM objects, as well as to most types of objects in Windows.

Creating an Object

Every object has code and data structures associated with it. This information is usually stored in the user part (below the 2GB line) of the process's address space. Although the same code is shared among all objects of the same type, each instance of an object has its own unique data area that is created when the object is created.

Objects are referenced through an object variable in your program. The object variable merely points to a particular instance of an object rather than storing the entire object itself. Figure 3.1 illustrates object creation.

Creating an object variable
in Visual Basic

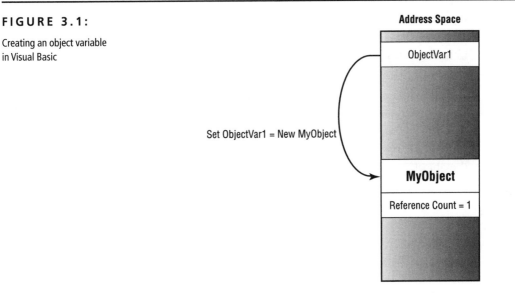

Address Space

ObjectVar1

Set ObjectVar1 = New MyObject

MyObject

Reference Count = 1

The Set statement with the New keyword is used to create a new instance of an object. This puts a pointer to the object in the specified object variable Object-Var1. Before the pointer is returned to the object variable, the code for the object must be loaded into memory, if it hasn't already been loaded. Then any initialization code associated with the object is run.

Each instance of an object has a reference counter that tracks the total number of times it has been referenced. In the example shown in Figure 3.1, because the object has just been created, the reference counter has a value of one.

NOTE   In Visual Basic, you define an object by using a class module. You create an instance of the object by using either the Dim or Set statement. I'll talk about this in detail in Chapter 4.

Using an Object

Once an object has been created and initialized, using the object isn't much different than making a function call, at least as far as your program is concerned. The object then performs the desired function and returns to the calling program when complete. Note that there are no real restrictions on the type of processing an object can do. It is quite common for one object to create another object, which in turn creates a third object.

After the object is created, it is possible to use multiple pointers to the same object. This doesn't mean that a new instance of the object is created; it means that you now have two pointers pointing to the same place. In Figure 3.2, you can see how the Set statement is used to create a second pointer to the same object. The reference count within the object is set to two, since there are now two pointers to the object.

FIGURE 3.2:

Using two objects that
point to the same object

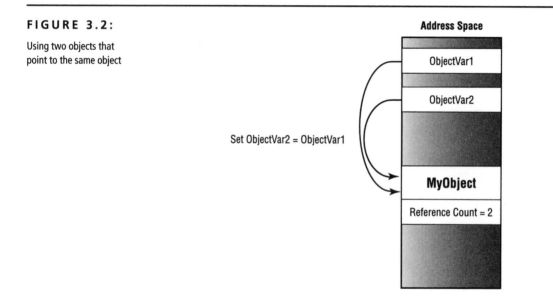

Deleting an Object

In theory, an instance of an object should be deleted when no more object variables are pointing to it. In practice, this is a little difficult to achieve. As new object variables point to the object, the counter should be incremented. When the reference is deleted by setting the object variable to Nothing, the counter should be decremented, as shown in Figure 3.3. When the counter reaches zero, the object is deleted, as shown in Figure 3.4.

FIGURE 3.3:

Deleting a reference to an object

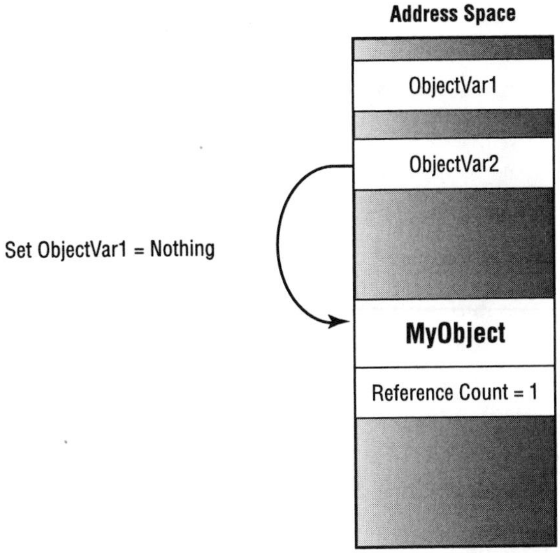

Address Space

Set ObjectVar1 = Nothing

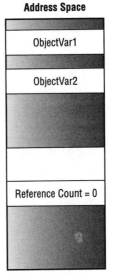

ObjectVar1

ObjectVar2

MyObject

Reference Count = 1

FIGURE 3.4:

The object is deleted when the reference counter becomes zero.

Address Space

ObjectVar1

ObjectVar2

Set ObjectVar2 = Nothing

Reference Count = 0

In practice, it's easy for the counter to become out of sync with the pointers. When this happens, you have one of two situations:

- You have a pointer to an object that no longer exists. Your program will die when you try to reference the object.

- You have an object that exists with no pointers to it. The resources owned by the object remain owned without a way to free them.

Neither of these situations is particularly desirable. Both usually can be prevented with good programming practices. For instance, you should never create an object that contains an object pointer to itself. If you try to destroy the object, COM will attempt to destroy any object it contains. Since the object points back to itself, you end up with a situation where COM will try to delete the object again and again, causing an infinite loop. Note that circular references like this do not always involve just one object. You can have a series of objects, where each object points to the next object in the chain, with the last object pointing back to the first. Deleting any of these objects will still cause an infinite loop.

NOTE   Visual Basic hides the counters and automatically handles them for you, so it's much harder to get the counters out of sync. However, you can still get into trouble if you create circular object references.

What's Inside a COM Object?

COM objects communicate to the world through a series of interfaces. Standard interfaces are generally used to access information about the COM objects. These interfaces include or perform various COM-related tasks. Custom interfaces are those interfaces designed by the user as COM objects.

The interfaces are implemented in one of two basic ways:

- *In-process object servers* run in the same address space as the client process. Using them doesn't add much more overhead to your application than calling a function or a subroutine.

- *Out-of-process object servers* run in a different address space. They come in two different flavors: local and remote. Using these objects is more expensive in terms of overhead; however, in the long run, they may actually help your application to run faster. While your program calls them like a function or a subroutine, a lot of work needs to be done to marshal your request to another process, wait for results, and then marshal the results in the same fashion as an in-process COM object.

These servers interact with your client program using the same statements, but underneath the covers, they are two radically different tools.

The next sections provide details about standard and custom interfaces. Then you'll learn more about in-process and out-of-process objects.

Interfaces

An *interface* is a contract between a COM server and a COM client. It specifies the methods, properties, and events that are used to communicate between the client and the server. This is perhaps the most important part of the COM object, because the interface isolates the internal workings of the COM object from how it is used by the client.

Every COM object presents at least two interfaces to the outside world. In most cases, more than two will be present because a number of interfaces are dictated by the COM architecture. As noted in the previous section, the interfaces can be divided into two groups: standard interfaces and custom interfaces.

Using Standard Interfaces

Standard interfaces are those defined by Microsoft. All COM objects are expected to implement IUnknown. IDispatch is required when you want to support late binding. The IUnknown interface returns information about the other interfaces in the object. The IDispatch interface is used to get the details about the various methods that exist in an interface. Other standard interfaces that may or may not be included in a COM object are IPersist, IPersistPropertyBag, IPersist-Stream, and IPersistInitStream. These interfaces are used to provide special services in Visual Basic programs.

The IUnknown Interface

The IUnknown interface contains three functions: QueryInterface, AddRef, and Release.

The QueryInterface function returns information about what the object can do. It uses an interface identifier as a parameter. If the specified interface exists, QueryInterface will return a pointer to an interface. This technique lets you dynamically determine what interfaces are available in a COM object.

The AddRef and Release calls handle reference counting. Reference counting lets the COM object keep track of the number of times the object was referenced. Each time you create a new reference to an existing COM object, the AddRef method needs to be called to increment the reference counter. The Release method does the opposite—it decrements the counter. It is useful to know that this interface exists, but Visual Basic takes care of calling the AddRef and Release methods when you use the Set statement to create a new object or to destroy an existing object.

Figure 3.5 illustrates the IUnknown interface in a sample COM library.

The IDispatch Interface

The IDispatch interface provides a set of methods that gets information about the methods of an interface and helps you use them. The GetIDsOfNames method is used to map the name of a method in a specified interface onto a dispatch identifier (also known as a DISPID). Then the DISPID can be used with the Invoke method to call the specified method.

The IPersist Interfaces

The IPersist, IPersistPropertyBag, IPersistStream, and IPersistInit-Stream interfaces are defined as part of the COM interface, but they are rarely implemented by C++ programmers. These interfaces allow the state of the object to be stored and retrieved in another instance of the object.

Visual Basic automatically implements these interfaces in ActiveX control projects to allow you to save and retrieve the control's property values while in design mode. Otherwise, the programmer wouldn't be able to set the property values in design mode.

FIGURE 3.5:

A sample COM library

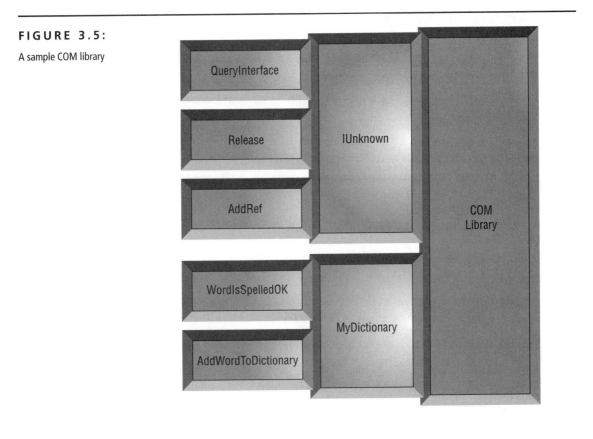

There are many other uses for the IPersist interfaces for a C++ programmer, such as creating OLE DB programs. However, Visual Basic programmers don't need to worry about these interfaces, because Visual Basic takes care of all the grungy details for you.

Using Custom Interfaces

Any interface not supplied by Microsoft is known as a custom interface. Calling an object's method involves using a normal subroutine call to one of the routines defined by the interface. Properties are accessed as either external variables or as a function that returns a value, depending on how the object designer implemented them.

Accessing Information through an Interface

An interface is a binary specification that allows you to locate a particular variable or function in the code module. This information is stored in a data structure called a virtual method table, or vTable. A vTable is merely an array of function pointers, where each pointer points to a particular method or property contained in the object.

Each function pointed to by the vTable contains not only the address of the function, but additional information, such as the name of the function, the data type it will return, and the name and data type for each of its parameters. This information is accessed through a method in the IDispatch interface called GetIDsOfNames.

Binding to an Interface

In order to use a COM object, you must find and load the library containing the object. Then you must create a link between the object variable you plan to use and the desired interface. This process is known as *binding*.

There are two basic types of binding: early and late. Each type has advantages and disadvantages.

In late binding, Visual Basic is unable to determine the type of the object you're using. This happens when you declare a variable as Object or Variant. At runtime, Visual Basic must use the GetIDsOfNames method to find the appropriate DISPID in the vTable. Once the DISPID is known, Visual Basic can use the Invoke method with the DISPID value to access the method or property.

With early binding, you must declare your object variable with a specific object type. With this information, Visual Basic is able to bind your variable to the object at design time, thus avoiding the extra overhead of searching for the object at runtime.

For most early bound objects, Visual Basic performs vTable binding in which Visual Basic computes the offset in the vTable and uses this information when you call methods or access properties. This makes the overhead for using an in-process object about the same as just calling a normal DLL function.

Visual Basic components always include a vTable, so you will always be able to perform vTable binding with your own Visual Basic code. However, some objects do not contain a vTable, so it isn't possible to perform vTable binding with them.

In those cases, Visual Basic obtains the DISPID value and uses the Invoke method, just as in late binding. This is known as DISPID binding. DISPID binding is not as efficient as vTable binding, but it is still more efficient than late binding.

NOTE   Using the New keyword in a Dim statement is not always a good idea. The New keyword implies that a new instance of the object will be created the first time you attempt to use it. However, since Visual Basic doesn't know which statement in your program will be the first to use the object, extra code is included before each object reference to see if the object exists and to create a new instance if it doesn't. This adds overhead to your program. While it isn't much extra overhead, if you reference the object inside a loop, it can add up quickly.

In-Process COM Objects

As you would expect, an in-process COM object is loaded into the same address space as your program. It is loaded from a regular DLL file, which contains a set of standardized functions and tables that allows you to load and use the COM object dynamically.

An ActiveX DLL file can contain one or more COM objects. Access to individual objects is done through a COM interface. As mentioned in the previous section, each COM object has a standard interface called IUnknown and may also have other interfaces.

Finding and Loading In-Process COM Objects

When an object in the COM library is accessed for the first time, the COM library is loaded into your address space, just like any other DLL. However, unlike DLL files, which require Windows to search in a number of places to find the file (as explained in Chapter 2), COM objects are quickly located by using a GUID.

A GUID (globally unique identifier) is a 128-bit (16-byte) number that is unique—not just in a specific computer, but in the entire world. This value is derived from a complex algorithm designed by the same people that developed the Distributed Computing Environment (DCE). The GUID generator uses your system's clock and the MAC address from your network interface card to create a value that is guaranteed to be unique on your computer. If your computer doesn't have a network interface card, the GUID will be created from a value based on your hard disk space and the total time since the computer was booted.

NOTE   The MAC address is unique for a network card. It's based on a combination of unique serial number from the network interface card manufacturer and a vendor identification number.

Each class or interface in a COM object is assigned a GUID. This value is known as CLSID for a class ID and IID for an interface ID. The CLSID listed below is for the ADO (ActiveX Data Objects) Data control.

```
{67397AA3-7FB1-11D0-B148-00A0C922E820}
```

When your program attempts to access a COM object for the first time, it searches the Windows Registry for the key CLSID value associated with the control. If this key isn't in your Registry, then the COM object isn't on your system. For instance, here is the key for the ADO Data control:

```
\HKEY_CLASSES_ROOT\CLSID\{67397AA3-7FB1-11D0-B148-00A0C922E820}
```

If it's in the Registry, all you need to do is look for the InprocServer32 subkey to find the name of the library to load. In the case of the ADO Data control, the file C:\Windows\System\MSADODC.OCX would be loaded, as shown in Figure 3.6.

FIGURE 3.6:

The ADO Data control's CSLID and related information

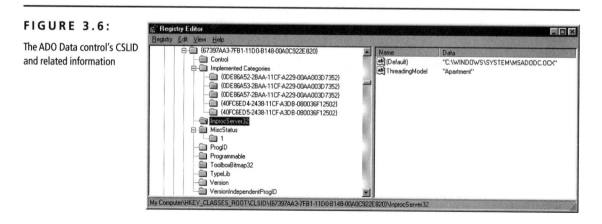

After the system has found the library, it uses the normal techniques I talked about in Chapter 2 to load the library into memory. However, loading the library doesn't make it ready to use. As with other types of DLLs, any library initialization needs to be done first. This usually includes allocating global variables and running any global initialization code. Note that this is different from the code used to initialize any particular object in the library.

Understanding In-Process Threading Models

Although COM supports several different threading models for in-process objects, Visual Basic only allows you to choose the single-threaded model or the apartment model. These threading models are designed specifically to prevent deadlocks from occurring while running COM objects.

The Single-Threaded Model

As its name implies, the single-threaded model allows only one thread to access a COM object. When you choose the single-threaded model, you are guaranteed that you can't have a deadlock, because only the thread that created the object can access it. This simplifies some of the implementation details of programming a COM object, but it can slow down the application.

NOTE   Windows requires additional resources to manage extra threads, so your application may actually run slower with multiple threads. However, if used properly, multiple threads allow your application to separate long-running background tasks from short-running foreground tasks. This will let your users think the application is running faster because it's more responsive, even though it's actually consuming more resources.

Internally, a single-threaded model is implemented as just one large apartment. So, when a multiple-threaded application tries to access a single-threaded control, one of two things will occur:

- If the thread happens to be the thread that created the object (also known as the *main* thread), processing will proceed normally, and the thread can process the request.

- If the thread trying to access the object isn't the main thread, it needs to ask the main thread to perform the request. This can have a significant impact on performance, because cross-thread marshaling is nearly as expensive as cross-process marshaling.

Figure 3.7 illustrates how a multiple-threaded application can use a single-threaded set of COM objects.

FIGURE 3.7:

When a multithreaded application uses a single-threaded model COM object

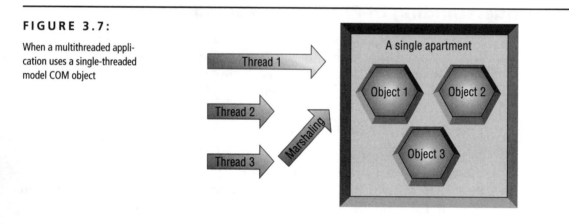

The Apartment Model

In apartment model threading, all of the objects created by a single thread "live" in an apartment and share their own private copy of the global data. This means that you can't use global data to communicate among multiple threads. In many ways, this approach is just like single threading, except that it is possible to service multiple independent threads with the same object. Figure 3.8 illustrates how a multithreaded application uses an apartment model set of COM objects.

This means that each thread can access the objects it creates, much like the main thread in the single-threaded model. Also, just like in the single-threaded model, if the thread that needs to access the object isn't the thread that created it, the request must be passed to the thread that created the object. This ensures that there are no conflicts caused by two threads trying to update the same information at the same time.

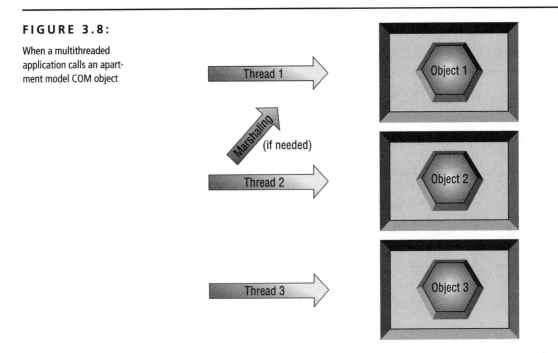

FIGURE 3.8:

When a multithreaded application calls an apartment model COM object

---

NOTE In C++ (not in Visual Basic), you can also use a free-threading model that permits multiple threads to access any COM object in the process. However, there isn't any synchronization between threads that are accessing the object. For some objects, this may not be a problem. On the other hand, if you need to make sure that only one thread is accessing an object at a time, you need to either choose a different threading model or supply your own synchronization method.

Because MDI (Multiple Document Interface) parent and child forms share data in ways that aren't thread-safe, you can't use MDI forms with apartment threading.

Out-of-Process COM Objects

An out-of-process object resides in its own address space, so essentially it's just another program running in Windows. However, unlike a typical Windows program, an out-of-process object doesn't need a user interface, although it can have one.

An example of an out-of-process COM library is Microsoft Excel. While you can run Excel just like a normal application, you can also use its facilities to perform tasks by accessing its object library.

Finding and Loading Out-of-Process COM Objects

Finding out-of-process objects is similar to locating in-process objects. The calling program supplies the object's CLSID, which is used to find information about the object in the Windows Registry. For example, the Registry key shown below for Microsoft Excel will find the information shown in Figure 3.9.

\HKEY_CLASSES_ROOT\CLSID\{00024500-0000-0000-C000-000000000046}

FIGURE 3.9:

Excel's CSLID and related information

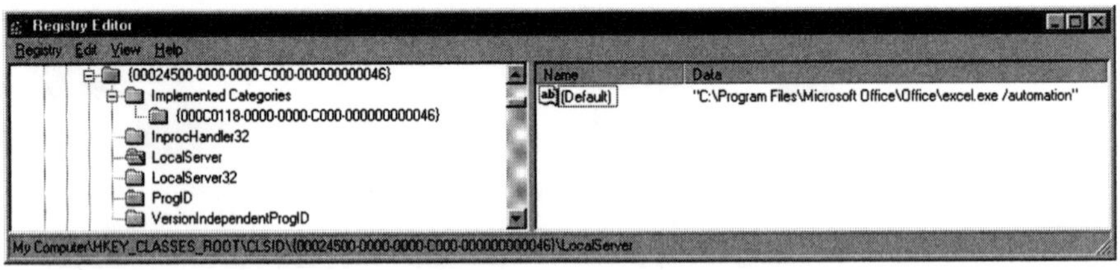

When you compare the subkeys listed in Figure 3.9 with those in Figure 3.6, you'll notice that that the `InprocServer32` has been replaced with an `InprocHandler32` and a `LocalServer32`. This is because you now need two components to handle the request.

Within your main application, you need a stub that will direct the requests to the appropriate out-of-process server. So the `InprocHandler32` points to the OLE32.DLL.

The `LocalServer32` key contains information about how to start the out-of-process server. In this case, all it does is run the Excel program file with a special command-line parameter that indicates that the user interface isn't required.

C:\Program Files\Microsoft Office\Office\excel.exe /automation

NOTE   Out-of-process COM servers are also known as Automation servers.

Just as an in-process library must be loaded before it can be used, an out-of-process server first needs to be loaded. While it is possible to load multiple copies of an in-process server that is shared among several applications, you actually need only one copy of the out-of-process server. You go through the same steps you use to load a regular application to load an out-of-process server; however, the out-of-process server isn't launched until it's first accessed.

Understanding Out-of-Process Threading Models

Out-of-process COM objects can use two different threading models in Visual Basic:

- One thread per object
- Multithreaded using a pool of threads

Both approaches to threading have their advantages and disadvantages, as explained in the next sections.

The One-Thread-per-Object Model

In the one-thread-per-object model, each time a new object is created, a new thread will be used to access it. When the object is deleted, the thread will be terminated also.

The downside to this approach is that if a large number of objects are used, a large number of threads will be created. This can have a negative impact on system performance.

The Pool-of-Threads Model

The other approach to assigning threads is to maintain a pool of threads that are assigned on a round-robin basis when you need to create a new instance of an object.

This concept is governed by the same set of rules that govern multiple-threaded in-process COM objects. When an object is created, only the thread that created it can access it. If another thread needs to access the object, then the request must be moved to the thread that created the object.

Also, each thread is assigned its own copy of the global area that is shared by all of the objects it creates. Given the round-robin nature of the object creation, it is possible that two objects created by the same process will be assigned to different threads and thus have different global areas, while two objects created by different processes may share the same thread and the same global area.

I'll talk about the pool-of-threads model in more detail in Chapter 7.

NOTE   Before you add a global variable to your object library, consider that the value stored there may not be the same for all instances of the object. Use global variables only for values that don't extend beyond the life of the object. For instance, you may want to use a global object variable to hold a pointer to a database connection object. Then you can share this among all of the objects in the library.

Running Out-of-Process COM Objects Remotely

If your computer is attached to a network, Windows includes the capability to run your object on another machine. The same interfaces that your program sees with a local out-of-process COM object still exist, but now they direct your request to another computer where the objects exist.

To direct your COM calls to another computer, COM uses a proxy component that intercepts your calls to methods and properties and passes them onto the remote computer using DCE Remote Procedure Calls (RPCs). The RPCs are received by another proxy, which passes them onto your ActiveX EXE, as illustrated in Figure 3.10.

FIGURE 3.10:

Accessing a remote out-of-process server

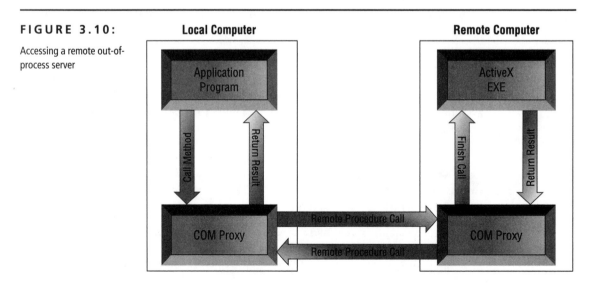

DCOM Objects

A DCOM object is similar to an out-of-process COM object, except you don't need to know the machine on which it runs. This is done by letting your application look on your local machine for the object, just as it normally would. However, instead of finding the information about your object on the local machine, it finds a reference to a remote machine where the object resides. Then the object is located in the Windows Registry using the same techniques used to locate an out-of-process server on your local machine. From there, RPCs are used to communicate between your program and the remote object.

The biggest advantage of using DCOM over running a COM object remotely is that your program doesn't need to know where the object is located. This information can be set and changed in the Windows Registry without affecting your program.

Finding DCOM Objects

When you install your application on a client system, the setup program will automatically create the entries in the Registry needed to find the object. These entries are nearly identical to the ones created for a regular out-of-process COM object. However, one additional subkey value called AllowRemoteActivation is added. If this subkey has a value of Y, it means that object can be created on a different system.

Which system actually holds the object depends on how the DCOM object has been configured. The DCOM Configuration utility (DCOMCNFG.EXE) allows you to specify where to find the application and other information. This information is stored under the same CLSID value, beneath the \HKEY_CLASSES_ROOT\AppID subkey in the Registry. Subkeys under this subkey include the remote system that will run the DCOM object (RemoteServerName), security information (AuthenticationLevel, AccessPermission, and so on), and which identity will be used to run the object (RunAs).

Running DCOM Objects

Once your object has been located, the same techniques used to allow a normal COM out-of-process server object to run on a remote system are used to run a

DCOM object. You continue to create and use DCOM objects in your application just as if the objects existed on your local system.

DCOM uses the same proxies and RPCs as used in running an out-of-process COM server on a remote computer. In fact, this is one of DCOM's strengths. You don't need to convert your current remote COM servers to use a different technology. You simply use the DCOM Configuration utility to add the definitions to the Registry. Then you can start using it. I'll talk about DCOM and the DCOM Configuration utility in detail in Chapter 8.

COM+ Objects

Like remote COM and DCOM objects, objects that run under the control of the COM+ transaction server are designed to be used over a network. These objects use an ActiveX DLL rather than an ActiveX EXE.

ActiveX DLLs are collected and stored on a computer system using special software that catalogs them and makes them available to your application. Additional software is used to provide an environment where the COM+ resources may be shared more efficiently and allows the work performed by an object to be grouped together as a single transaction. Other facilities, such as a queuing model and an in-memory database (as described in Chapter 1) are also included to improve the performance and capabilities of your application.

There isn't sufficient room to cover all of the pieces of how COM+ works in a single chapter. I'm going to spend the second half of the book (Parts 3 and 4) discussing how COM+ works, as well as how to use it with your Visual Basic programs.

Final Thoughts

COM, DCOM, and COM+ objects are all based on the same low-level technology. The only difference between them is how a client program locates them. COM objects are located by using the Windows Registry on the local computer. If you use COM objects on a remote computer, you need to know on which computer the object resides. On the other hand, DCOM objects include information on the local computer that points to the remote computer containing the object. COM+ objects are also found based on information kept on the local computer.

COM+ objects build on this foundation by adding special features that handle issues such as support for load balancing and resource sharing, operating under the support of a transaction server. This ensures that either the object completed its task successfully or the work is undone so that it looks like the transaction never ran. As I said earlier, instead of releasing MTS version 3, Microsoft's marketing folks decided to change the name to COM+. This reflected its integration into the Windows 2000 Professional operating system as a basic service.

Knowing how COM, DCOM, and COM+ objects work in a Windows program gives you a lot of insight into when you should use which type of object. You understand the trade-offs between extra overhead imposed by some of the object types and the performance that can be gained by moving the object away from your application. For example, one of my favorite ways to speed up processing in an application is to launch a background program to handle long-running tasks. Why tie up a user's display while a big report is being generated? You can easily build an out-of-process server to run the report and have it periodically report its status back to the main program.

CHAPTER

FOUR

4

Building Class Modules in Visual Basic

- Parts of class modules

- Module-level variables

- PropertyGet, Let, and Set routines

- Method routines for objects

- Events from objects

- The Object Browser

In the previous chapters, I've covered everything from how COM has evolved through all of the theory behind how Windows runs programs and COM objects. However, all of this information is useful only when you can apply it to a Visual Basic program. This is where the Visual Basic class module comes into play.

You use class modules to create object templates in Visual Basic. Class modules were originally designed to allow programmers to build objects in regular Visual Basic programs. Starting in Visual Basic 5, you used the same collection of statements to create COM objects, in the same way that programmers can build COM objects using Visual C++.

Programming with Class

The class module in Visual Basic is where you define an object's template. Within the class, you set up the properties, methods, and events that the class will offer to outside users. This corresponds to the interface of a COM object. Your class module also contains any internal data structures and routines that will help you with your code.

> **NOTE**   When building a class module, you need to remember that a class is only a template that represents how the object will work when it is actually created. You need to explicitly create an instance of the object elsewhere in your program—by using the **New** keyword in a **Dim** or **Set** statement or by using the **CreateObject** function—before you can use that object.

Class modules have four main pieces, each of which plays a different role in how your object is used:

Event declarations   These are subroutine definitions that allow your object to call a subroutine in the program that created the object (of course, the programmer using your object needs to create a subroutine using this definition for the event to work). You should be familiar with events from using controls in your program. But realize that events aren't restricted to controls. They can be used in any type of object.

Module variables   These are variables that are declared at the start of your module and can be accessed by any routine in the module. In addition, if you declare a variable `Public`, it can be accessed outside the class module as a property of the class.

Property routines   These are functions and subroutines that allow you to programmatically verify values and return values from the class. As far as the object's client is concerned, there is no difference between a property routine and a `Public` module-level variable. However, you can use a routine to ensure that only valid values are assigned to a property or to make the property read-only or write-only.

Method routines   These are functions and subroutines typically used by a client program to signal the object to perform some action. Method routines usually return information to the client through one or more property values, or by returning a value directly via one of the parameters or the value of the method. However, methods can also return by raising an event.

The next sections explain the class module and its pieces in more detail. Then I'll show you how it all fits together in a simple application.

Elements of the Class Module

A class module is similar to any other module in Visual Basic. It's merely a collection of subroutine, function, variable, and option declarations. It also includes a few other features that help it support object programming. A class module is not an object; rather, it provides the framework to create your own objects. Like an object, however, a class module has some predefined properties and events that you will need to understand.

NOTE   Here, I cover only the names and properties that are common to all class objects. Some of the class objects (such as the ActiveX DLL class objects) have more properties. I'll discuss these in Part 2, when I talk about the various forms of ActiveX class objects.

The Class Name

Setting the class name property specifies the name that the object will be known by in the client program. It's important that you choose a unique but meaningful name for your class. This is how you will identify the object in your program. For instance, setting the `Name` property to `Stack` means that you can create an instance of the `Stack` object with the following statement:

```
Dim s As Stack
```

Initialization and Termination Routines

Because a class module represents an object that is created on demand at runtime, it's highly desirable to be able to perform some processing before the client program begins to use the object and after it has finished with it. This is done in the `Class_Initialize` and `Class_Terminate` routines.

The `Class_Initialize` routine is called once the object has been loaded into memory, but before the object reference has been returned to the program that created the class object. I like to use this event to initialize all of my module-level variables that need specific initialization, create some objects that will be used by the class, or perform some processing that only needs be done when the object is created (such as opening a database).

After the last reference to the class object is set to `Nothing`, the `Class_Terminate` routine is called. You use this event to set any object references to `Nothing` and close the database that you opened in the `Class_Initialize` event.

WARNING   If the program that creates this class blows up unexpectedly, the `Class_Terminate` routine won't be called. This can cause problems if your objects require this routine to clean up properly. For example, if you use `Class_Initialize` to retrieve some information and `Class_Terminate` to save it, make sure that the `Class_Initialize` event has code to handle the situation where the information from the last use wasn't saved.

The Public, Private, and Friend Keywords

Within a module, you can control the visibility of the variables, functions, subroutines, and properties by declaring them as `Public`, `Private`, or `Friend`. These keywords can be used in place of the Dim statement or in front of any Property, Sub, or Function statement.

- The Public keyword indicates that a variable or routine can be referenced from anywhere in the Visual Basic project. By default, any function, subroutine, or property will be public.

- The Private keyword indicates that the variable or routine is local to the module. It can't be referenced from outside the module. Any variables declared with the Dim statement are assumed to be private.

- The Friend keyword indicates that the routine is visible anywhere in the project, except the routine will not be visible to the controller of an instance of an object. This means you can call the routine directly from anywhere in your Visual Basic project, but if you create an object, the routine is not a valid method.

NOTE Very rarely will you need to use a Friend routine in a Visual Basic class module. The only case where you might want to use a Friend routine is when you have a collection of class modules that are interrelated and have some common functions. However, even then, you could do the same thing by putting the common routines into their own module.

Module Variables

Variables declared outside the routines in a module are called *module-level variables*. They are available to every routine in the module as normal variables.

Public versus Private Variables

If a variable is declared Public, the variable will be visible outside the class module as a property. The one advantage a Public module-level variable has over property routines (discussed in the next section) is that accessing a module variable is much faster than accessing a property routine.

By declaring a module-level variable `Public`, you allow the programmer using your class object to change the property without notifying your object of the change. If you need to verify that the property was assigned a proper value or need to take some action when the property changes, use a `Property Let` or `Property Set` routine, as described in the next section.

`Private` variables are useful for storing information that is associated with an instance of an object. Each new instance of the class object will have its own unique set of module variables. You can use these variables to hold data associated with an instance of an object.

Module Variable Declaration Syntax

To declare a module variable, use the following syntax:

`[Public|Private|Dim]` *variable* `[,` *variable*`]` ...

In this syntax, *variable* means

`[WithEvents]` *varname*`[([`*subscripts*`])]` `As` `[New]` *typename*`]`

where:

- *varname* is the name of the variable you want to create.

- *subscripts* specifies array size:

  `[`*lower* `To]` *upper* `[,[`*lower* `To]` *upper*`]` ...

  where *lower* means the lower bound of the array and *upper* means the upper bound of the array. If *lower* isn't specified, it will default to zero or the value specified in the `Option Base` statement. Each *lower* and *upper* pair constitutes a dimension of the array. Visual Basic supports arrays with up to 60 dimensions.

- *typename* is the variable's type.

`Public` implies that the variable will be visible as a property value for anyone using the class object. Selecting `Private` or `Dim` means that the variable will be visible only within the class module.

The WithEvents keyword indicates that the variable is an object variable that has events. Without this keyword, any events triggered in the object will be ignored. The WithEvents keyword isn't valid when the variable is an array or with an object that doesn't use events.

The New keyword is used to automatically create an instance of the object specified in *typename* the first time the object is referenced. If the New keyword isn't present, you must explicitly create a new instance by using the Set statement.

If you don't specify a valid type for *typename*, Visual Basic will assume that the variable is of type Variant. This will allow you to store nearly any value in the variable.

> **NOTE** When you define your variables with a valid type, Visual Basic will check the variable each time you use it to be sure that it has the correct type.

Property Routines

Property routines come in three flavors: Property Get, Property Let, and Property Set. These routines allow you to implement property assignments as a set of code rather than allowing the programmer to directly access a module-level variable. Property routines have the advantage of allowing you to perform error checking before a property value is assigned, making a property read-only, or triggering an action when a property value is changed.

The Property Get routine is basically a function that returns the value of a property. Property Let and Property Set are subroutines that allow you to assign a value to a property.

> **NOTE** You can make a property read-only by not including a Property Let or Property Set routine. You can make a property write-only by not including a Property Get routine.

Property Get Syntax

The Property Get routine returns the value of the property to the calling program.

```
[Public|Private|Friend] [Static] Property Get property [(arg [, arg]…)]
➡ [As typename]
```

where:

- *property* is the name of the property.

- *arg* is short for

```
[Optional] [ByVal|ByRef] [ParamArray] argname [()] [As typename]
➡ [=default]
```

  argname is the name of an argument, *typename* is a valid Visual Basic data type, and *default* is used to specify the default value of an optional argument.

- *typename* is the property type.

Public, Private, or Friend describes the visibility of the property function. Public properties are visible from everywhere in your Visual Basic project. Private properties are visible only in the module in which they are defined. Friend properties are visible throughout the Visual Basic project, but can't be referenced through an instance of a class object.

Using the Static keyword means that any local variables in the property routine will be preserved from one call to the next. This is similar to declaring every local variable in the routine to be Static.

The ByVal keyword means that the argument is passed by value to the property routine, and any changes made to a ByVal argument will not be seen by the calling program. ByRef means that a pointer to the value is passed instead, and any changes made in the ByRef argument are seen by the calling program. If neither ByVal nor ByRef is specified, then ByRef is assumed.

The ParamArray keyword is optional and must be used only in front of the last argument in the list of arguments. It can't be used in combination with the ByVal, ByRef, or Optional keywords. It specifies that the last argument is a Variant array that contains as many parameters as the caller chooses to specify. You can use the For Each statement to examine each value in the array, or you can use the LBound and UBound functions to determine the number of elements present.

The `Optional` keyword means that the argument may be skipped. You can use the `IsMissing` function to determine if a value was supplied to the argument, or you can assign a default value to the argument using the `=default` clause.

Although you can specify a list of arguments to the `Property Get` routine, typically you won't bother. Most properties don't have or need arguments. It will just confuse most programmers using your class object. If you need to return a value based on a set of arguments, consider using a method function (discussed later in this chapter).

If you specify arguments in a `Property Get`, `Property Let`, or `Property Set` statement, they must match those in all of the other `Property` statements. This means the arguments must be in the same order, must have the same names, and must have the same data types. If the arguments don't match, an error will occur.

NOTE   If you do choose to include a set of arguments in a `Property Get` statement, consider designing them so that the arguments appear to be subscripts into an array, rather than just a set of arguments. This concept helps to reinforce the notion that the property is just a module variable that has been made available for other programs to access.

Before you leave the `Property Get` routine, you must assign a value to *property*. This is the value that will be returned to the client program. You can exit the `Property Get` routine by using the `Exit Property` statement or by reaching the `End Property` statement.

Property Let and Property Set Syntax

The `Property Let` routine is called when a client program assigns a non-object value to a property. The `Property Set` routine is called when a client program assigns an object value to a property.

```
[Public|Private|Friend] [Static] Property [Let|Set] property ([arg,
➡ [arg,]…] value [As typename])
```

where:

- *property* is the name of the property.

- *arg* has the following syntax:

```
[Optional] [ByVal|ByRef] [ParamArray] argname [()] [As typename]
➡ [=default]
```

argname is the name of an argument, *typename* is a valid Visual Basic data type, and *default* is used to specify the default value of an optional argument. If any arguments are specified, they must be the same as in the `Property Get` statement; otherwise, an error will occur.

The keywords used in these statements have the same meanings as those in the `Property Get` statement.

NOTE   Making your property routine `Private` means that you can't access the routine from outside the class module. This defeats the purpose of defining a property routine, so unless you're adding a property routine that you don't want anyone to access, don't use `Private`.

The last argument in `Property Let` and `Property Set` statements, called *value* in the syntax description above, is the value that will be assigned to the property. *Value* can be either a normal variable (`Property Let`) or an object reference (`Property Set`). Even though the definitions of *arg* and *value* may look similar, every `Property Set` and `Property Let` statement must include a definition for *value*. This definition always follows any arguments, and its data type must correspond to the data type specified for the `Property Get` routine.

In these statements, the property corresponds to the variable on the left side of the equal sign, and *value* corresponds to the expression on right. If you need to use a `Set` statement to perform the assignment, then you need to code the `Property Set` statement. Otherwise, you should use the `Property Let` statement.

As with the `Property Get` statement, you can exit the `Property Let` and `Property Set` routines early by using the `Exit Property` statement, or you will leave the routine by reaching the `End Property` statement.

Method Routines

Method routines are nothing more than regular functions and subroutines that are buried in a class module. They are almost identical to the property routines just discussed, because the property routines are simply a special form of functions and subroutines.

The primary difference between method routines and the property routines is how the programmer using the class perceives them. Properties are perceived as static values that are used to determine how the class object works. Methods are viewed as performing operations against an object.

Like the property routines, you can declare functions and subroutines to be `Private`, `Public`, or `Friend`. In the case of method routines, you should take advantage of `Private` routines. These routines are local to the class module and can't be called from outside the module.

NOTE   As the interface to your class object evolves over time, you may find that you need to create a new method to perform a specific task. Rather than having two methods containing similar code, consider creating a private routine that can be called by the original method and the new method. This means that you have one copy of the code that does the real work, while you have a couple of simple routines that simply intercept the request and pass it along to the common routine.

I'm not going to cover the syntax of functions and subroutines here, since you should already be comfortable with how to create them. However, here are some considerations when you're designing your methods:

- Where possible, combine multiple requests into a single call by using `Optional` arguments or `ParamArray` argument. The cost to call a method often can be much higher than the cost to perform the actual work. Thus, having the ability to perform multiple requests in a single call can save considerable resources.

- Use `Optional` parameters with default values where possible to simplify the code the average programmer needs to write to use your object. This is especially true if the parameter uses the same value most of the time.

- Use meaningful names for the arguments of a method. This information will appear in many places, such as in the Object Browser and the tip boxes in the Visual Basic Editor.

- Identify (at least internally) the properties that may be changed by the method. This may help to eliminate confusion about how the method works.

- For methods where there is a possibility of failure or error, provide a clear path for returning the cause of the failure. This may be through a property, a function value that is returned to the controlling program, or an event. While the programmer has the right to ignore this information, it is better to give the programmer the ability to make that choice.

Event Declarations

Event declarations allow your class object to call a subroutine in a client program. Using events is a good idea because they provide a way to inform the client program using your object about what is happening within your object. This way, the client program doesn't need to check your object's properties every so often to see what is happening.

Event Declaration Syntax

To use an event in a class object, you use the following syntax to define the event's name and the list of values that will be passed to the client's program.

```
[Public] Event eventname [(arg [, arg] … )]
```

where:

- *eventname* is the name of the event.

- *arg* is short for

```
[ByVal|ByRef] argname [()] [As typename]
```

argname is the name of an argument, and *typename* is a valid Visual Basic data type.

By default, all event declarations are public, so whether or not you include the keyword Public is up to you. However, you can raise events only in the class module in which they are defined.

An event does not need to have any arguments. The client program can access the object's properties to get or set information about the state of the object while executing the code in the event subroutine. However, in many cases, it is useful to pass arguments to the event. You might choose to use arguments rather than properties to pass along information that is temporary in nature.

For each argument you specify, you can choose how it is passed to the client. By default, the arguments are passed by reference, so the client's code can change the value you specify. You can also explicitly specify the ByRef keyword to make it clear that the event can change the value you specify. When the event is called, a pointer, rather than the value itself, will be passed to the variable you specify.

If you pass a constant or use an expression for the argument, a temporary copy of the value is made, which can be changed by the client's code. Obviously, any changes to this value will be lost when the client's code finishes and control is returned to your object.

If you precede the argument name with ByVal, the argument will be passed by value. This means that an independent copy of the value is passed to the event, thus preventing the client program from changing the value.

RaiseEvent Syntax

To trigger the event, you use the RaiseEvent statement with the following syntax:

```
RaiseEvent  eventname [( value [, value] …)]
```

where:

- *eventname* refers to the event defined in the Event statement.

- *value* is a variable, constant, or expression whose type corresponds to *typename* specified for the argument in the Event statement.

A Classy Little Application

Now that you understand the pieces of a class module, let's look at a simple little application that implements a stack using a class module. Figure 4.1 shows the Stack application window.

NOTE   You can find this program, as well as all of the other examples in this book, on the book's web site at www.Sybex.com. You can also download the programs in this book from my web site at www.JustPC.com.

FIGURE 4.1:

The Stack program

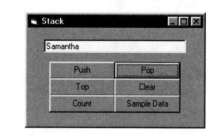

This program consists of two modules: a normal module associated with the form, called Form1, and a class module that holds the Stack object.

Setting Up the Stack Interface

A stack is simply a first-in-last-out (FILO) method of arranging information. You can think of a stack as a series of plates placed one on top of the other. While you can add a plate to or remove a plate from the top of the pile, you can't directly access any of the plates below that. To get to the plate on the bottom, you need to remove every plate on top of it first.

Stacks are often used in computers because they allow you to set aside something that you are currently doing, perform something else, and then return to exactly where you were. Visual Basic is based heavily on stacks; the local variables for a subroutine or function are stored in a stack. When you call a new subroutine, its local variables are placed on the stack on top of the calling subroutines. When the new subroutine finishes, it removes its local variables, leaving the original subroutine's variables on the top.

The Stack class implemented here is very simple. It holds objects of type Variant, so that you can store any Visual Basic variable on the stack. Table 4.1 lists the properties, methods, and events available in the Stack object.

TABLE 4.1: The Stack Interface

Name	Type	Description
Clear	Method	Initializes a stack
Count	Property	Returns the number of entries in the stack

Continued on next page

TABLE 4.1 CONTINUED: The Stack Interface

Name	Type	Description
Error	Event	Triggered on stack overflow or underflow
Pop	Method	Returns and deletes the current entry from the top of the stack
Push	Method	Adds a new entry to the top of stack
Top	Property	Holds a copy of the current top of stack value

Using the Object Browser

When programming with class objects, I find one of the most useful tools for viewing the structure is the Object Browser. This tool allows you to see all of the properties, methods, and events supported by an object. To start the Object Browser, press the F2 key or choose View ➤ Object Browser from the main menu.

The Object Browser provides a view of all of the objects and controls available to your program. Alternatively, you can specify the library you wish to view. In Figure 4.2, I choose Project1, which limits the display to the objects found in the Stack program. As you can see in the Classes section of the display, the only two objects in this project are the Form1 and Stack objects. I clicked the Stack object to display all of the members of the Stack class.

> **NOTE**   Because the Stack object is part of the active program, you will see all of its members listed here, including the ones marked Private. However, you won't be able to see the private members of external objects.

You can also use the Object Browser to search for a particular class or member by specifying a value in the Search Text box (located below the Project/Library box at the top-left corner of the window). The Search Results section is directly below the Search Text box. Clicking an entry in the Search Results box displays the related information in the Classes and Members lists below. Information about the property, method, or event appears at the very bottom of the Object Browser. Figure 4.3 shows an example of choosing Pop in the Search Results box.

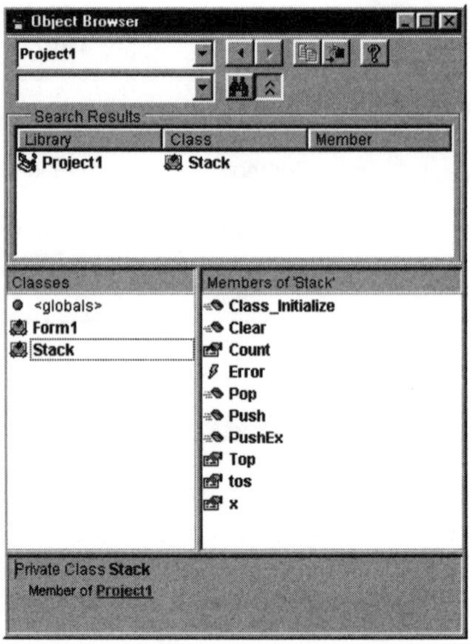

FIGURE 4.2:

Viewing the Stack object
with the Object Browser

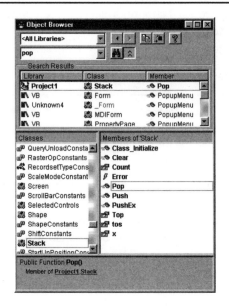

FIGURE 4.3:

Searching for the Pop
method

NOTE When I need to know what members are available in an object or a control, I use the Object Browser to locate the object or control. Then I can scan the items in the Members list to find the method I'm looking for. Selecting the member will display the syntax for it, plus a short description.

Building the Stack Class

There are many different ways to start building an object, but I usually start out by defining the data structures I plan to use inside the object. In this case, we will use an array with an index pointer to the highest occupied stack location. If there aren't any values in the stack, we'll set the pointer to –1.

Stack Declarations

Listing 4.1 contains the module-level declarations for the Stack class. The Variant array x is where we keep the data for the stack, and the variable tos contains the top-of-stack pointer. This class had two other declarations: the property Top and the event Error.

Listing 4.1:   Declarations for the Stack class

```
Option Explicit

Private x(127) As Variant
Private tos As Long

Public Top As Variant

Event Error(ByVal ErrNum As Long, ByVal ErrMsg As String)
```

Top is used to hold the current value of the top of stack. I did this mostly to let you see how a public variable can be accessed from outside the class module. Because this is a separate variable, each time we add or delete something from the stack, we need to adjust its value. Also, because it is public, the program using the object could change its value, so it would no longer have the same value as the top of stack. A better solution would be to use a Property Get routine that would extract the top of stack directly from the array and wouldn't let the user directly modify the value.

The Error event is triggered anytime we encounter a stack overflow, which happens when we attempt to push more than 127 elements on the stack. Likewise, a stack underflow occurs when we attempt to remove an element from an empty stack. It returns two values: an error number and its corresponding error message. I like using events to communicate errors because they can be easily ignored if they're not important.

Initializing the Stack

When an instance of the class object is created, the Class_Initialize routine will be called. In this object, we merely need to set the tos variable to –1, as shown in Listing 4.2.

Listing 4.2:   **The Class_Initialize event of the Stack class**

```
Private Sub Class_Initialize()

tos = -1

End Sub
```

Note that there is a corresponding Class_Terminate event that will be called just before the object is destroyed. If we had created some objects local to this module in Class_Initialize, the Class_Terminate event would be the ideal place to ensure that they have been properly destroyed.

Adding a Value to the Stack

The client program uses the Push method to add a value to the stack. To make this routine a little more interesting, I decided that I would let the user call this routine in two different ways:

- The user can assign a value to the Top property and then call the Push method to place the value onto the stack.

- The user can call the Push method with the value he or she wants added to the top of the stack.

Listing 4.3 shows the Push method.

Listing 4.3:   **The Push method of the Stack class**

```
Public Sub Push(Optional a As Variant)

If tos + 1 >= UBound(x) Then
   RaiseEvent Error(1, "Stack overflow.")

ElseIf IsMissing(a) Then
   tos = tos + 1
   x(tos) = Top

Else
   tos = tos + 1
   x(tos) = a
   Top = a

End If

End Sub
```

In order to handle the two conditions, we need to declare the parameter that will hold the value to be added to the stack as Optional. This means that we can use the IsMissing function to see if a value is present, and then choose whether to look for the value in the parameter a or in the variable Top.

The first thing we do inside the routine is to ensure that adding the new value won't overflow the storage in the x array. We check the next available location with the upper bound of the array. If it's greater than or equal, we use the RaiseEvent statement to trigger the error event.

Next, we use the IsMissing function to determine where we get the value for the stack. Then we can increment tos and assign the value to the array element it points to. Note that when we get the value from the parameter a, we also need to assign the value to the Top variable.

Taking a Value from the Stack

Popping a value from the stack is similar to pushing a value onto the stack. We need to check to make sure that the operation is valid and then do the work. In this case, we check to see if the top-of-stack pointer tos is set to –1. If it is, we'll use the RaiseEvent statement to trigger the Error event with a stack underflow error. Listing 4.4 shows how the value is popped from the stack.

Listing 4.4:   **The Pop method of the Stack class**

```
Public Function Pop() As Variant

If tos = -1 Then
    RaiseEvent Error(2, "Stack underflow.")

Else
    Pop = x(tos)
    tos = tos - 1
    Top = x(tos)

End If

End Function
```

If we know we have at least one value in the stack, all we need to do is to save the current value into the property Top as the value of the function itself, and decrement the top-of-stack pointer (tos).

Extending the Stack Class

Eventually, programmers usually want to improve their projects. Suppose that we've decided to enhance the Stack class after the original interface was designed. We want a method that will allow us to push multiple items onto the stack in a single call. Rather than changing the existing routine, we can add a new routine called PushEx (for Push Extended). This routine takes advantage of the Param-Array feature that allows us to accept a variable number of parameters in a single subroutine call.

The PushEx routine, shown in Listing 4.5, starts out by declaring a ParamArray called a in the Sub statement. Then we declare a variable z as type Variant and use it in a For Each loop that will examine every element in the array a. If the element would cause a stack overflow, we return that message to the calling program and exit the routine; otherwise, we add it to the top of the stack. Finally, we set the Top property to the last value added to the top of the stack.

NOTE   Calling a method in a COM object can take up to 20 times the resources than calling a local subroutine. In order to minimize this overhead, consider adding routines like `PushEx` to your class modules. This approach allows you to combine a number of method calls into a single method call, which could make a big impact on the performance of your application.

Listing 4.5:   **The PushEx method of the Stack class**

```
Public Sub PushEx(ParamArray a() As Variant)

Dim z As Variant

For Each z In a
    If tos + 1 >= UBound(x) Then
        RaiseEvent Error(1, "Stack overflow.")
        Exit Sub

    Else
        tos = tos + 1
        x(tos) = z

    End If

Next z

Top = x(tos)

End Sub
```

Using the Stack Class

Using the Stack class in a program isn't difficult. The following sections review the basics of creating and deleting an object, as well as explain how to use the various properties and methods in the Stack class.

Creating and Deleting a Stack Object

Because the Stack class has an event, we need to declare it a little differently than most objects. We need to include the WithEvents clause in the Private statement to allow us to use an event:

```
Private WithEvents s As Stack
```

Using this clause presents some limitations:

- It prevents us from using the New keyword in the statement to automatically create a new instance of the Stack class.

- It prevents us from creating an array of Stack objects.

- It means that the object can't be declared inside a subroutine or function. It must be declared at the module level.

However, these limitations are a small price to pay for using events in the program.

> **NOTE**
>
> If you don't need to use the events in your application, you don't need to declare the object using the WithEvents keyword. Even if you do include the With-Events keyword, you still don't need to define the events. Whenever the object raises an event, your program will simply ignore it.

Once the Stack variable has been defined, it's a simple matter to create a new instance of the variable using the Set statement with the New keyword.

```
Set s = New Stack
```

Finally, when you're finished with the object, use the Set statement to delete the object.

```
Set s = Nothing
```

Pushing and Popping the Stack

Using the Push and Pop methods from the Stack class isn't terribly complicated once you've seen the code for those routines. To pop something from the stack, use code like this:

```
Text1.Text = s.Pop
```

When you push a value onto the stack, you have a few choices:

- You can choose to assign a value to the Top property and then call the Push method, as in the following code:

```
s.Top = "Samantha"
s.Push
```

- You could combine these two steps into a single step:

```
s.Push "Samantha"
```

- Using the PushEx method allows you to push multiple items on the stack in a single statement, like this:

```
s.PushEx "Wayne", "Jill", "Christopher", "Samamtha"
```

Final Thoughts

The Microsoft developers leveraged many of the concepts already in Visual Basic when they implemented class modules. This makes it much easier for Visual Basic programmers to create their own objects. Given how easy it is to create class modules, I'm surprised that more programmers don't use them.

From my point of view, I like the idea of creating reusable class modules. It lets me be lazy. After all, why should I rewrite code for something I already wrote?

When I started using Visual Basic, I took the time to create a regular module that contained all kinds of utility routines that I would use across the application. This made it easier for me to build my applications—I already had standard routines to perform common tasks, such as opening a database or reading a recordset. Now, I just create class modules containing the routines I want to share among the programs in my application.

PART II

Programming COM with Visual Basic

CHAPTER

FIVE

Creating ActiveX DLL Objects in Visual Basic

- ■ A definition of ActiveX DLLs

- ■ Practical uses of ActiveX DLLs

- ■ An ActiveX DLL with Win32 API function calls

The previous chapters provided the theory and background material. Now it's time to move onto the real thing. In this chapter, you'll learn about using ActiveX DLLs. As a practical example, we'll build an ActiveX DLL that includes several useful Win32 API function calls.

What Is an ActiveX DLL?

An ActiveX DLL is a really just a collection of one or more Visual Basic class modules. It uses the same basic programming structures as class modules (described in Chapter 4). There are some minor differences, but they are mostly in the properties associated with the class module and the ActiveX project, rather than in the actual statements you'll use to build your application.

A class module is not the only thing you can store in an ActiveX DLL. You can also store regular functions and subroutines, forms, controls, property pages, and nearly anything you can include in a normal Visual Basic program. The one exception is an MDI (Multiple Document Interface) form.

So is an ActiveX DLL just a catchall for any Visual Basic code that you want to put into a common library? Yes! Just remember two things:

- You can't run an ActiveX DLL directly, so you can't use it to hold your main program.

- If you don't need to share your code with another program, why bother putting in a code library?

SDI versus MDI

Okay, I admit it. I don't like MDI-based applications, including Visual Basic. The first thing I do with Visual Basic is switch the development environment from MDI (Multiple Document Interface) to SDI (Single Document Interface). I just choose Tools ➢ Options from the main menu and check the SDI Development Environment check box on the Advanced tab of the Options dialog box.

Continued on next page

I find the MDI environment too constraining, since I usually have anywhere from four to ten applications running at the same time. I often want to look at a window containing information from one application while I'm in another application. I find the nontransparent background of an MDI form wastes space on my Desktop, since I can't see the forms beneath it.

I realize this issue can be elevated to a religious war (witness all of the discussions that resulted from Word 2000 shifting from an MDI environment to an SDI environment). I suggest that you keep an open mind and try both. Then you can make your own choices.

Why Use an ActiveX DLL?

Along the way, most programmers collect a set of routines that they use over and over again when they write their programs. Some of these routines can be very complex; others may implement hidden Windows functions. You may use some of these routines all of the time and use others infrequently.

Most programmers either copy these routines from the last program that used them or share a source file between applications. These approaches have several disadvantages.

If you're like me, when you copy code from one program to another, you invariably make changes to it. Often, these changes are necessary for the routine to work in your new application, but sometimes these changes simply make the routine work better. Unless you propagate your improvements back to the original program, they may be lost.

Also consider the problems that you will encounter if you find an error in the routine. You'll need to locate every program that contained the routine and make the same fix. This can be a time-consuming mess, especially if you changed the routine when you copied it from program to program.

Using a common library is also hazardous to your sanity. The routines are pulled into your program, but unless you take special steps to prevent changes to the routine, you can have one programmer destroying the work done by another. You may change the routine in the common library to fix a problem with one program, and inadvertently introduce a new bug into a different program. If you don't bother to recompile all of your programs that use the common library at the same time, you may not be aware of the problem for quite some time.

NOTE   With Visual Basic, you can share the same source file between multiple programs by choosing Project ➤ Add File and selecting your common source code library. I suggest that you mark the file as read-only and make changes to it only when you're certain that it's not being used elsewhere.

A better way to share code is by taking a little time and creating your own ActiveX DLL. You could move the common routines you use now to an ActiveX DLL and simply share the DLL. Because the DLL is object code, it can be easily distributed and independently updated. The normal COM mechanisms force you to create and maintain a well-defined interface. Visual Basic can detect when that interface was changed and let you know that you have a problem.

There are only two disadvantages to using an ActiveX DLL. One is that there is a slight performance penalty. For most applications, this will go unnoticed. The second is that you're forced to think about the design of your functions more than if you included them directly in your program. But a little extra work on the front end will prevent problems and save time in the long run. That should be one of the goals of a lazy programmer.

Building an ActiveX DLL

One of the more dangerous things you can do in Visual Basic is to call the Win32 API function calls directly. Often, you need to do some unusual things to make the calls work properly. However, sometimes you don't have a choice. For instance, many organizations are spread across the world, yet there isn't a convenient way for a Visual Basic programmer to know which time zone an application is running in. All of Visual Basic's date and time routines are relative to the system clock, not UTC (also known as Universal time, Greenwich Mean Time, or GMT). This information is only available to the Win32 programmer.

The UTC time is only one example of a function that's available with the Win32 API but isn't included in Visual Basic. Have you ever wanted to run a second program, and perhaps wait for it to return? Maybe you would like to be able to find out which program is associated with a particular file type. In this chapter, we're going to include these functions, along with the UTC time information, in an ActiveX DLL called WinUtil.

TIP For more information about Win32 APIs, see *The VB Developer's Guide to Win32 API* by Steve Brown (Sybex, 1999).

To create the WinUtil ActiveX DLL, start Visual Basic and double-click ActiveX DLL on the New tab of the New Project dialog box, as shown in Figure 5.1. You'll automatically get a class module, called Class1, where you can begin coding your COM object.

FIGURE 5.1:

Choosing to create a new ActiveX DLL project

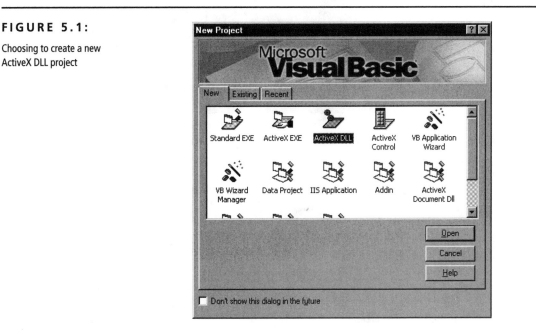

Setting the Project's Properties

Before you start to write code, you should take the time to set the various properties that will control how the COM object works. These are in the Project Properties dialog box, which you can display by choosing Project ➤ Project1 Properties (or whatever name you choose for your project) from the main menu. Figure 5.2 shows the Project Properties dialog box for the new ActiveX DLL project.

FIGURE 5.2:

Updating project properties

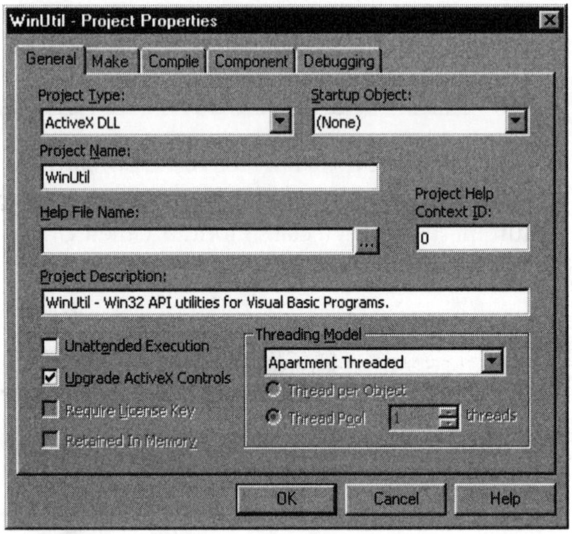

Adjusting General Settings

In the General tab of the Project Properties dialog box, there are a few things you should change. First, you should set the Project Name field to a meaningful name that describes your object. This value will be used in the Windows Registry to locate your DLL. Next, you should supply a meaningful description in the Project Description field. This description will be displayed when you use the Object Browser or in the References dialog box.

The default values for the rest of the fields on this tab are fine. If you want to run some code when you load the entire DLL into memory, you can select Sub Main as the Startup Object. Note that you need to include this routine in a regular Visual Basic module that isn't associated with any of the class modules that actually make up the COM object.

Check the Unattended Execution check box if you want to direct any messages to a log file rather than to the user. For now, you will probably want to display message boxes and other information on the screen. This will help you debug the application. (Later, when we start building COM+ transactions in Part III, you will probably want to enable this feature to log any problems.)

Unless you need single-threaded objects, leave the Threading Model option set to Apartment Threaded. This is the most efficient threading model for an ActiveX DLL.

Setting Make Information

One problem with creating independent object code libraries such as an ActiveX DLL is that you can't easily look at the source code to identify what's in the file. The Make tab of the Project Properties dialog box, shown in Figure 5.3, allows you to define a bunch of information that describes your component.

FIGURE 5.3:

Setting information for your ActiveX DLL

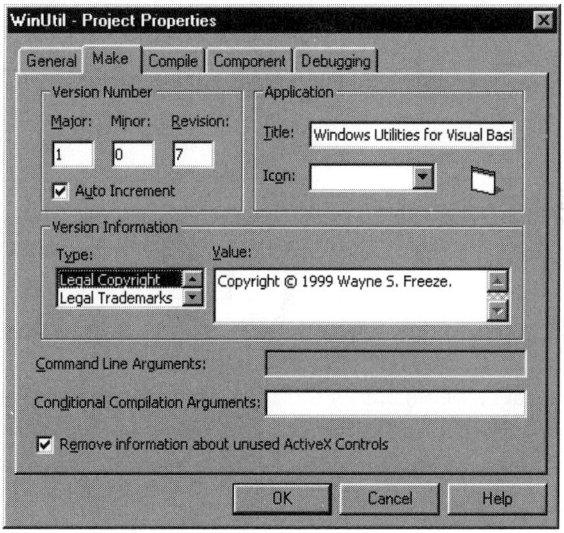

After you've entered this information, you can view it as part of the file's properties, as shown in Figure 5.4. For example, you can right-click the filename in

Windows Explorer and select Properties from the pop-up menu. You can also view the values you specify on the Make tab by examining the various properties of the App object.

Of the pieces of information available, probably the most important is the version number. This will help you identify which version of the ActiveX DLL you are using in a production application. By checking the Auto Increment check box in the Make tab, the version number is automatically incremented after you create a new copy of the DLL file. This allows you to compile and test your objects as many times as you want in the development environment and then freeze that version number when you are satisfied with it.

The Version Information group of the Make tab lets you specify values for your company name, the file's description, the legal copyright, and the product's name. You can also include trademark information and general comments. As with the rest of the information, you can view these entries by displaying the file's properties in Windows Explorer.

For every executable file you distribute, I strongly recommend including your company's name in the Company Name field and a value for Legal Copyright, such as "Copyright © 1999 Wayne S. Freeze."

Setting Compile Options

Most of the settings on the Compile tab, shown in Figure 5.5, control which compile-time optimizations should be used. Other than making sure that Compile to Native Code is set (which should be the default value anyway), I wouldn't bother changing any of the radio button or check box settings. However, I do recommend changing the DLL Base Address value at the bottom of the tab.

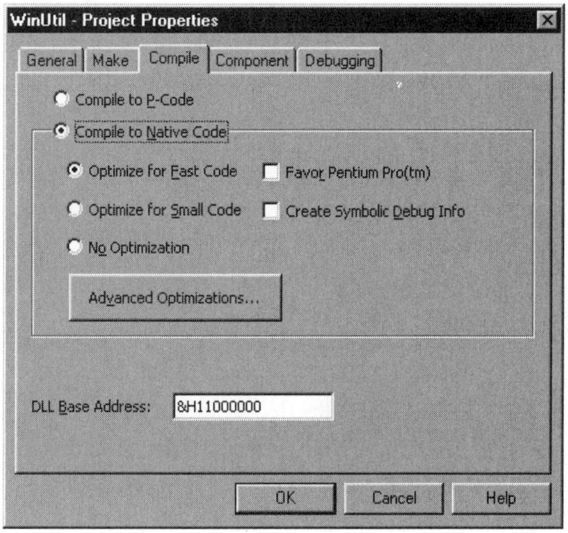

FIGURE 5.5:

Setting compile properties

Each DLL file you create for an application should have a different base address. Otherwise, Windows will need to relocate your DLL if the default base address value conflicts with an already active DLL in your address space. You should change the default value from &H11000000 to some other value, such as &H3A000000. This will help to improve the time it takes to load the DLL file at runtime. Just make sure you use a unique address for each DLL file you include to avoid DLL address conflicts.

Setting Component Options

On the Component tab, shown in Figure 5.6, you determine how changes to your COM object's interfaces are handled. There are three main choices that determine how your object relates to any programs that may use it:

- No Compatibility generates new class IDs and interface IDs each time you compile your code. This means that any existing applications that access your COM object will not be able to locate it the next time you recompile it. This is useful when you've changed the way your objects work and want to prevent older programs that referenced the objects from using them.

- Project Compatibility allows you to debug and make changes to your programs without generating new class IDs and interface IDs each time you run your program in the Visual Basic development environment. Only those classes that aren't binary compatible with the previous version will get new class IDs. The rest of the interface definitions will remain the same. (Project Compatibility worked differently in Visual Basic 5—any change in an interface would generate new class IDs and interface IDs for every class in the project.)

NOTE   To make a clean break with a previous version of your ActiveX DLL, select No Compatibility and recompile the object module. Then select Project Compatibility and recompile again. This ensures that no GUIDs from the previous object remain, but allows you to develop and test your changes under the more friendly Project Compatibility rules. If you plan to use the same name for your DLL, you should unregister your old DLL before compiling the new one to prevent the old GUID from pointing to the new DLL.

- Binary Compatibility forces Visual Basic to scan for and detect changes in the binary COM interface in the specified file. There are three different levels that can be assigned:

    Version Identical means that there were no changes to the interface.

    Version Compatible means that there were no changes to any of the previously existing interface definitions, but new objects, properties, or methods may have been added.

Version Incompatible means that there was a change to at least one of the existing interface definitions.

NOTE   Version Identical, Version Compatible, and Version Incompatible refer only to the interface, not the code behind the interface. Thus, you could completely rewrite the COM object, but as long as the interface remains identical with the previous version, it will be classified as Version Identical.

FIGURE 5.6:

Setting component compatibility

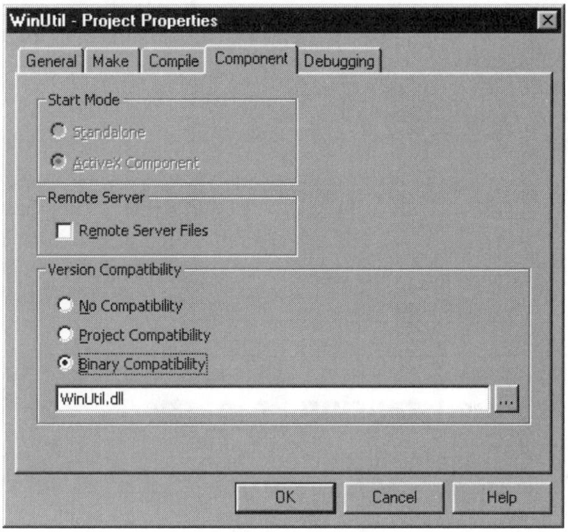

Setting Class Module Properties

Once you've set the project-level properties, you should review the properties for each class module in your ActiveX DLL. Figure 5.7 shows the class module properties for TimeInfo, with the five properties that you can change. The DataBinding-Behavior and DataSourceBehavior properties relate to database issues that I'll cover in Chapter 9. MTSTransactionMode covers how the objects will work under the COM+ transaction server, which I'll begin talking about in Chapter 10. This leaves two properties that I want to talk about here: Instancing and Persistable.

FIGURE 5.7:

Reviewing class module
properties

The Instancing Property

Instancing determines the level of availability of the COM object. This property
can have one of the following settings:

Private   Even though your object may have Public members, if
Instancing is set to Private, no programs outside your ActiveX DLL
can access it.

PublicNotCreatable   This means that programs can use the object but
can't create it. This is useful when you want to return objects containing
data to a container program, but you don't want the program to create
new instances of the object. It is also useful when you want to create an
interface that will be used by an object using the Implements keyword.

MultiUse   This means that other programs can create new instances of
your object and use them as they desire. This is the default setting in
Visual Basic.

GlobalMultiUse   This is similar to MultiUse, except that the properties and methods of the class can be used without explicitly creating an instance of the object first. Visual Basic will automatically create an instance of the object the first time it is used. Because you lose control over when this object is created, you could potentially end up with many more instances of this object than you need or want. Unless you have a specific need to use this feature, I recommend that you avoid it.

The Persistable Property

The Persistable property allows you to decide whether you want your object to keep properties between instances. If you set the property to Persistable, then the InitProperties, ReadProperties, and WriteProperties events and the PropertyChanged method are added to the class object. These tools work with the PropertyBag object to save information from one instantiation of your object to the next.

Creating the TimeInfo Class

The first class object for our project is TimeInfo. The purpose of this object is to return information about the current time zone. Primarily, we're interested in converting the local time to UTC time and back again. It's useful to know the name of the current time zone, so we'll include that information as well. Table 5.1 shows the elements of the TimeInfo interface.

TABLE 5.1: The TimeInfo Interface

Name	Type	Description
DaylightBias	Property	Returns the number of hours to add to daylight savings time to get UTC time
Refresh	Method	Updates the information in the object
StandardBias	Property	Returns the number of hours to add to standard time to get UTC time
TimeZoneName	Property	Returns the name of the time zone as configured in Windows
TimeZoneType	Property	Indicates if the time zone is currently in standard time or daylight savings time
UTCBias	Property	Indicates the current bias to be added to local time to get UTC time

TimeInfo Module-Level Declarations

Like all Visual Basic programs that use Win32 API, the TimeInfo class requires quite a few definitions in order to make the calls. These definitions are shown in Listing 5.1. Most of the definitions are required to use the GetTimeZoneInformation Win32 API routine. This includes the Const statements, the Declare Function statement, and the Type definitions.

Listing 5.1   Header information for TimeInfo

```
Option Explicit

' Win32 API Definitions

Const TIME_ZONE_ID_UNKNOWN = 0
Const TIME_ZONE_ID_STANDARD = 1
Const TIME_ZONE_ID_DAYLIGHT = 2

Private Declare Function GetTimeZoneInformation Lib _
    "kernel32" _
    (lpTimeZoneInformation As TIME_ZONE_INFORMATION) As Long

Private Type SystemTime
        Year As Integer
        Month As Integer
        DayOfWeek As Integer
        Day As Integer
        Hour As Integer
        Minute As Integer
        Second As Integer
        Milliseconds As Integer
End Type

Private Type TIME_ZONE_INFORMATION
        Bias As Long
        StandardName(31) As Integer
        StandardDate As SystemTime
        StandardBias As Long
        DaylightName(31) As Integer
        DaylightDate As SystemTime
        DaylightBias As Long
End Type
```

```
' Local information for the TimeInfo Class

Private tz As TIME_ZONE_INFORMATION
Private tztype As TimeZoneValues

Public Enum TimeZoneValues
    UnknownTime = TIME_ZONE_ID_UNKNOWN
    StandardTime = TIME_ZONE_ID_STANDARD
    DaylightSavingsTime = TIME_ZONE_ID_DAYLIGHT
End Enum
```

NOTE   For your own sanity, always use the `Option Explicit` statement at the top of each module. The variables, functions, and constants you use for Win32 API calls are long and easy to misspell. When you use `Option Explicit`, Visual Basic will let you know when an identifier hasn't been defined, which often means that you misspelled it. You can automatically add `Option Explicit` in any new modules by checking Require Variable Declaration in the Options dialog box (select Tools ➢ Options from the main menu).

To get these definitions, you can use the API Text Viewer utility included with Visual Basic, shown in Figure 5.8. You just need to enter the name of the constant, type, or function definition, and it will be displayed on the form. Then including the definition is a simple copy-and-paste operation.

WARNING   When copying the definition of the `TIME_ZONE_INFORMATION` field, you need to change the array dimension from 32 to 31 for the `StandardName` field and the `DaylightName` field. Otherwise, the API call will not work properly.

After the Win32 API definitions, we declare two variables:

- `tz` with the type `TIME_ZONE_INFORMATION`, which will hold the data retrieved from the `GetTimeZoneInformation` function

- `tztype` as `TimeZoneValues`, which will indicate whether the time zone is currently on daylight savings time or standard time

FIGURE 5.8:

The API Text Viewer

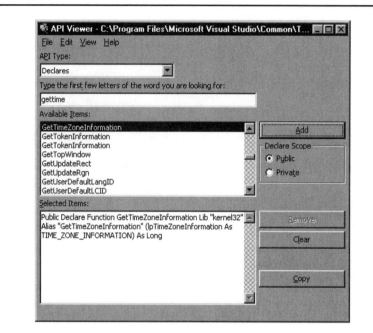

Then we define an enumerated value called TimeZoneValues, which describes whether the current time zone is daylight savings time or standard time. Because it is possible that the type of time zone may be unknown, we also include a value for unknown. These values are derived from the Win32 API constants included in Listing 5.1.

Initializing and Refreshing

When an instance of the TimeInfo object is created, the Class_Initialize event will call the Refresh method to get the time zone information from Windows. The Refresh method, shown in Listing 5.2, merely calls the GetTimeZoneInformation Win32 API routine. The return value from the function contains the type of time zone (standard time or daylight savings time). The tz argument will hold a data structure containing the rest of the time zone information.

Listing 5.2	**Getting a copy of the time zone information**

```
Public Sub Refresh()

tztype = GetTimeZoneInformation(tz)

End Sub
```

Getting the Bias

The three routines that return the number of minutes you need to add to get UTC are similar. Listing 5.3 show the routine that returns the UTC bias. Note that UTCBias simply goes to the private variable tz, which is a structure, and returns the Bias element. Because there isn't a corresponding Property Let or Property Set statement, this property is read-only.

Listing 5.3	**Getting the UTC bias**

```
Property Get UTCBias() As Long

UTCBias = tz.Bias

End Property
```

Getting the Time Zone Type

Listing 5.1 includes a user-defined type called TimeZoneValues. This type simply indicates whether the time zone is on standard time or daylight savings time. Listing 5.4 displays the code of the TimeZoneType routine. It merely converts the value tztype to the enumerated type TimeZoneValues and returns it to the calling program.

Listing 5.4	**Returning the time zone type**

```
Property Get TimeZoneType() As TimeZoneValues

TimeZoneType = tztype

End Property
```

NOTE
When defining values for a property, consider using enumerated types rather than constants. The enumerated type values will show up when the user types in code that uses your object. If the values are predefined and the user just needs to select them from a list of values rather than typing them, there is less chance for errors when entering a property value.

Getting the Time Zone Name

Getting the name of the time zone is probably the most complex part of this object, as you can see in Listing 5.5. This is mostly because of the way Windows stores text. Each character is stored as a double-byte character or integer. We use the Chr function to grab just the lower byte and append the character to a temporary string before returning it to the user.

Listing 5.5   Getting the time zone name

```
Property Get TimeZoneName() As String

Dim i As Long
Dim t As String

t = ""
If tztype = TIME_ZONE_ID_STANDARD Then
    Do While tz.StandardName(i) <> 0
        t = t & Chr(tz.StandardName(i))
        i = i + 1
    Loop

ElseIf tztype = TIME_ZONE_ID_DAYLIGHT Then
    Do While tz.DaylightName(i) <> 0
        t = t & Chr(tz.DaylightName(i))
        i = i + 1
    Loop

Else
    t = "Unknown Time Zone"
```

```
    End If

    TimeZoneName = t

    End Property
```

Creating the RunMe Class

Visual Basic allows you to run a program or execute a DOS command using the Shell function. Unfortunately, the Shell function doesn't offer many options when it comes to running a program. Hence, I decided we should include a RunMe class in WinUtil.

Table 5.2 lists the elements included in the RunMe interface. To use this object, we assign a value to FileName and then use the AssociatedProgram method to get the name of the program that would open the specified file. The ExecuteFile method opens the file in FileName using its associated program. The Execute method simply runs the executable program.

TABLE 5.2: The RunMe Interface

Name	Type	Description
AssociatedProgram	Method	Returns the filename of the program that will be executed for a given file
Error	Property	Returns the most recent error number
Execute	Method	Runs the specified program
ExecuteFile	Method	Opens the application associated with the specified file
FileName	Property	Holds the name of the program or the file you wish to execute
Priority	Property	Describes the priority of the program to be run
ProcessId	Property	Returns the process identifier of the currently running program

RunMe Module-Level Definitions

There are a number of module-level definitions for RunMe that deal strictly with the Win32 API stuff, which I won't go over here. You can look at the sample program for those details. However, there are a few definitions for private variables to the class that you need to know about:

- Fname holds the current filename.

- LastErr holds the last error encountered.

- ProcId holds the process identifier of the program just started.

- Priority supplies the default priority for starting a new process.

These module-level definitions are shown in Listing 5.6.

Listing 5.6   **Module-level definitions for RunMe**

```
Private FName As String
Private LastErr As Long
Private ProcId As Long
Private ProcessPriority As Long
```

Setting the Default Process Priority

The Priority property is implemented as a pair of Property Get/Property Let statements. This allows us to verify that the value being passed to the property is valid. Listing 5.7 shows how we check each of the possible values for process priority and set the default value only when a new value is valid. This means that we can assume that the private variable ProcessPriority always has a valid value.

Listing 5.7   **The Priority Property Let routine**

```
Public Property Let Priority() a As Long

If a = NORMAL_PRIORITY_CLASS Or _
    a = IDLE_PRIORITY_CLASS Or _
    a = HIGH_PRIORITY_CLASS Then
```

```
    ProcessPriority = a

End If

End Property
```

Returning the current value for the Priority property is merely a matter of returning the private value. Listing 5.8 shows the Property Get routine.

Listing 5.8   The Priority Property Get routine

```
Public Property Get Priority() As Long

Priority = ProcessPriority

End Property
```

Executing a Program

One of the techniques I like to use when creating methods is to take advantage of default values for parameters. The Execute method, shown in Listing 5.9, is a good example of this. It has the two parameters FileName and Priority, neither of which is required. If these values aren't supplied, then the Execute method will look to the values already set in the FName local variable (which is the FileName property) and the ProcessPriority module variable (which is the Priority property).

Listing 5.9   The Execute method

```
Public Sub Execute(Optional FileName As String, _
    Optional Priority As Long)

Dim p As PROCESS_INFORMATION
Dim s As STARTUPINFO
Dim pHandle As Long
Dim r As Long

s.cb = Len(s)
s.dwFlags = 0
```

```vb
    s.lpDesktop = vbNullString
    s.lpReserved = vbNullString
    s.lpTitle = vbNullString

    If Not IsMissing(FileName) Then
        FName = FileName
    End If

    If Not IsMissing(Priority) Then
        If Priority = NORMAL_PRIORITY_CLASS Or _
            Priority = IDLE_PRIORITY_CLASS Or _
            Priority = HIGH_PRIORITY_CLASS Then

            ProcessPriority = Priority

        End If
    End If

    LastErr = 0

    r = CreateProcess(FName, vbNullString, 0, 0, True, _
        ProcessPriority, 0, vbNullString, s, p)
    If r <> 0 Then
        r = CloseHandle(p.hThread)
        If r <> 0 Then
            r = WaitForInputIdle(p.hProcess, INFINITE)
            r = CloseHandle(p.hProcess)

        End If
    Else
        LastErr = GetLastError()

    End If

    ProcId = p.dwProcessId

End Sub
```

This routine takes advantage of the IsMissing function to determine if a parameter is missing. If it is, then we assign the value to the local variable we're using to hold the value, thus making it the default value for the next time we run the Execute method. Once we update the properties with the new values, we're ready to begin running the program.

We begin running the program by setting the LastErr local variable to zero. This assumes that everything will work properly. Next, we use the CreateProcess Win32 API to start the program specified in the module variable FName at the priority specified by the module variable ProcessPriority.

If the call to CreateProcess works fine, r will contain a nonzero value. Then we close the handle to the process and check for a nonzero value for r again. Next, we wait for the new program to finish loading by waiting for it to request input using the Win32 API call to WaitForInputIdle. If that works, then we know that everything is fine and can return. Otherwise, we set LastErr to the value of the Win32 API routine GetLastError, which the user can inquire using the Error property.

What's in a Name?

By now, you may have figured out that I don't believe in Microsoft's naming conventions for Visual Basic. I believe they are too cumbersome, because you don't really need the complete type information buried along with a variable name. In many cases, the length of the prefix can exceed the rest of the variable name, which makes it difficult to determine which variable you're using.

In general, I group variables into two different categories, depending on scope. For purely local variables, I usually use the shortest possible names, such as r for result or i for index. I do this for two reasons:

- I'm more likely to use these variables more often and in more complex expressions, which reduces the amount of typing.

- The shorter variable names lead to shorter lines, which tend to fit better in books without manually forcing a line break. Since the scope of these variables is limited to a single routine, it isn't hard to determine their meaning just by looking at the code.

Variables whose scope exceeds that of a local routine should have meaningful names that reflect their role in the program. These variables will be used in many different places, so

Continued on next page

you want to be clear about what they do and how they should be used. You may even want to include comments near the variable declaration just to make sure that you know how to properly use the variable.

Properties, methods, and parameters to both properties and methods fall into the second category. Use meaningful names! Also, remember that Visual Basic will prompt you using IntelliSense for many of these things, so using clear names is even more important when creating objects, properties, and methods than module-level variables.

Testing the ActiveX DLL

Now that you've built your class modules in one project, you will want to test your application. The best way to do this is to add a second project to your Visual Basic development session. Then you can test both the ActiveX DLL and the test program together before you compile your program into object code.

Adding Another Project

To add another project to your current development environment session, choose File ➢ Add Project. You see the familiar dialog box that allows you to create a new project or choose an existing or recent project. Select a new Standard EXE project, as shown in Figure 5.9, and click Open. You'll now have two different programs in your Visual Basic development session.

The development environment will automatically create a project group for you that encompasses both your original ActiveX DLL project and the new Standard EXE project. You can look at this new structure in the Project Explorer window, as shown in Figure 5.10. From this window, you can select any of the forms, classes, controls, and other elements and edit them directly, just as you can when you have only a single project.

Selecting Run ➢ Start from the main menu or pressing F5 will automatically start both projects. However, because the WinUtil project is the default project, trying to run the program isn't going to accomplish much. You need to change the default project from WinUtil to Project2. To do this, right-click Project2 in the Project Explorer window and choose Set as Start Up. Then run the program. This starts the `Project2` Standard EXE program, which in turn will create the COM objects from `WinUtil` as needed.

FIGURE 5.9:

Adding a new project to your development session

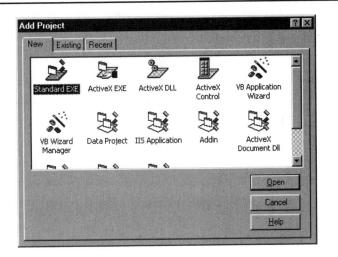

FIGURE 5.10:

Viewing your projects in the Project Explorer window

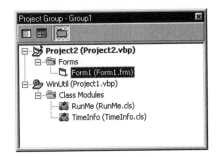

Building the Test Program

Like most test programs, the one we built here isn't fancy. It's designed mostly to demonstrate that the objects work. Our test program has two main sections, one for each object class, as shown in Figure 5.11. The `TimeInfo` section displays information about the current time zone whenever the Get Time Zone Information button is clicked. The RunMe section has three buttons, which invoke the AssociatedProgram, Execute, and ExecuteFile methods using the text box above them as input.

Adding a Reference to WinUtil

Just because your ActiveX DLL and your test program are both open at the same time in the Visual Basic development environment doesn't mean you can automatically use the objects from the ActiveX DLL. You need to explicitly include them by using the References dialog box.

Select the test program in the Project Explorer dialog box and then choose Project ➤ References to display the References dialog box, shown in Figure 5.12. The references that have a check mark are the COM objects that are available in your application. The first four—Visual Basic For Applications, Visual Basic runtime objects and procedures, Visual Basic objects and procedures, and OLE Automation—are selected by default. Attempting to remove any but OLE Automation will cause an error.

Immediately after these references will be the ActiveX DLLs included in your current project group, listed by their project name. In this case, all we need to do is to put a check mark next to WinUtil and click OK to make the object references available to the test program.

FIGURE 5.12:

Adding WinUtil to the text
program

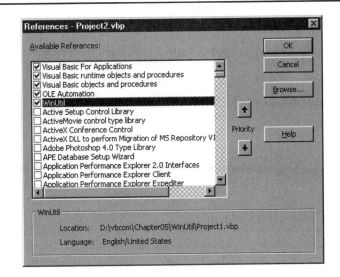

Using the TimeInfo Object

Clicking the Get Time Zone Information button triggers the Command1_Click
event shown in Listing 5.10. This routine begins by creating a new instance of the
TimeInfo object using the tinfo object variable. When the new instance of the
object is created, it will automatically initialize itself with the current information
about the time zone. This allows us to immediately pull the name of the current
time zone from the TimeZoneName property and display it in the Text1 text box.
We display the bias to UTC from the UTCBias property in the Text2 text box.

Listing 5.10	The Command1_Click event

```
Private Sub Command1_Click()

Dim tinfo As TimeInfo

Set tinfo = New TimeInfo

Text1.Text = tinfo.TimeZoneName

Text2.Text = FormatNumber(tinfo.UTCBias, 0)
```

```
Set tinfo = Nothing

End Sub
```

When we're finished with the `TimeInfo` object, we set `tinfo` to `Nothing` to free the resources owned by the object. While this isn't strictly necessary, it is good form. However, if we didn't explicitly release the object, Visual Basic would automatically decrement the reference counter when the end of the routine is reached as part of returning from the routine. Because there was only the one reference to the object, the object would automatically be deleted.

Using the RunMe Object

All three of the `CommandButton` events are similar to each other, so I'll talk only about the `Execute` example. You can look at the sample program to see how the `AssociatedProg` and `ExecuteFile` methods work.

In Listing 5.11, you can see that we just create a new instance of the `RunMe` object in the `Dim` statement. Compare this to Listing 5.10, where we define the object variable using the `Dim` statement and use the `Set` statement to create an instance of it with the `New` keyword. Both ways are acceptable; which you choose is up to you.

NOTE   If your object has events, such as the example in Chapter 4, you must include the `WithEvents` keyword in the `Dim` statement and use a separate `Set` statement with the `New` keyword to create an instance of the object. The `New` keyword is illegal in the `Dim` statement.

Listing 5.11   **The Command3_Click event**

```
Private Sub Command3_Click()

Dim p As New RunMe

p.Execute Text3.Text

Set p = Nothing

End Sub
```

This routine includes the name of the file (from the Text3 text box) as part of the call to the method, but not the value for priority. Looking at Figure 5.13, you can see how Visual Basic will prompt you for the parameters for the method. This is why picking meaningful names for your parameters is important. The right names will make a world of difference to anyone using your DLL.

FIGURE 5.13:

Visual Basic will automatically prompt you for the method's parameters.

Using the ActiveX DLL

Once you've tested your ActiveX DLL and you're satisfied that it works properly, you're ready to begin using it. However, before you begin using it in regular applications there a few steps you need to take first. You need to compile your ActiveX DLL, register it, and then add it to a project. While these steps may be obvious to many of you, I want to take some time to go over them and offer some new insights into the process.

Compiling the ActiveX DLL

Compiling your ActiveX DLL isn't much different from compiling a regular Visual Basic program. The only complicating factor is that you need to choose which project you want to compile from the Project Explorer window first; then you can choose File ➢ Make WinUtil.DLL (or Make whatever project name you used) from the main menu. Also, there will be a File ➢ Make Project Group menu item, which will compile every project in the Visual Basic development environment.

After you start to compile your DLL, you'll be prompted for the name of the file where the object code will be saved, as shown in Figure 5.14. Choosing a filename and pressing OK finishes the compilation process.

FIGURE 5.14:

Compiling your ActiveX DLL

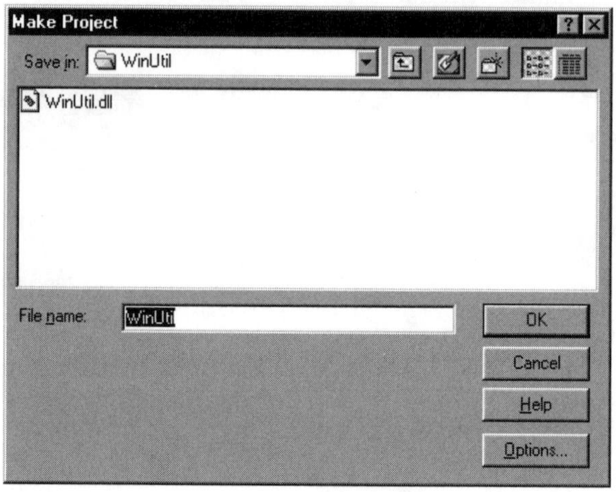

In the Make Project window, notice the button in the lower-right corner labeled Options. Clicking this button will display the Make and Compile tabs of the Project Properties dialog box, discussed earlier in this chapter. This is an excellent time to review the version number associated with this build, especially if you didn't check the Auto Increment check box earlier.

Registering Your ActiveX DLL

When you compile your ActiveX DLL, all of the necessary entries into the Windows Registry are made automatically, so you can begin using your DLL immediately on the same machine you used to compile it. However, if you plan to use the DLL on another machine, you need to add all of the appropriate entries into the Registry. This is done using the RegSvr32 program.

The RegSvr32 program calls the DLLRegisterServer routine that is included in most COM objects. You don't need to worry about this routine, because Visual Basic automatically includes it when it creates the DLL. This routine contains all of the necessary information to create the entries in the Registry.

To register your ActiveX DLL manually, simply choose Start ➤ Run and enter **RegSvr32**, followed by the filename of your ActiveX DLL, something like this:

```
RegSvr32 d:\VBCOM\Chapter05\WinUtil\WinUtil.DLL
```

You'll see a message box letting you know if the DLL was registered.

NOTE   I often find myself using the `Dir` command to look for a file in a directory or the `MkDir` command to create a new directory. (Old habits die hard, I guess.) Like those commands, the RegSvr32 utility just begs to be run from a DOS window. Of course, others may argue that it's easier to simply select Start ➤ Run, type **RegSvr32**, and drag and drop the file you want to register into the Run dialog box.

If you're finished with the ActiveX control, you clean up the Registry entries it added by using the same command, but adding the /U option, as shown below.

```
RegSvr32 /u d:\VBCOM\Chapter05\WinUtil\WinUtil.DLL
```

As before, a message box will appear with the results of the process.

The RegSrv32 program includes several other command-line options. You can display the complete list by running RegSvr32 without any additional options. The /S option is useful if you want to call the RegSvr32 program from your setup program. This option will suppress all of the message boxes when the program is run.

Adding Your ActiveX DLL to a New Program

Now that the DLL is ready to use, it's a simple matter to add it to your Visual Basic application. Select Project ➤ References from the main menu to display the list of COM objects that you can use in your Visual Basic program. (Figure 5.12, earlier in the chapter, shows the References dialog box.)

To add your ActiveX DLL, search the list looking for the value you supplied in the Project Description field of the General tab of the ActiveX DLL's Project Properties dialog box. (If you didn't supply a value for this field, Visual Basic will use your project name by default.) If you don't see it, don't panic. You can click the Browse button and locate the physical file on your hard disk using the Add Reference dialog box, shown in Figure 5.15. Clicking OK will add the reference to the list of references and also place a check mark next to it. Now you're ready to begin programming.

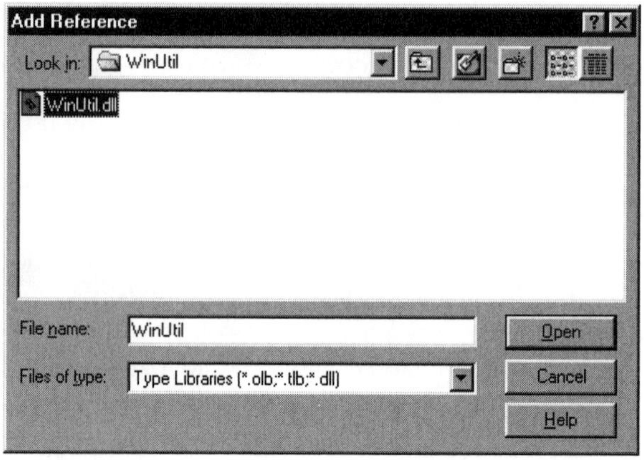

FIGURE 5.15:

Adding a new COM object
to your project

Final Thoughts

Using ActiveX DLL files in your application is a good idea for several reasons:

- Your application is more modular. You can modify one of the DLL files without needing to change others that are not affected by the modification. This also means that you only need to distribute the changed files, rather than the entire application.

- Other programming languages, such as Visual C++ or Visual FoxPro, can use your DLL files. Because ActiveX DLL files are binary-compatible, you can choose the best programming language for the task at hand.

- Because you can dynamically load an object in an ActiveX DLL by using the `CreateObject` function, you can create applications that have optional components. If the `CreateObject` function fails at runtime, you can continue running your application without the optional component.

CHAPTER

SIX

6

Creating ActiveX Controls

- ActiveX control characteristics

- The UserControl object

- A sample ActiveX control

- Property pages

- An About box for an ActiveX control

The programmers' dream after Microsoft added support for VBXs back in Visual Basic 3 was to be able to build their own controls. They wouldn't be limited to just those controls that Microsoft chose to include in Visual Basic, and they wouldn't need to buy somebody else's controls. Yet now that this capability is available, I believe that most programmers don't bother.

This chapter explains how to create your own ActiveX controls using Visual Basic. After you've seen how easy it is to create your own controls, you will definitely want to take advantage of this capability.

What Makes an ActiveX Control Different?

Unlike an ActiveX DLL, which is primarily a collection of objects with their properties and methods, an ActiveX control is designed to provide a plug-in component that can be easily added to a Visual Basic form, just like the controls Microsoft includes with Visual Basic. Also unlike an ActiveX DLL, an ActiveX control has both a runtime aspect and a design-time aspect. You need to be able to handle issues such as resizing your control, setting and remembering property values, and using property pages. ActiveX controls are also implemented in Visual Basic using a User-Control object rather a regular class object. Yet under the wrappers, an ActiveX control is still a regular COM object.

ActiveX Control Project Properties

When you consider that the only real difference between an ActiveX control and an ActiveX DLL is how they are used in your program, you shouldn't be surprised that the project properties are identical. After all, ActiveX controls and ActiveX DLLs are both in-process COM objects.

All of the trade-offs I talked about in Chapter 5 apply equally to an ActiveX control and an ActiveX DLL. The one exception is a license key.

License Keys

Let's assume that you've built a useful ActiveX control. Now you want to distribute it to others. You have all the copyright information included in the actual object code, but you may want a little extra protection. Microsoft added a feature called a *license key*, which allows you to prevent others from using your ActiveX control in their own programs without your permission.

By default, ActiveX controls are unrestricted. This means that anyone can use them in any fashion, including programmers who may add the control to their Visual Basic projects and distribute the control as part of their applications. By checking the Require License Key check box on the General tab of the Project Properties dialog box, as shown in Figure 6.1, you can prevent anyone from using the control improperly. When the control is initialized, it will check to see if it is properly licensed. If it isn't, an error message will be displayed and the control won't operate.

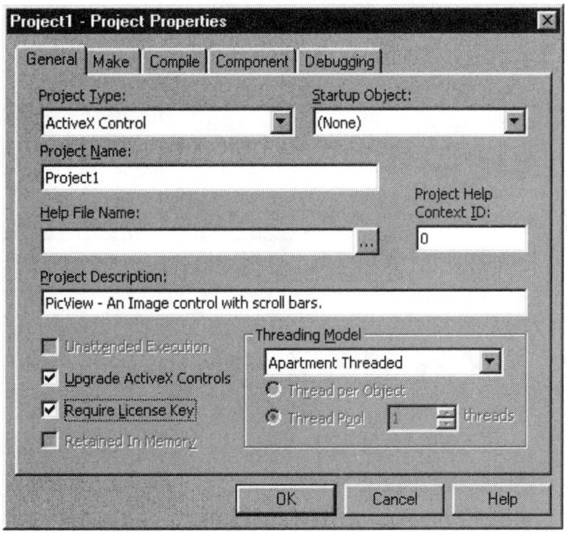

FIGURE 6.1:

Check the Require License Key check box on the General tab of the Project Properties dialog box to prevent improper use of your control.

NOTE   Licensing requirements work both ways. If you are building your ActiveX control using other ActiveX controls, you must make sure that you have the right to redistribute the other controls to your clients. Any control supplied in the Professional Edition of Visual Basic may be redistributed as part of another control (except for the DBGrid control), as long as you meet Microsoft legal requirements for redistribution (that is, you must add significant and primary functionality to your control; see the Microsoft licensing agreement for complete details).

The license key is stored in either the Windows Registry or in the program that is using the control. If the license key is stored in the Registry, any program on that system may use that control. Otherwise, the key must be stored in each application that uses the control. This happens automatically when you compile your application.

If you are distributing only the ActiveX control, the Package and Deployment Wizard will automatically generate a .VBL file that will hold the license key. When the user runs the setup program, the license key will be added to the Windows Registry automatically.

WARNING   Don't give away the key. Installing the licensing key into the Registry allows the person to redistribute your control. Be certain you want to let the user have the right to redistribute your control before you install the license key into the Registry.

The UserControl Object

An ActiveX control is based on the UserControl object. This object has features from both a Form object and Class object. Many of the properties, methods, and events you have in the Form object carry over to the UserControl object. This is because the UserControl object presents a visual interface for a user to interact with. As with a class object, you can create your own properties by using Property Get, Property Let, and Property Set routines. You can also define your own events by using the Event statement. To implement methods, you create regular subroutines and functions.

Containers, Constituents, and Other Stuff

Although an ActiveX control may resemble a Form object, an ActiveX control cannot exist by itself. It must exist in some kind of *control container*.

The most common control container is the Form object, but other controls, such as the Picture control and the Frame control, can serve as control containers. You also can take advantage of any other ActiveX or intrinsic controls. These controls are known as *constituent controls*. By using constituent controls as building blocks, you can create your own specialized controls or create new controls with more functionality. Of course, if you desire, you also can create your own control from scratch using the elements of the UserControl object.

Many of the properties, methods, and events associated with the UserControl object aren't under your direct control. These elements come from the container of the control and are known as Extender properties, methods, and events. The exact set of elements will vary from container to container. You can access this information via the Extender object.

> **NOTE**
>
> If there is a conflict between an Extender property or method and one of the properties or methods you include in your control, the Extender element will override the one your wrote.

The AmbientProperties object provides information about the container object. This information is useful because it gives you hints about how the control's container looks. This allows you to set property values that are similar to those in the container (such as fonts and colors). It also provides information for the control to use, such as the control's name and how the control is being used.

UserControl Properties, Methods, and Events

The UserControl object implements a number of properties, methods, and events. Many of these are familiar to you, but quite a few are new. Rather than go through these elements one at a time, I've grouped them together in terms of the functions they perform.

The Design-time Life Cycle

When someone attempts to incorporate your control into a program, a number of things happen. The sequence below outlines the various design-time events that are triggered and the kinds of actions your program should take:

1. UserControl_Initialize occurs when an instance of your control is created. This can happen many times during a development session.

2a. UserControl_InitProperties occurs when the control is placed on a Form or in another container for the first time. You should use this event to set all of your property values to their default values.

2b. Once the control has been created and the properties have been initialized, the UserControl_ReadProperties event occurs in place of the UserControl_InitProperties event. You should restore the current properties for the control from the PropertyBag object.

3. UserControl_Resize occurs each time that the control is created or its size changes. If you need to rearrange or resize the constituent controls, this is the place to do it.

4. UserControl_Paint occurs each time that the control needs to be redrawn.

5. UserControl_WriteProperties occurs each time that Visual Basic wants to save the property values. This may happen just before the container program is run or simply because the user has clicked the Save button.

6. UserControl_Terminate occurs just before the control is destroyed.

During the course of a development session, instances of your control will be created many times. Each time someone opens a form with your control on it, resizes the control on the form, or simply sees what it looks like, a new instance of your control is created.

TIP You can check the UserMode property of the AmbientProperties object to determine if the control is being used at design-time by a programmer or at run-time by a user.

The runtime life cycle pretty much follows the design-time life cycle, including the `ReadProperties` event, which is used to initialize the control. The `WriteProperties` event never occurs, however, because there isn't a need to save the property values after executing your program.

Transparent Background

One of the nicer features of an ActiveX control is the ability to draw a control that has any shape. The trick is that the control still resides in a rectangular window, but you can make the background of the control invisible, allowing other controls to show through.

Setting the `BackStyle` property to `Invisible` (or the value 2) allows anything that is drawn behind the control to show through. The `MaskPicture` property contains an image that is drawn in two colors: the color specified by `MaskColor` determines the locations that should be drawn as transparent, and the color specified by `BackColor` determines which part of the image should be displayed on the screen. The image itself is stored in the `Picture` property of `UserControl`. Note that you must set `WindowLess` to `True` for this to work.

Transparent backgrounds cause complications because you are now responsible for determining when the mouse is over your control and when it isn't. Using the `HitBehavior` property determines how your control will respond to mouse events. You can force all mouse events to be handled by the control's container by specifying a value of 0. A value of 1 means that Windows should send only those mouse events that occur where the `MaskPicture` is set to `MaskColor`. When `HitBehavior` has a value of 2, it means that mouse events will be triggered in the control when the mouse is over any areas that have been painted.

The `HitTest` event works with the `HitBehavior` property to provide more information about how to handle mouse events. This event occurs when the mouse pointer is over the rectangular window associated with your control. You have three choices:

- You can decide if the cursor is over the actual control. In this case, the mouse messages will be received by your control.

- You can decide that the mouse is outside your control. In this case, the mouse messages are passed to a control that is beneath your control in `ZOrder`.

- You can decide that the mouse is close to your control, but not over it. In this case, Windows will pass the mouse messages to the control beneath yours. If none of these controls accepts the mouse message, Windows will redirect the message to the topmost control in the ZOrder that returns a close hit.

The ClipBehavior property determines how the various painting tools work on your control. If ClipBehavior is set to 0, you can draw anywhere inside the rectangular area of the control. When ClipBehavior is set to 1, Windows will draw on only those areas in MaskPicture where the color is set to MaskColor.

The AmbientProperties Object

The AmbientProperties object contains a set of suggestions from the control's container for various property values in your control. For instance, the Back-Color property contains the suggested background color for your control. Note that you don't need to use this information, but it may be helpful to the programmer using your control.

NOTE The AmbientProperties object is not available when the UserControl_Initialize event is triggered, but it is available when the UserControl_InitProperties and UserControl_ReadProperties events are fired.

Not all of these properties are implemented in all control containers, but reasonable default values will be returned if the property isn't available. Some of the more interesting properties are listed below.

BackColor/ForeColor   Provides standard color settings for your control.

DisplayName   Contains the name your control should display when it issues an error message. Typically, this is the name of the control as specified by the user.

Font   Contains a Font object with recommended defaults for your control. For instance, if a programmer changed the default font information on a Form object, this information would be made available to your control, so you could use the same font, rather than the font you chose at design time.

LocaleId   Contains the locale identifier for the control's container.

TextAlign   Describes how any text should be aligned in your control.

UIDead   Is True when Visual Basic doesn't want your control to respond to messages. Typically, this occurs when programmers are debugging their program and have entered break mode.

UserMode   Is True when the control is being used at runtime. False means that the control is being used at design time.

The Extender Object

Many of the properties, methods, and events a programmer will see in your ActiveX control don't come from your control, but are supplied by the control's container. These are known as Extender properties, methods, and events.

You can reference these properties and methods by using the UserControl .Extender property. Like the AmbientProperties object, the Extender object isn't available until the InitProperties or ReadProperties event occurs.

The actual properties that are available from the Extender object will vary depending on the control's container. If there is a conflict between an Extender property and one you explicitly coded into your control, the Extender will always take precedence. The following properties always will be available from the Extender object, no matter what the control's container is:

Cancel   Is True when the control is the default cancel control for the container.

Default   Is True when the control is the default control for the container.

Enabled   Is True when the control will respond to user requests.

Name   Contains the name of the control, as defined by the programmer.

Parent   Contains an object reference to the control's container.

Visible   Is True when the control is visible to the user.

The Form object contains a number of other properties that are available from the Extender object. Note that with the exception of Height and Width, none of these properties are available for the user control at design time.

CausesValidation   Is True if shifting to another control should cause a Validation event.

`Container` Returns an object reference to the control's container.

`Height` Contains the height of the control.

`Index` Contains the index of the control when the control is a member of a control array.

`Left` Contains the relative placement of the control from the left edge of the control's container.

`Object` Returns an object reference to the `UserControl` object without the properties and methods from the `Extension` object.

`Parent` Returns an object reference to the control's container.

`TabIndex` Contains the relative position of the control in the container's tab order.

`TabStop` Is `True` if the tab should stop on this control.

`Tag` Contains user-defined data associated with a particular instance of the control.

`ToolTipText` Contains a string that should be displayed when the mouse cursor hovers over the control for a second or so.

`Top` Contains the relative placement of the control from the top edge of the control's container.

`WhatsThisHelpID` Contains a context ID reference for a help file.

`Width` Contains the width of the control.

TIP
If one of the **Extender** properties overrides a property or method you created in your control, you can always use the **Object** property to access your own code rather than the **Extender**'s routine.

In addition to the above properties, there are a number of methods that are available, including `Drag`, `Move`, `SetFocus`, `ShowWhatsThis`, and `ZOrder`. Also, the `Extender` object manages the following events: `DragDrop`, `DragOver`, `GotFocus`, `LostFocus`, and `Validate`.

Building a Simple ActiveX Control

I've always thought that Visual Basic should include an image control with scroll bars. This control would display any size image in a fixed area, and we would not need to worry about resizing the image to fit the window. It would also be dynamically resizable so that it could be placed on a separate form and resized as the user desires. Of course, this control should have its own property pages and an About dialog box, just like any other control. It should support the same properties, methods, and events that are available in most common controls.

I call this control PicView. As you might guess, it is based on the Image, HScroll, and VScroll intrinsic controls supplied with Visual Basic.

> **NOTE**   The source code for the PicView control can be downloaded from the Sybex web site at **www.sybex.com** or from my web site at **www.JustPC.com**.

Designing the PicView Control

The first step in building a control is deciding which properties, methods, and events you want your control to support. In this case, we essentially want to replace the Image control with one that includes a little more functionality. Table 6.1 lists the key properties of the PicView control.

TABLE 6.1: The PicView Interface

Name	Type	Description
Click	Event	Occurs when the user presses the left mouse button while the cursor is over the control
HLargeChange	Property	The value added to or subtracted from HValue when the user clicks the area between the scroll bar slider and a scroll arrow
HMin	Property	The value associated with the extreme left position of the scroll bar
HMax	Property	The value associated with the extreme right position of the scroll bar

Continued on next page

TABLE 6.1 CONTINUED: The PicView Interface

Name	Type	Description
HScroll	Event	Occurs whenever the scroll button is moved
HSmallChange	Property	The value added to or subtracted from HValue when the user clicks a scroll arrow
HValue	Property	Determines the relative position of the horizontal scroll bar
ImageHeight	Property	Returns the total height of the image
ImageWidth	Property	Returns the total width of the image
LoadPic	Method	Loads an image into the control from a disk file
Picture	Property	Sets or returns a reference to the underlying Image control's Picture property
Refresh	Property	Refreshes the image displayed in the control
RightClick	Event	Occurs when the user presses the right mouse button while the cursor is over the control
Scroll	Event	Occurs whenever the image is scrolled (called after HScroll or VScroll)
Stretch	Property	Stretches the image to fill the space available in the control
VLargeChange	Property	The value added to or subtracted from VValue when the user clicks the area between the scroll bar slider and a scroll arrow
VMin	Property	The value associated with the extreme top position of the scroll bar
VMax	Property	The value associated with the extreme bottom position of the scroll bar
VScroll	Event	Occurs whenever the scroll button is moved
VSmallChange	Property	The value added to or subtracted from VValue when the user clicks a scroll arrow
VValue	Property	Determines the relative position of the vertical scroll bar

As you can see, many of the properties, methods, and events are derived from the Image, HScroll, and VScroll controls. For instance, the HScroll and VScroll events are really just the Scroll events from the HScroll and VScroll controls, just like the Picture property is derived from the Image control's Picture property.

I've also included properties that will let the client program determine the actual size of the image (ImageHeight and ImageWidth). This kind of information can be useful to application developers, who may want to adjust the size of the image based on their application's requirements.

The Stretch property basically sets the Stretch property in the underlying Image control, so that the entire image fills the PicView control. Simply set the Stretch property to True to fill the control; set it to False to restore the image to its normal size.

I've added a LoadPicture routine that will let you load an image from a disk file using the LoadPic method.

Just to make things more interesting, I've added a routine, called RightClick, which I wish Microsoft would include with its controls. While I know that it's easy to use the MouseUp event to detect when the user has pressed the right mouse button, this type of event raises a few interesting issues when building an ActiveX control. I'll talk about those issues a little later, when I discuss the RightClick routine in more detail.

Drawing the PicView Control

The PicView control consists of four Visual Basic intrinsic controls: Image, HScrollBar, VScrollBar, and CommandButton. These controls are placed on the UserControl window, as shown in Figure 6.2.

The trick to making this control work is to load an image into the Image control and then use the boundaries of the UserControl object to clip the edges of the image, so that only the part of the image the user wants to see is visible. The scroll bars and the command button float on top of the Image control.

In many applications, you can leave the area between the horizontal and vertical scroll bars blank. However, in this case, leaving that area blank will allow the Image control underneath to show through. The easiest solution to this problem is to add a small control in the corner where the scroll bars meet. I like to use a CommandButton control because its 3D effect looks pretty, plus I can use it to toggle the Stretch property.

FIGURE 6.2:

Drawing the PicView control

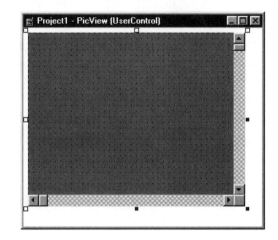

Of course, every control should have its own unique icon that will be displayed in the toolbox. This icon isn't really an icon—it's merely a bitmap file. You can use any 16 × 15 pixel .BMP, .JPG, or .GIF file you choose. Simply create the image using your favorite drawing package and then assign it to the ToolboxBitmap property of the UserControl object.

Coding the PicView Control

The PicView control is a relatively simple control, with most of the code devoted to setting and returning property values from the controls it is made up from. The only parts of the code that are more than a couple of statements long are those devoted to stretching the image, changing the size of the control, and scrolling.

Module-Level Declarations

The module-level declarations for the PicView control are shown in Listing 6.1.

Listing 6.1   **The PicView module-level definitions**

```
Option Explicit

Const ScrollBarSize = 255
```

```
Private PicHeight As Single
Private PicWidth As Single
Private VBar As Single
Private HBar As Single
Private Stretched As Boolean

Event Click()
Event HScroll()
Event RightClick()
Event Scroll()
Event VScroll()
```

We save the full size of the image in the Image control in the PicHeight and PicWidth variables once the image has been loaded. This means that we can change the size of the Image control and always be able to restore it to what it was originally.

The VBar and HBar variables are used to hold the current width of the vertical and horizontal scroll bars. If the scroll bar is invisible, then we set the corresponding variable to zero; otherwise, this value will hold the value from the Scroll-BarSize constant.

NOTE   Sometimes I find it useful to keep a copy of a property of an object in a module-level or local variable. In the case of VBar and HBar, these values can be derived from the properties of the VScroll and HScroll controls. However, getting this information requires a couple of lines of code and checking two different properties. Keeping a local copy of these values means that they can be accessed with much less overhead and also simplifies the code required to use the information.

Finally, the Stretched variable holds the state of Stretch property. True means that the image will be stretched to fit the entire area of the UserControl object, and False means that the image will be shown in normal size.

Loading the Image

The LoadPic method is used to load an image file into the Image control using the LoadPicture function, as shown in Listing 6.2. We use the optional parameter feature to let the application programmer call the LoadPic without a filename to load an empty image into the control.

Listing 6.2   **The LoadPic method**

```
Public Sub LoadPic(Optional PictureFile As String)

Image1.Stretch = False
Stretched = False

If IsMissing(PictureFile) Then
   Image1.Picture = LoadPicture()

Else
   Image1.Picture = LoadPicture(PictureFile)

End If

PicHeight = Image1.Height
PicWidth = Image1.Width

Reposition

End Sub
```

This routine begins by setting the Image1.Stretch property to False. This means that the first time an image is loaded, it will always be shown normally. Since the Stretched variable mirrors the value of the Stretch property, we need to set that variable to False also.

Next, we call the appropriate LoadPicture routine, depending on whether a value was passed in PictureFile. Then we save the image's height and width into PicHeight and PicWidth. Finally, we call the Reposition routine to adjust the scroll bars and other nice things, as explained in the next section.

Repositioning the Control

The Reposition routine, shown in Listing 6.3, is an internal routine used in a number of different places within the control to recompute various aspects of how the control is sized and displayed. Although this routine was designed primarily to be called by the Resize event, we end up calling it whenever the size of the Image1 control changes.

Listing 6.3   The Reposition subroutine

```
Private Sub Reposition()

If (PicWidth > UserControl.Width - VBar) _
    Or Image1.Left < 0 _
    Or Stretched Then

    HScroll1.Visible = True
    HBar = ScrollBarSize

Else
    HScroll1.Visible = False
    HBar = 0

End If

If (PicHeight > UserControl.Height - HBar) Or _
    (Image1.Top < 0) Or _
    Stretched Then

    VScroll1.Visible = True
    VBar = ScrollBarSize

Else
    VScroll1.Visible = False
    VBar = 0

End If

HScroll1.Top = UserControl.Height - HBar
HScroll1.Width = UserControl.Width - VBar

VScroll1.Left = UserControl.Width - VBar
VScroll1.Height = UserControl.Height - HBar

Command1.Top = HScroll1.Top
Command1.Left = VScroll1.Left

End Sub
```

The `Reposition` routine begins by determining if the horizontal scroll bar should be displayed. The scroll bar should be displayed if the width of the image is greater than the width of the control, less the width of the vertical scroll bar. However, the scroll bar should not be displayed if the `Image` control is even with the left edge of the control or the image has been stretched to fill the control. Displaying the scroll bar is merely a matter of setting the `HScroll1.Visible` property to `True` and setting `HBar` to `ScrollBarSize`. Hiding the scroll bar is accomplished by setting the `Visible` property to `False` and `HBar` to zero.

After we apply the same logic to the vertical scroll bar, we need to adjust the sizes and positions of the scroll bars and the command button. If `HBar` is zero, then the horizontal scroll bar will be placed outside the edge of the `UserControl`, where it won't be visible to the user. If `HBar` is greater than zero, the scroll bar will be displayed inside the visible part of the `UserControl` and aligned with the bottom edge.

We do the same thing with the vertical scroll bar and then locate the command button at the corner of the two scroll bars. Thus, the command button will be visible only if both scroll bars are visible.

Scrolling the Image

We use the same basic logic for scrolling the image with both the horizontal scroll bar and the vertical scroll bar, so I'm just going to cover the vertical scroll bar. This routine is shown in Listing 6.4.

Listing 6.4   The VScroll1_Change event

```
Private Sub VScroll1_Change()

Dim gap As Single
Dim Scroll As Single

gap = Image1.Height - UserControl.Height + HBar
Scroll = VScroll1.Value / VScroll1.Max
Image1.Top = -(gap * Scroll)

RaiseEvent VScroll
RaiseEvent Scroll

End Sub
```

Basically, this routine needs to adjust the Top property of the Image control based on the relative value of the scroll bar slider. We do this by computing the size of the image that isn't displayed and saving the result in gap. Then we compute the percentage (Scroll) that value must be scrolled by taking the ratio of the Value and Max properties. Finally, we multiply the two values together and make it negative, so that we'll move the Image control up relative to the top of the UserControl.

After we adjust the image, we fire the VScroll and Scroll events. This lets the client program know whenever the user moves the image in the control.

Stretching the Image

Stretching the image mostly involves setting the Stretch property of the Image control. However, I decided that whenever the user stretches the image, we need to move the image so that the upper-left corner is in the upper-left corner of the control. This ensures that the entire image is visible. This Property Let routine is shown in Listing 6.5.

Listing 6.5   **The Stretch Property Let routine**

```
Property Let Stretch(s As Boolean)

Stretched = s

If Stretched Then
    Image1.Top = 0
    Image1.Left = 0
    VScroll1.Value = 0
    HScroll1.Value = 0
    Image1.Width = UserControl.Width - HBar
    Image1.Height = UserControl.Height - VBar
    Image1.Stretch = True

Else
    Image1.Height = PicHeight
    Image1.Width = PicWidth
    Image1.Stretch = False

End If

End Property
```

Here, we receive the new value for Stretch and save it into Stretched. Then if we need to stretch the image, we move the image to the upper-left corner of the control by setting the Top and Left properties to zero. Then we need to set the scroll bar Value properties to zero, or the sliders won't match the image's new position. Finally, we reset the Image control's Height and Width properties to match the available space on the control and set the Stretch property to True.

To undo the stretch operation, we merely restore the image's real height and width from PicHeight and PicWidth, respectively, and set the Image1.Stretch property to False.

Right-Clicking Away

Detecting a right-click is easy. You simply use the Mouseup event to determine when the user released a mouse button and fire the event for the appropriate button, as shown in Listing 6.6. However, this isn't the entire solution when building a UserControl.

Listing 6.6   The UserControl_Mouseup event

```
Private Sub UserControl_Mouseup(Button As Integer, _
   Shift As Integer, X As Single, Y As Single)

If Button = vbRightButton Then
   RaiseEvent RightClick

ElseIf Button = vbLeftButton Then
   RaiseEvent Click

End If

End Sub
```

A UserControl object works just like a Form object in that the UserControl's Mouseup event will be triggered only when the mouse pointer is directly over an unoccupied part of the control. Since it's quite likely that the Image1 control will occupy the entire area of the control (or at least the area remaining after the scroll bars and the command button), we need to trap the Mouseup event in the Image control as well. Since we already have the code to handle `Mouseup` event in the `UserControl` object, we merely pass the same values to the `UserControl_Mouseup` routine, as shown in Listing 6.7. This also means that if we change how the event is processed in the future, we only need to change one event.

Listing 6.7   **The Image1_Mouseup event**

```
Private Sub Image1_Mouseup(Button As Integer, _
    Shift As Integer, X As Single, Y As Single)

UserControl_Mouseup Button, Shift, X, Y

End Sub
```

Adding Information about Your Properties, Methods, and Events

When you use the Object Browser, you will notice that most properties, methods, and events include a short description of what they are and how they work. Figure 6.3 shows an example of this information for one of the `PicView` control's properties.

It's easy to add descriptions using the Procedure Attributes tool. To start the Procedure Attributes tool, make sure your control is visible on your display. Then select Tools ➢ Procedure Attributes from the main menu. This brings up the Procedure Attributes dialog box, shown in Figure 6.4. Choose the name of the property, method, or event from the Name drop-down list and then add your description in the Description box.

If you have created a help file that provides information about your control, you can fill in the Project Help File and Help Context ID boxes in the Procedure Attributes dialog box. Then when someone clicks the Help button, Visual Basic can display the help information for your control.

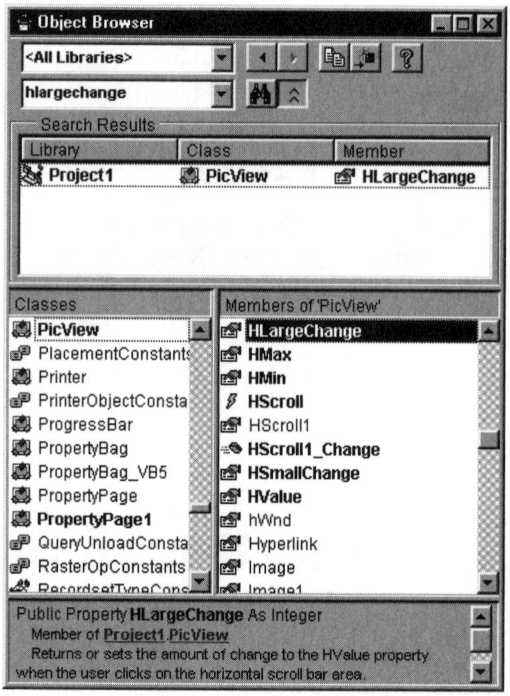

FIGURE 6.3:

Viewing information about
a property in the Object
Browser

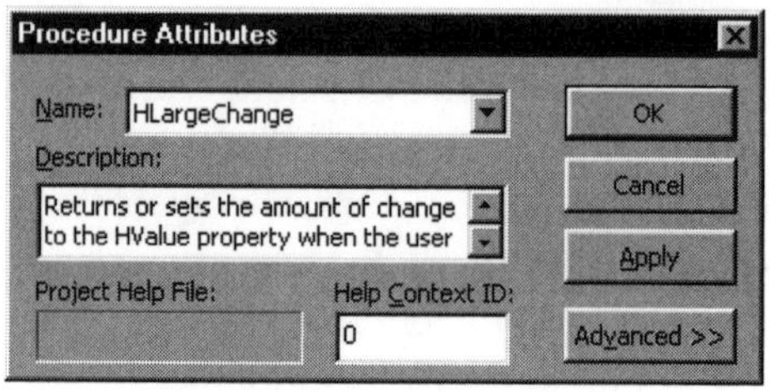

FIGURE 6.4:

Using the Procedure Attributes dialog box

Creating Property Pages

Property pages are an easier way for a Visual Basic programmer to view and set
properties for an ActiveX control. In some cases, the property pages merely

provide a prettier way to enter information than the Properties window. In other cases, the only way that you can enter a value for a property is to use a property page.

By using property pages, you can verify that the values programmers enter are correct. You can also provide visual cues to programmers that will help them set up the proper relationship between multiple properties.

NOTE   A good example is worth 1,024 bytes. You are probably familiar with the Microsoft Windows Common Controls in Visual Basic, especially if you've ever used the `Toolbar` control. Take a look at the property pages associated with that control for some ideas about how you might implement your own property pages.

Using Standard Property Pages

Visual Basic includes four standard property pages that allow the programmer to enter information about pictures, colors, fonts, and data formats. You can easily add any of these four property pages to your control project by viewing the Properties window, selecting the `PropertyPages` property, and clicking the ellipsis at the end of the entry. The Connect Property Pages dialog box appears, as shown in Figure 6.5.

FIGURE 6.5:

Connecting standard property pages to your control

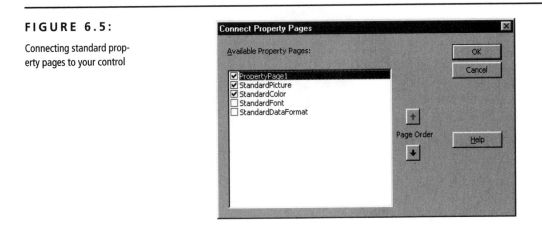

This dialog box lists all of the available property pages in your project. Simply check the property pages you want to display. However, merely checking the standard property pages isn't sufficient. If you displayed one of these property pages for your control now, you would see a window with a lot of blank spaces. You need to associate the property with the appropriate property page by using the Procedure Attributes dialog box.

In the Procedure Attributes dialog box, select the property you want to modify and click the Advanced button to display the entire dialog box. Then choose the property page you want to be associated with this property from the Use this Page in Property Browser drop-down list. Figure 6.6 shows the dialog box with the Picture property and StandardPicture property page selected.

FIGURE 6.6:

Assigning a property to a property page

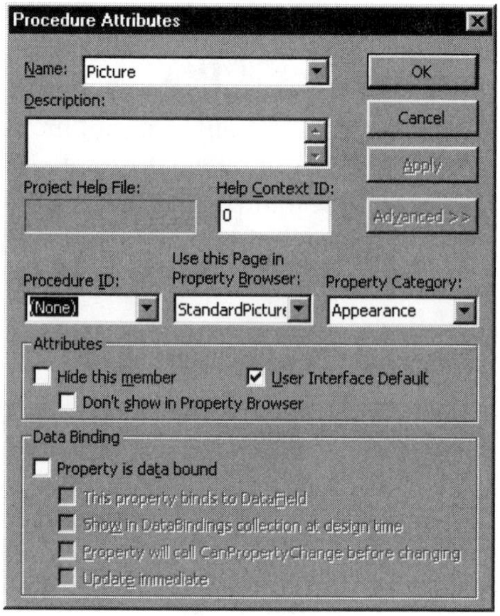

The result is that the Picture property is listed on the Picture property page, as shown in Figure 6.7.

NOTE   When creating properties that use pictures, colors, and fonts, you need to use the proper data type. Use Picture for pictures, OLE_COLOR for colors, and Font for fonts.

FIGURE 6.7:

FIGURE 6.7:

The Picture property on the
Picture property page

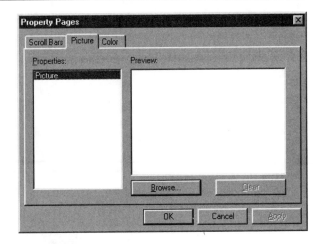

Designing a Property Page

A PropertyPage object is similar to a Form object in that there is a place for you
to put controls to display and accept various property values. Typically, you'll
use a Label control paired with a TextBox control to display a property, but there
aren't any restrictions on the kinds of controls you can use. You might want to use
a Frame control with a series of OptionButtons when the user has a limited list of
choices. A ComboBox control may prove a better choice when you have a longer
list of values to display. For example, when you have a property that uses an enumerated type, use a ComboBox control to list each of the property values by value
and type. This will help the programmer remember the constant's name.

Being the lazy programmer, I drew a simple property page listing the key properties for the horizontal and vertical scroll bars. As you can see in Figure 6.8, this
property page uses ten separate TextBox controls and ten more Label controls.

Figure 6.9 shows what application programmers using the control will see
when they display the property page at design time. Notice that the size of
the property page will be adjusted automatically to match the size of the largest
property page and that the name of the property page will appear on the tab
associated with the page.

FIGURE 6.8:

A simple property page

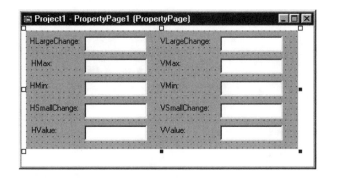

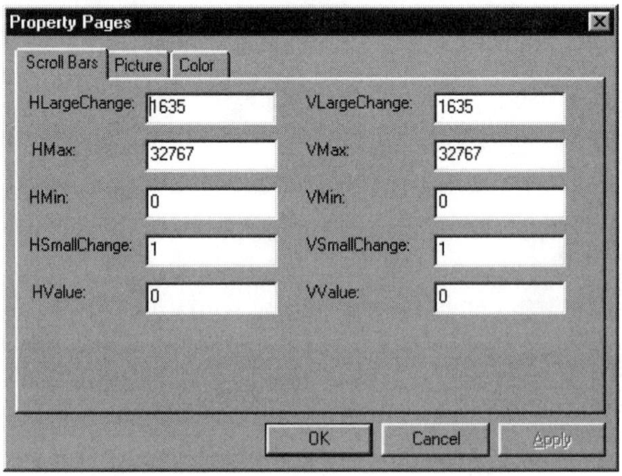

FIGURE 6.9:

Using the simple
property page

> **NOTE**   Since a property page represents a single page in a series of tabbed pages, you shouldn't add a set of tabbed pages to a property page.

Understanding Property Page Properties and Events

When programming a property page, there are two properties and two events you need to understand. These four elements dictate how you display and change property values in your control:

- The SelectedControls property contains all of the controls that are currently selected on the user's Form or other container.

- The Changed property indicates that one or more property values for the selected controls have been updated but not yet applied.

- The SelectionChanged event occurs when the set of selected controls changes.

- The ApplyChanges event occurs after the user clicks the OK or Apply button at the bottom of the Property Pages dialog box.

Loading the Current Set of Properties

Whenever a user selects your control, a SelectionChanged event occurs. This event happens the first time a property page is displayed and every time the user changes the set of selected controls after that. You use this event, shown in Listing 6.8, to copy the current property values from the control to the property page.

Listing 6.8	The PropertyPage_SelectionChanged event

```
Private Sub PropertyPage_SelectionChanged()

Text1.Text = SelectedControls(0).HLargeChange
Text2.Text = SelectedControls(0).HMax
Text3.Text = SelectedControls(0).HMin
Text4.Text = SelectedControls(0).HSmallChange
Text5.Text = SelectedControls(0).HValue
Text6.Text = SelectedControls(0).VLargeChange
Text7.Text = SelectedControls(0).VMax
Text8.Text = SelectedControls(0).VMin
Text9.Text = SelectedControls(0).VSmallChange
Text10.Text = SelectedControls(0).VValue

End Sub
```

This routine makes the assumption that only one control will be selected at a time while the property page is displayed. If more than one control is selected, then only the property values for the first control will be updated. This is a fairly good assumption—users rarely select and attempt to change the properties for multiple controls.

Detecting Changes

At the bottom of the property page are three buttons: OK, Cancel, and Apply. The OK and Cancel buttons are enabled, but the Apply button becomes enabled only when a property value has been changed.

You need to set the Changed property to True, as shown in Listing 6.9, whenever a property value is changed. This is also a good place to check the property value to make sure that it is acceptable before acknowledging the change. Note that you need to do this for each property you display on your property page. In the example, there are ten properties displayed, so we need to code ten separate events.

Listing 6.9	The Text1_Change event

```
Private Sub Text1_Change()

If IsNumeric(Text1.Text) Then
    Changed = True

Else
    MsgBox "Invalid property value for HLargeChange"

End If

End Sub
```

TIP	You may want to use a control array if you have a large number of similar controls. You need only one copy of the Changed event to handle all of the controls in the array.

Applying Changes

Listing 6.10 shows how to copy the new property values back to the control. Note that we don't need to bother keeping track of the property values that changed and those that didn't. We can simply copy all of the values on the property page back to the control, whether they've changed or not.

Listing 6.10   The ApplyChanges event

```
Private Sub PropertyPage_ApplyChanges()

SelectedControls(0).HLargeChange = Text1.Text
SelectedControls(0).HMax = Text2.Text
SelectedControls(0).HMin = Text3.Text
SelectedControls(0).HSmallChange = Text4.Text
SelectedControls(0).HValue = Text5.Text
SelectedControls(0).VLargeChange = Text6.Text
SelectedControls(0).VMax = Text7.Text
SelectedControls(0).VMin = Text8.Text
SelectedControls(0).VSmallChange = Text9.Text
SelectedControls(0).VValue = Text10.Text

End Sub
```

Looking at Other Interesting Properties and Events

There are a few other properties and events that may be of some interest to you when coding complex property pages.

- The Caption property contains a string that will be displayed on the property page's tab.

- The EditProperty event occurs when a programmer clicks the ellipsis at the end of a property displayed in the Properties window. You can use this event to set the focus to the associated control on your property page.

- The StandardSize property can be used to set the property page to a standard size, either 101×375 (small) or 179×375 (large), or to a custom size.

Handling Multiple Selected Controls

When dealing with multiple selected controls, you need to handle the situation where some controls have a different value for a property than other controls. To be absolutely safe, you need to examine each of the controls and identify the properties that have different values. These values should be displayed by using blank text boxes or some other technique to communicate to the programmer that there isn't a single value for all of the selected controls. Properties that have a single value for all of the selected controls should be displayed normally. The best place to put the code to handle this situation is in the SelectionChanged event, since this event will be called each time the user changes the selected controls.

Then, in the ApplyChanges event, you need to identify the changed properties and apply them to all of the controls in the SelectedControls object. Note that you'll also need to handle the situation where the developer enters a value into a field that was previously displayed as blank. This implies that the programmer now wants all of the selected controls to have the same value for that particular property.

Adding an About Box

Nearly every ActiveX control includes an About box that you can view by clicking the (About) entry in the Properties window. Usually, this dialog box will contain the name of the control, the name of who built it, and the all-important copyright and licensing information. This is also a useful place to put registration information if you're building a shareware control.

The key to making the About box work is that you add a standard Form object to your control and display it on request. If you're really lazy, you can use the sample About form supplied with Visual Basic; however, if you do, you will also get a bunch of code that will launch Microsoft's system information program. Instead, I'm going to show you how to do this the old-fashioned way.

Creating the About Box

An About box can be as simple or as complex as you want. Figure 6.10 shows a plain About box, whose looks certainly could be improved. However, this box does provide all of the information that should be included.

As we saw in Chapter 5, you can define a lot of information about your COM object using the Project Properties dialog box. This includes the title of the application, the version number, copyright, trademark, and other information. You can even put a description of the control in the Comments section of the Project Properties dialog box.

FIGURE 6.10:

A simple About form

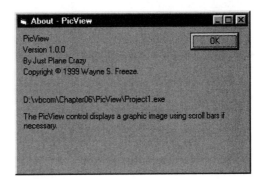

Visual Basic allows you to extract this information using the App object. This means that you can create a generic About box form that merely displays the information from the App object.

Listing 6.11 shows the Form_Load event for the sample About box.

Listing 6.11   The Form_Load event for AboutBox

```
Private Sub Form_Load()

FormHeight = Me.Height
FormWidth = Me.Width

Me.Move (Screen.Width - FormWidth) / 2, _
    (Screen.Height - FormHeight) / 2

Me.Caption = "About - " & App.Title
Label1.Caption = App.Title
Label2.Caption = "Version " & _
    FormatNumber(App.Major, 0) & "." & _
    FormatNumber(App.Minor, 0) & "." & _
    FormatNumber(App.Revision, 0)
Label3.Caption = "By " & App.CompanyName
Label4.Caption = App.LegalCopyright
Label5.Caption = App.LegalTrademarks
Label6.Caption = App.Path & "\" & App.EXEName & ".exe"
Label7.Caption = App.Comments

End Sub
```

The routine begins by saving the height and width of the form. We use this information in the Form_Resize event to prevent the user from changing the size of the About box. Then we use the Screen object and the form's size to move the form to the center of the screen.

After moving the form, we use the information in the App object to fill in the various label fields on the form. This way, information like the version number is the same as that associated with the binary object code. This means that we only need to update the version on the object code to update the About box information.

Hooking the Window to the Control

Now that we've created the form for the About box, we need to connect the form to the control and have it appear in the Properties window. To do this, we add a little routine called ShowAboutForm to the UserControl object. This routine is shown in Listing 6.12.

Listing 6.12   The ShowAboutForm method

```
Public Sub ShowAboutBox()

AboutBox.Show vbModal
Unload AboutBox
Set AboutBox = Nothing

End Sub
```

The ShowAboutForm routine merely shows a Visual Basic form object called AboutBox on the screen. Everything will pause until the form returns because we display the form modally. Once the form returns, we unload it and then set the form object to Nothing to recover the resources that are associated with it. If we didn't go through these last two steps, the development environment would become littered with unused resources that couldn't easily be collected.

Final Thoughts

One subject I skipped over in this chapter was the use of wizards and templates. Visual Basic comes with several different wizards that will help you perform tasks ranging from creating your ActiveX control to building a property page. You can also find templates for About forms and various types of ActiveX controls.

There is value to be gained from using these tools. However, for learning about ActiveX controls, I believe that it is more important to understand the fundamentals. These tools often create complex pieces of code, which may prove useful but can be difficult to extend or debug. After you learn how to build a simple control, you should experiment with these tools and see the actual code they generate.

CHAPTER
SEVEN

7

Creating ActiveX EXE Objects

- A definition of an ActiveX EXE

- The CreateObject and GetObject functions

- A sample ActiveX EXE server

- Asynchronous processing

- Multipurpose programs

Have your users ever had to wait a long time for a function in your application to finish, when they could be doing other useful work? Wouldn't it be nice to start a long-running task in the background and check it periodically to make sure that it is working properly? Don't you wish you could split your application across more than one computer?

If you answered yes to any of these questions, then you need an ActiveX EXE application. This chapter describes how to create an out-of-process ActiveX program in Visual Basic.

What Makes an ActiveX EXE Different?

An ActiveX EXE program is similar to an ActiveX DLL, but an ActiveX EXE doesn't run in your current address space. It runs by itself in its own address space. More technically, an ActiveX EXE is an out-of-process server, and an ActiveX DLL is an in-process server.

> **NOTE**
>
> ActiveX EXEs are often referred to as Automation applications. This is a holdover from the days when COM was known as OLE. ActiveX EXEs were also known as OLE servers, because they were designed to respond to requests from other client applications.

Other than that distinction, there isn't a significant difference between an ActiveX EXE and an ActiveX DLL. Both are COM objects, which are built in Visual Basic using class modules. You can easily move the class modules from an ActiveX DLL to an ActiveX EXE and back again, without changing a single line of the client's code.

In developing your own applications, you may find that choosing between the two types of ActiveX projects isn't always the easiest thing to do. Communications between a client and server are much more efficient in an in-process server than in an out-of-process server. However, an out-of-process server has the ability to be run on a different computer, thus allowing you to dedicate a computer to providing a middle tier when developing client/server programs.

You can also use this technique to create instances of objects in a remote ActiveX DLL file. Since the DLL is an in-process server, it can't run as a stand-alone process.

Windows contains a default surrogate host that can be used for this purpose, but you must edit the Windows Registry directly to create all of the proper definitions for this to work. For this reason, I recommend avoiding this approach to creating remote objects and sticking with ActiveX EXE programs.

Programming with More Class

If you thought we were finished with subject of programming classes, you were wrong. I want to discuss how you can use the `CreateObject` and `GetObject` routines to access a COM object. I also want to talk about why you might want to use an ActiveX EXE instead of a regular EXE.

Object Creation and Access

Up until now, we've used two basic techniques to create a new instance of an object. We either used a `Set` ... `New` statement to create a new instance of an object we already declared or used a `Dim` ... `New` statement to create a new instance of an object immediately. Declaring a variable as an object by using the `Dim` statement merely classifies the variable as a pointer to a specific object type. It does not create an instance of the object. In fact, the object variable has a value of `Nothing`, which means that it doesn't point anywhere.

In Visual Basic, object variables are declared as type `Variant`, type `Object`, or a specific object type such as `FileSystemObject` or `Recordset`. You can create as many instances of an object as you want. Each time, new storage is allocated so that the newly created object is independent of any previously created instances of the object. You can also use multiple pointers to point to the same object, by using the `Set` statement to assign one pointer value to another object pointer value.

TIP Although you can declare an object as `Variant` or `Object`, you should try to declare the variable with the actual object type. This allows Visual Basic to check its type more closely when it is used in calculations. This practice also has the side effect of helping you edit the program, because Visual Basic will provide you with a list of choices for properties and methods as you type your statement. It also will have better performance at runtime.

An object is destroyed in Visual Basic by setting its pointer to `Nothing`. However, if you have multiple pointers to the object, each of those pointers must be set to `Nothing` before the object will cease to exist.

Visual Basic supports a couple of other ways to create or gain access to an object. These are the `CreateObject` and `GetObject` functions. These functions both return pointers to objects, but they differ in how they work. `CreateObject` works like the `New` keyword, but it has the ability to create an object on a remote system. `GetObject` attempts to reuse an existing object where appropriate and is geared toward processing object information that is stored in a file. Although the `CreateObject` and `GetObject` functions are typically used to start ActiveX EXE applications, they also can be used to create instances of objects contained in ActiveX DLLs.

The CreateObject Function

The `CreateObject` function is similar to the `Set … New` and `Dim … New` statements. It creates a new instance of the specified object and returns an object reference that you can assign to an object variable with the `Set` statement.

NOTE   You must use the `CreateObject` function in VBScript. This is because VBScript doesn't support the `New` keyword in either the `Dim` statement or the `Set` statement.

The syntax for the `CreateObject` function is:

```
Set objectvar = CreateObject(class [,server])
```

where:

- *objectvar* is the name of an object variable that will hold a pointer to the newly created object.

- *class* is the name of the object class to be created.

- *server* is the name of the machine where the object should be created. If *server* isn't specified, it will default to your local machine.

One feature of the `CreateObject` statement that isn't available by using the `New` keyword is the ability to create the object on a remote computer. `CreateObject` is the only way to create an object on another computer using just standard COM techniques. If the remote computer doesn't exist or its security prevents you from accessing the object, a runtime error will occur, and the object will not be created.

TIP

DCOM allows your program to automatically find objects on remote computers without explicitly specifying where the object is located in your application program. I'll cover DCOM in more detail in Chapter 8.

The GetObject Function

The `GetObject` function is similar to the `CreateObject` function in that it returns a reference to an object, but its purpose is significantly different. It is designed primarily to open files that were created with object-oriented programs such as Microsoft Excel or Word. As part of opening the file, `GetObject` also runs the application associated with the file's type.

The syntax for the `GetObject` function is:

```
Set objectvar = GetObject([filename] [,class])
```

where:

- *objectvar* is the name of an object variable that will hold a pointer to the newly created object.

- *filename* is the complete name of the file to be opened, including path information.

- *class* is the name of the object class to be created and is in the form of *application.object* (for example, `Word.Application` or `Excel.Application`).

At least one of the parameters (*filename* or *class*) must be specified, or a runtime error will occur.

WARNING

Specifying the filename of the application's executable will cause a runtime error. You must specify the path to a file whose file type is associated with the specified application. For instance, `c:\MyWorkSheet.XLS` is a valid value for *filename*, as is `MyDoc.DOC`. However specifying `c:\Program Files\Microsoft Office\Office\Excel.EXE` for *filename* will not work.

Specifying a value for *filename* causes the GetObject routine to search the Windows Registry for the program associated with the file. Then it launches the program (if it isn't already running) and causes the program to load the file. Finally, it will return an object reference to your program, which you can use to access the object in your program.

If your application supports multiple ways to open a file containing object information, you can use the *class* parameter to clarify which object you want to use to open the file. This is strictly an application issue, and you are free to specify a value for *class*, even if there is only one choice.

By specifying an empty string for *filename*, a new instance of the object will be created. It's up to you to use the appropriate properties and methods provided by the application to save the file. Note, however, that you must specify the appropriate value for *class* in order to create the object.

If you omit a value for *filename*, GetObject attempts to return an object reference to the currently active object. If the application containing the object isn't running, a runtime error will occur.

Threading Models

When you build your ActiveX EXE, you have a choice of two threading models:

- One thread per object created
- A pool of threads

You specify the threading model in the Project Properties dialog box, shown in Figure 7.1 (choose Project ➤ Project Properties from the main menu to display this dialog box).

The One Thread per Object Model

One thread per object means exactly that. Each object that is created will run in its own thread in the address space. This can cause performance problems, depending on how many objects are active at the same time. So unless you have a specific reason to use this threading model, I suggest that you choose the thread pool model.

FIGURE 7.1:

Choosing a threading
model for your ActiveX EXE

FIGURE 7.1:

Choosing a threading
model for your ActiveX EXE

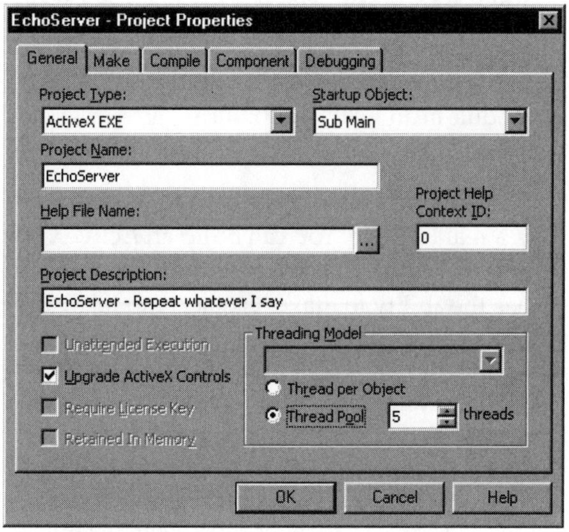

The Thread Pool Model

In the thread pool model, you can specify the number of threads that will be available in the address space. Each instance of an object will be assigned to the pool of threads on a round-robin basis.

If you set the number of threads too high, you essentially have the same situation as with the one thread per object model, resulting in adverse performance due to too many threads. In general, this value should be at least as large as the number of processors you have in the system. This means that each thread in the address space could be active at the same time. The value you use will depend on what those threads are actually doing. If your objects spend most of their time performing I/O, then you may want to increase the number of threads. If your system is heavily loaded, you may want to decrease the number of threads.

The only way to find the optimum number of threads is to monitor your application and your system. If all of the processors are running at maximum capacity, try reducing the number of threads. If there is a lot of unused CPU time, try increasing the number of threads. Of course, there is no advantage to increasing the number of threads beyond the number of objects that you expect to create. If you expect to create only one object at a time, then a thread pool of one will be sufficient.

An ActiveX EXE Can Have Forms, Too

As you saw in the previous chapter, you can include a bunch of other things in an ActiveX file, besides just a collection of class objects. You can use nearly any other module in an ActiveX EXE file (or an ActiveX DLL file) except for an MDI Form object (which I don't consider a loss anyway, since I don't like MDI applications in general).

An ActiveX EXE can be started independently of another application, because it is a real EXE file. You can build an ActiveX EXE application that displays forms and works just like a normal EXE program. The difference is that an ActiveX EXE has the ability to make its object model available to other applications. If you don't think this is a useful concept, consider that this is the same programming model that Microsoft uses for Word, Excel, Visual Basic, and other products.

> **TIP**
>
> One useful side effect of having a bunch of COM objects in your application is that it makes it easy to add support for VBScript. For complete details on how to add VBScript to your application, see Chapter 13 in the *Expert Guide to Visual Basic*, written by someone who is too modest to mention his name and published by the same great outfit that published this book.

Building an ActiveX EXE

To demonstrate what you can do with an ActiveX EXE, I decided that we would do something different than we have done in the previous chapters. While practical applications are interesting, sometimes they don't always allow room to communicate various techniques. The application in this chapter doesn't try to do anything really useful. It just echoes the string that is passed to it. To make up for the lack of usefulness, we will go about building the application in a useful way.

How the EchoClient Program Works

The EchoClient program, shown in Figure 7.2, has six main buttons. Clicking the Create Object button will create an instance of the EchoServer program by using the CreateObject function. Clicking the Release Object button sets the object to Nothing and releases all of its resources. The other buttons perform various tasks that I'll cover as I talk about the various routines.

About the Project Files

There are two project files associated with this application, EchoServer and EchoClient. Unlike the previous projects, where both the ActiveX component and the demo program are included in the same project group, I left these as separate projects. You can either load them in two separate Visual Basic development sessions or compile the EchoServer and install it into your system so that the EchoClient program can find it.

As with all the other examples, the source code for the EchoClient and EchoServer programs can be downloaded from the Sybex web site at www.sybex.com or from my web site at www.JustPC.com. Just follow the links to this book and download the zip file associated with this chapter. The complete source code for both projects is included in the zip file. I strongly recommend downloading the source code, since I'm only going to refer to the interesting routines in this chapter. Having the complete program also lets you see all of the individual components and their property settings, plus it makes it easier to try different things with the application.

You may be thinking, "I don't need no simple samples." However, as with any computer book, you should spend a few minutes trying the sample applications. Sometimes you may wonder why I did something one way versus another. In many cases, the reason I did something is a matter of personal style. In other cases, it might be due to the fact that it worked properly one way and would not work the other way. The sample programs give you a point from which to experiment. Modifying a working program to try different ideas is always the laziest way to do something (and often the best way). So go ahead and take advantage of my work.

At the top of the EchoClient form there are two input areas. The area on the left contains the text that is to be echoed. On the right is an area that you can optionally use to specify the name of the computer where the ActiveX EXE file can be found. Beneath the buttons is an area where the result of various functions will be displayed. The exact contents of this area depend on which button was pressed.

Notice in Figure 7.2 that the Create Object button is disabled. This figure shows an active session with the object. I've echoed the string Hello! on the computer named Mycroft. If I were to click the Release Object button, all of the buttons except for Create Object would become disabled. The Create Object button would be enabled to create a new instance of the object.

NOTE   Because this is just a test program, I don't do much in the way of error checking to prevent runtime errors. Aside from enabling and disabling the buttons, I don't bother checking for errors. I would rather let the runtime errors interrupt the program and debug from there.

The EchoServer Object

We use the CreateObject function to create the EchoServer.Echo object, as shown in Listing 7.1.

Listing 7.1   **The Command1_Click event in EchoClient**

```
Private Sub Command1_Click()

If Len(Text3.text) = 0 Then
    Set MyEcho = CreateObject("EchoServer.Echo")

Else
    Set MyEcho = CreateObject("Echoserver.Echo", Text3.text)

End If

Command1.Enabled = False
Command2.Enabled = True
Command3.Enabled = True
```

```
Command4.Enabled = True
Command5.Enabled = True
Command6.Enabled = True

End Sub
```

If the Text3 text box contains a blank value, then we assume that we want to start the EchoServer program on the local machine; otherwise, we'll pass the value as the name of the remote computer. Note that if the object isn't available on the remote computer, we'll get a nasty error message from Visual Basic saying that the Automation server isn't available.

After we create a copy of the Echo object, we enable and disable the appropriate command buttons. This simply prevents users from clicking the wrong button at the wrong time.

Missing Object Files

If you're running both your client and server programs in the development environment, you may occasionally see the message "Connection to type library or object library for remote process has been lost. Press OK for dialog to remove reference." Then the dialog box shown in Figure 7.3 appears.

FIGURE 7.3:

The missing object file

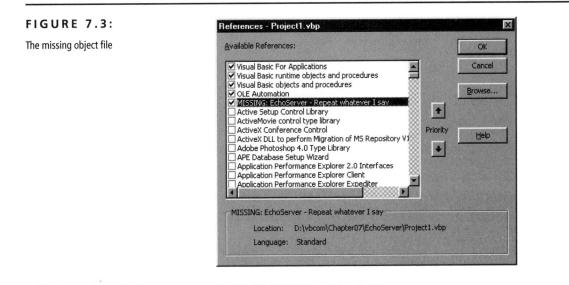

This message is generated when the server program isn't running and the client program needs to access the object's definitions. You can correct this problem by unchecking the missing object file and closing the References dialog box. Start your ActiveX EXE running and switch back to the client application. Open the References dialog box again by choosing Project ➢ References and select the object reference again.

Another way to correct this problem is to go to the Program Properties dialog box for the server program, click the Component tab, and Select Project Compatibility. This will prevent the problem from occurring while you're running programs in the Visual Basic development environment.

The EchoText Method

The EchoText method, shown in Listing 7.2, is a simple function. It merely returns a string that repeats the input string three times. This is part of the EchoServer class module.

Listing 7.2 **The EchoText method in EchoServer**

```
Public Function EchoText(text As String) As String

EchoText = text & vbCrLf & text & vbCrLf & text & vbCrLf

End Function
```

To call this function, we use the routine shown in Listing 7.3, which is triggered when the user clicks the Echo Text button. Note this routine doesn't look any different than it would to call an ActiveX DLL object.

Listing 7.3 **The Command4_Click event in EchoClient**

```
Private Sub Command4_Click()

Text2.text = MyEcho.EchoText(Text1.text)

End Sub
```

Asynchronous Processing

Now that you've seen that there isn't anything special about using an ActiveX EXE program compared to using an ActiveX DLL, I want to talk about how to do asynchronous processing using an out-of-process COM object. Even though an out-of-process COM object runs in its own address space, your client program waits until the property or method it called finishes. This means that only one part of your program is active at the same time. If you stop to think this through, it makes a lot of sense. As far as your program is concerned, it must wait for the method or property routine to complete before it can continue.

> **NOTE**   Asynchronous processing allows you to start a task running in a different address space while monitoring its progress. This allows you start something that is going to take a long time to finish and freeze your user's application.

What we need is a way to start a routine without waiting for it to return. Unfortunately, like some other things in Visual Basic, this task needs a little help from some Win32 API routines. The approach I'm going to outline here is somewhat convoluted, but it has the advantage of working on nearly any Windows platform, including Windows 95 and newer and Windows NT 3.1 and newer. However, a better approach is to use COM+ message queues, which I'll cover in Chapter 13.

Design Overview

One way to start a new thread in any application is to use a timer. In a normal Visual Basic program, you can use the Timer control to trigger the Timer event, which will run independently of the rest of your program. You need to trigger the Timer event only once, because you can call your long-running task from there. But since the ActiveX EXE doesn't rely on a form, we can't use the Timer control.

There ie a pair of Win32 API calls called SetTimer and KillTimer that we can use to accomplish the same thing as the Timer control without needing a form. The only problem with these routines is that we can't use them from inside a class module. So our approach is as follows:

- A method inside the Echo class module calls a routine in a general module.

- The routine in the general module uses the SetTimer routine to trigger a subroutine in the general module.

- The subroutine kills the timer using the KillTimer routine and then triggers a method in the Echo class to perform the processing.

- The method uses the RaiseEvent statement to trigger an event in the client program.

Starting in the Client

In response to the user clicking the Echo Message button, the Command5_Click event will be fired. This event, shown in Listing 7.4, uses the same instance of the Echo object that I talked about earlier. It passes the text from the Text1 text box using the EchoMsg method.

Listing 7.4   **The Command5_Click event in EchoClient**

```
Private Sub Command5_Click()

MyEcho.EchoMsg Text1.text

End Sub
```

Then onto the Server

In the EchoMsg method, shown in Listing 7.5, we save the text message into a private, module-level variable called Message for use later. Then we call a routine in the general module called StartTask and pass the routine a reference to this instance of the Echo object using Me.

Listing 7.5   **The EchoMsg method in EchoServer**

```
Public Sub EchoMsg(text As String)

Message = text
StartTask Me

End Sub
```

To Start the Task

In StartTask, shown in Listing 7.6, we save the object reference into a private, module-level variable called TimerObject. Then we call the SetTimer routine, using a delay of ten milliseconds and passing the address of another routine in the general module called OneShot. The SetTimer routine will return a value that we'll save in a module-level variable called TimerId. We'll use this value in a minute to kill the timer once the new thread has started.

Listing 7.6	The StartTask routine in EchoServer

```
Public Sub StartTask(ReturnObject As Object)

Dim delay As Long

Set TimerObject = ReturnObject

delay = 10

TimerId = SetTimer(0, 0, delay, AddressOf OneShot)

End Sub
```

After the timer has been set, this routine, as well as the EchoMsg routine and the Command5_Click event, will return. The user will again be able to interact with the EchoClient program.

Part of the trick here is that because we can't use the AddressOf operator in a class module, we need to create both the StartTask and the OneShot routines in a separate general module. The SetTimer routine will return immediately after setting the timer. This makes it possible to return to the calling program without waiting for the actual timer to start.

When the Timer Fires

In the OneShot routine, shown in Listing 7.7, you'll notice a rather complex header. This header information is required by the SetTimer routine. However, from our point of view, all of this information can be ignored.

TIP   For more information about Win32 APIs, see *The VB Developer's Guide to Win32 API* by Steve Brown (Sybex, 1999).

Listing 7.7   **The OneShot routine in EchoServer**

```
Private Sub OneShot(ByVal hWnd As Long, _
    ByVal uMsg As Long, ByVal idEvent As Long, _
    ByVal dwTime As Long)

KillTimer 0, TimerId

TimerObject.AsyncTask

Set TimerObject = Nothing

End Sub
```

The first thing we do inside this routine is to kill the timer using the `KillTimer` routine. We only needed the timer to start up a new thread. Once the thread was started, we don't need it to fire again. Note that we used the `TimerId` value from the `StartTask` routine to identify which timer we wanted to kill.

Once the timer has been killed, we use the object reference we saved in `StartTask` to call the `AsyncTask` method. This task will perform the actual processing. When the `AsyncTask` method completes, control will return here, and we'll set the local reference to the object to `Nothing`. This should not destroy the object, because we already have another pointer to this object in the `EchoClient` program.

WARNING   Destroying objects while running asynchronously can be dangerous to your application. Typically, you will destroy an object by setting every object variable to `Nothing`. This will destroy your object even if it is actively processing information. Note that Visual Basic will automatically set all object variables declared locally in a subroutine (or function or property routine) to `Nothing` when you exit the routine. To be safe, you may want to declare any object variables that are used for asynchronous processing at the module level of your application.

The AsyncTask Will Run

Listing 7.8 shows the AsyncTask method that simulates some processing and returns some information to the EchoClient. This routine begins by setting the module-level variable EchoCounter to 1. Then it computes a time value that is 15 seconds from now by using the DateAdd and Now functions.

Listing 7.8   **The AsyncTask method in EchoServer**

```
Public Sub AsyncTask()

Dim i As Date

EchoCounter = 1

i = DateAdd("s", 15, Now)

Do While i > Now
   DoEvents
   EchoCounter = EchoCounter + 1
Loop

RaiseEvent EchoMessage(Message)

End Sub
```

Next, we sit in a DoEvents loop until the 15 seconds are up. While we're in the loop, we increment EchoCounter. When our time is up, we return information in the module-level variable Message to the EchoClient program using the EchoMessage event.

And Return via the EchoMessage Event

The MyEcho_EchoMessage event, shown in Listing 7.9, simply receives the message and displays it on the screen using the MsgBox function.

Listing 7.9 **The MyEcho_EchoMessage event in EchoClient**

```
Private Sub MyEcho_EchoMessage(text As String)

MsgBox text

End Sub
```

While I Was Waiting

There are two more pieces to this puzzle. These pieces are used while the asynchronous processing is running. Listing 7.10 contains the property routine Counter. This routine just returns the module-level variable EchoCounter to the calling program.

Listing 7.10 **The Counter property routine in EchoServer**

```
Property Get Counter() As Long

Counter = EchoCounter

End Property
```

Listing 7.11 contains the code necessary to display the current value of the Counter in the Text2 text box.

Listing 7.11 **The Command6_Click event in EchoClient**

```
Private Sub Command6_Click()

Text2.text = FormatNumber(MyEcho.Counter, 0)

End Sub
```

Note that these routines work together to inquire about the current value of counter. They can be called while the code in AsyncTask is running. This is a perfect way to track the progress of the asynchronous process.

Designing Multipurpose Programs

It is important to remember that an ActiveX EXE program can also be used as a regular EXE program. This can be useful when building multipurpose programs that contain a user interface and an exposed object model.

Start Mode

An ActiveX EXE can be started in two different ways:

- When you start the program through the COM interface. This is the way that COM objects are normally accessed.

- You can run your ActiveX EXE program directly. In this case, the Sub Main routine will be called when the program is first started. If this routine isn't present or the Startup Object is set to (none), then your program will immediately terminate.

You can tell how your program was started by checking the App.StartMode property. A value of vbSModeStandalone (or the value 0) means that the program was started as a normal Visual Basic program. A value of vbSModeAutomation (or the value 1) means that the program was started as a COM object. This property is read-only at runtime, but you can set it by selecting the desired start mode on the Component tab of the Project Properties dialog box while in development mode, as shown in Figure 7.4.

NOTE   Setting the Start Mode entry in the Project Properties dialog box only affects the way your component is started within the Visual Basic development environment. Once you've compiled your project into an EXE file, the value of this property is determined by how you started the program, either by starting it directly (vbSModeStandalone) or by letting COM create it (vbSModeAutomation).

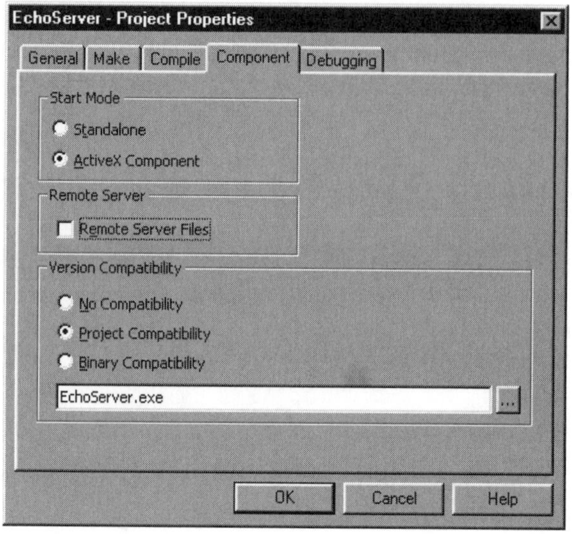

FIGURE 7.4:

Setting the StartMode
property in Visual Basic

Sub Main and the About Box

When your ActiveX EXE is run as a stand-alone program, you may want to provide some information about it. You can do this by showing an About box, like the one we created for the PicView control in Chapter 6, whenever the program is run directly. Listing 7.12 demonstrates how to display the AboutBox form when the App.StartMode property says that the program is being run in stand-alone mode. Figure 7.5 shows the About box for EchoServer.

Listing 7.12   The Main routine in EchoServer

```
Public Sub Main()

If App.StartMode = vbSModeStandalone Then
    AboutBox.Show 0

End If

End Sub
```

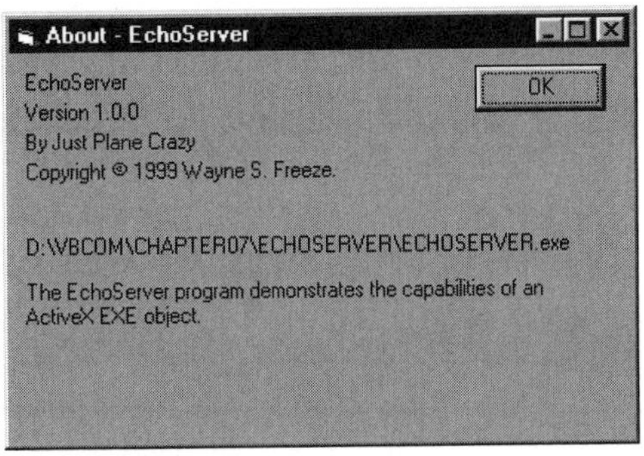

FIGURE 7.5:

The EchoServer's About box form

> **NOTE**　Don't forget to set the Startup Object to Sub Main on the General tab of the Project Properties dialog box. Otherwise, the Sub Main routine will never be called.

Sub Main and a Real Application

If you can display an About box from the Sub Main routine, then you can create a real application just as easily. The key here is to keep the Sub Main routine small and quick. This routine is called each time a new instance of a COM object is created. If this routine takes too long to run, it could result in a COM error, because the COM subsystem may interpret the delay as your component being unresponsive.

Use the Sub Main to launch a Form object, much as we just did with the About-Box form. You can build a normal Visual Basic application in the form.

Finishing Your ActiveX EXE Server

After you finishing debugging your ActiveX EXE server, you need to compile and add its information permanently in the Windows Registry. So far, this information was added temporarily while the program was running in the Visual Basic development environment. When the program stopped, the information about how to access the objects was removed from the system.

Compiling Your Server

You compile your out-of-process server into an EXE file in the same way that you compile any other Visual Basic program. Choose File ➤ Make Project from the main menu and compile away.

As with the other ActiveX program types, you can review the Project Properties on the Make and Compile tabs by clicking the Options button in the Make Project dialog box. This is a good way to make sure that you've filled out the version information and set the version number to a new value. Figure 7.6 shows the Make tab of the Project Properties dialog box for the EchoServer application.

FIGURE 7.6:

Checking your ActiveX EXE project properties

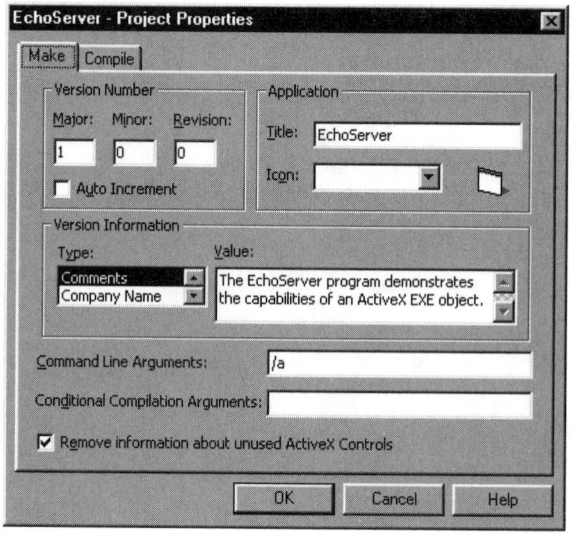

Installing Your Server

If you compiled your ActiveX EXE server on the same computer where you plan to run it, you're finished. Visual Basic automatically takes care of adding all of the appropriate information to the Windows Registry when it compiles the program.

If you plan to install the out-of-process server on a different machine, you have two alternatives:

- You can use the Packaging and Deployment Wizard to create a distribution package.
- You can copy the EXE file to the remote computer and run it using the `/regserver` switch, which will automatically create the proper entries in the Windows Registry:

      D:\EchoServer /regserver

NOTE   Registering your out-of-process COM server using the `/regserver` command-line option overrides the normal way your program works when it's manually started. Neither the `Sub Main` nor the `Class_Initialize` routines will be called. Only the registration logic included in the EXE file by Visual Basic will be run.

To remove the server from your system, use the following command:

    D:\EchoServer /unregserver

This will remove all of the entries related to the server from the Registry.

Accessing Remote Objects

As you saw in Listing 7.1, all you need to do to access remote objects is to include the name of the remote system in the `CreateObject` function. However, this applies only to a Windows 95/98–based system. Window NT and Windows 2000 systems have security issues that need to be addressed.

First, DCOM needs to be enabled on the computer containing the remote copy of the object, and it may need to be enabled on the local computer as well. I'll cover this information in more detail in the next chapter, which is about DCOM.

Second, you need to install the ActiveX EXE program on the remote system. On a Windows 95/98 system that has been enabled for DCOM, all you need to do is install the file on the computer, and you're ready to run. On a Windows NT system, however, you need to consider security in a much more rigorous fashion. Again, I'll cover this in more detail in the next chapter.

Finally, you need to code the machine name of the remote computer into your application. You can provide a field for the user to enter the name of the remote computer. However, it's usually a bad idea to rely on users to supply this information. It would be better to find another way to get the machine name into your program. One way is to use the Windows Registry to hold the name of the remote system. You could get the information by using the GetSetting function and specifying the appropriate key. You could even build a simple program whose purpose is to get the machine name from the Registry, allow you to edit it, and then put it back again.

Final Thoughts

Asynchronous processing as I outlined in this chapter can be a useful tool. It can also be a dangerous one. In today's world, there isn't much use for batch processing. However, users still want reports that take a long time to complete. One way of generating a report is to put the report into a separate program and just let users run it whenever they want a copy of it. However, this means that the user needs to know about multiple applications. Most users are better off loading just one application and clicking the appropriate button from there to perform the desired function.

With the WinInfo ActiveX DLL we created in Chapter 5, you could use the RunMe routines to launch the program from your current application. This has the advantage of simplicity, but running the program would add a new task to the Windows Taskbar and leave yet another window open on the user's Desktop.

A better alternative would be to create an out-of-process server using the asynchronous processing routines discussed in this chapter to launch an independent address space that is tightly managed by your current application. It's very easy to set properties in the COM object to direct how it will run. You can even peek inside the object to monitor its progress while it executes and report this information back to the user.

If you combine the ability to run the remote object on a different machine with the out-of-process server approach, you can implement a multiple-tier client/server application. You could create an application server dedicated to running the ActiveX EXE COM object. Then multiple client programs could make synchronous and asynchronous requests to the application server to perform various tasks, such as validating data or applying business rules to a set of data.

CHAPTER

EIGHT

8

Moving from COM to DCOM

- A definition of DCOM

- The DCOM Configuration utility

- Windows 2000 considerations

- Windows 95/98 considerations

- Suggestions for troubleshooting common DCOM errors

Moving from COM to DCOM isn't really all that difficult. Even though COM has the ability to run objects on remote computers, you may need to use the DCOM Configuration utility in order to configure your computer to handle remote COM objects properly.

In terms of the technology, DCOM has no special programming requirements. It uses the same tools that I've already covered in Chapter 7. Nearly all of the work done with DCOM revolves around using the DCOM Configuration utility and setting security permissions using the normal operating system utilities.

This chapter describes the issues of moving an ActiveX EXE program from a COM environment to a DCOM environment.

How Is DCOM Different?

DCOM uses the same tools and techniques that already exist in Visual Basic's ActiveX tools. In fact, there are no differences in how you build a COM out-of-process server versus how you construct a DCOM out-of-process server. The programs are identical.

DCOM Configuration

What makes DCOM different from COM is that DCOM has a special tool called the DCOM Configuration utility. This tool allows you to tweak how and where out-of-process servers are created by directly editing the Registry entries associated with a normal COM out-of-process server.

Using this utility, you can define where the out-of-process server is located, so you no longer need to specify the name of the remote computer in the Create-Object function. It also allows you to use the New keyword in the Set and Dim statements to create remote COM objects.

Another use for the DCOM Configuration utility is to control how the object is secured. It can work with the Windows NT operating system security to build tighter security rules.

Design Considerations for DCOM Objects

Although you can use any COM object remotely with DCOM, you may want to rethink your object's design before you begin using it in production. Design trade-offs that were acceptable in a normal COM object may or may not make sense when using the object across a network.

First and foremost, you need to keep in mind that you have two programs that are talking to each other across the network. No matter how the two computers are connected, you can't move data between them as fast as you can move data inside a single computer. Also, if you're using a typical 10BaseT or 100BaseT network, you need to share the available bandwidth with every other computer on the network. So even if the network was sufficiently fast to handle the communications between the two computers by themselves, it won't scale up if your network is handling tens or hundreds of computers. Thus, the number one rule of networked applications is to minimize the amount of information passed from one computer to another.

The second issue is related to the first. Each time you send a message from one computer to another, there is a lot of other information that is automatically included with the message. The size of this overhead is relatively independent of the message size. So sending one large message is much more efficient than sending one hundred smaller messages. This leads to the number two rule of networked applications: After you've minimized the amount of information you need to send between the computers, you should send it in as large chunks as practical.

Here are a few tips that will help you translate these ideas into Visual Basic.

- Minimize the amount of data sent between computers by transferring only the information you actually need.

- Use the `ByVal` keyword to send information in one direction only. Without this keyword, DCOM will need to return the value even if the value wasn't modified.

- Use ADO disconnected `Recordset` objects to transfer information between machines. ADO uses custom marshaling to improve performance when communicating over a network.

- Use methods that can set multiple properties rather than setting the properties individually.

Running the DCOM Configuration Utility

There are two different versions of the DCOM Configuration utility: one for Windows 2000 and NT and the other for Windows 95 and 98. The differences between the two versions relate mostly to how the utility handles security.

Because Windows 95/98 systems don't really have much in terms of a security subsystem, security on a DCOM object is pretty much limited to a yes or no proposition. Either your username has permission to access the object or it doesn't. Access can be controlled globally or for a particular DCOM object.

Windows 2000/NT security is a totally different story. You can grant access to the object, permission to launch the object, and permission to edit the configuration. As with the Windows 95/98 version, these permissions can be applied system-wide or to a particular object.

Setting Windows 2000/NT Options

You can start the Windows 2000 version of the DCOM Configuration utility by selecting Start ➤ Run and entering **DCOMCNFG**. You'll see the Distributed COM Configuration Properties dialog box, shown in Figure 8.1. The dialog box has four main tabs: Applications, Default Properties, Default Security, and Default Protocols. Each of these tabs is covered in the following sections, starting with Default Properties and leaving Applications for last.

DCOM Default Properties for Windows 2000/NT

The Default Properties tab, shown in Figure 8.2, allows you to configure how DCOM will operate on your system. The most important property is Enable Distributed COM on This Computer. This value *must* be checked to run DCOM on your system.

The Enable COM Internet Services on This Computer check box enables support for a transport protocol known as Tunneling Transmission Control Protocol (Tunneling TCP). This allows you to communicate over TCP port 80, which is the default port for Web browsers. This makes it easier to communicate through proxy servers and firewalls. However, since COM Internet Services (CIS) objects are created using Visual C++, this feature shouldn't be enabled for Visual Basic 6 applications.

FIGURE 8.1:

The DCOM Configuration utility for Windows 2000/NT

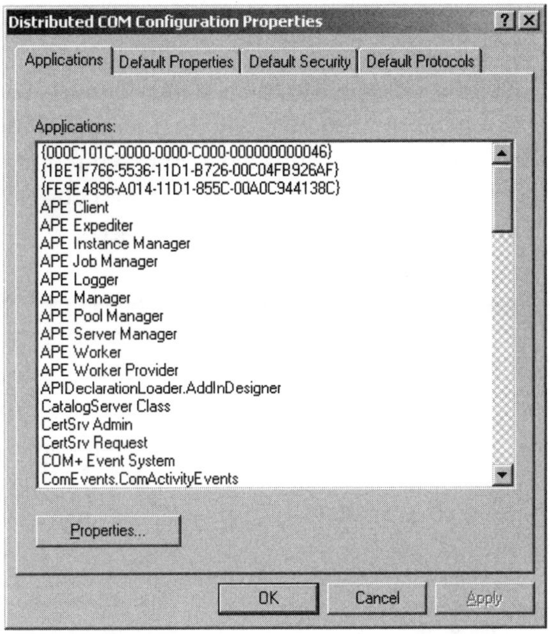

FIGURE 8.2:

The Default Properties tab for Windows 2000/NT

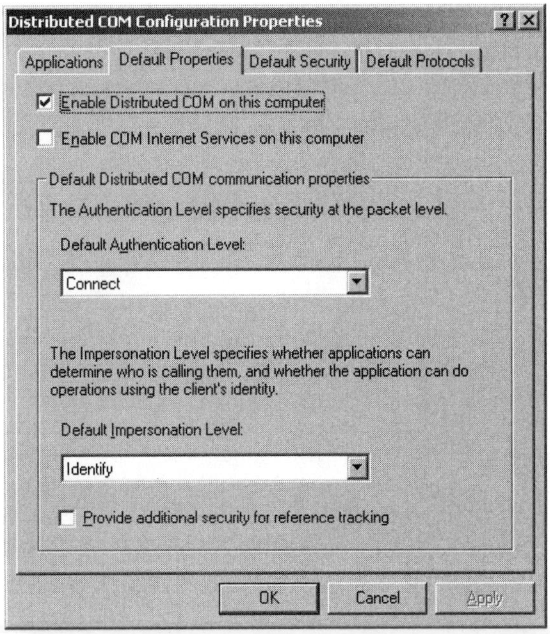

The Default Authentication Level setting determines how much security checking is done. Table 8.1 lists the levels that are available. In general, you should set this level to either None or Connect (which happen to be the only choices available for Windows 95/98 systems). None is best when you're developing and testing an application. This eliminates many of the most common DCOM errors you'll encounter while developing your application. Then you can focus on the errors related to developing the COM object rather than trying to figure out why Windows refuses to create your object.

TABLE 8.1: Default Authentication Level Settings

Value	Description
None	No security checking is performed. This should be used when the Default Impersonation Level is set to Anonymous.
Default	The default level of security checking is used. For Windows 2000/NT, this is the same as specifying Connect.
Connect	Security checking is done when the connection is first established with the server. This option will work with only connection-oriented networking protocols.
Call	A security check is performed on each call.
Packet	The sender's identity is encrypted with each packet.
Packet integrity	The sender's identity and signature are encrypted in each packet to ensure that packets arrive at the server unchanged.
Packet privacy	The data, the sender's identity, and the sender's signature are all encrypted to ensure maximum security.

WARNING   Someone may take advantage of an open door, so never operate a production server with the Default Authentication Level set to None. Someone could quite easily subvert the normal operating system security by accessing a COM object such as Microsoft Excel, which in turn can be used to access the operating system's files.

The Default Impersonation Level setting describes how the username will be mapped onto the server. Table 8.2 lists the settings that are available for this option. A value of Anonymous implies that no security checking will be done and is recommended for testing. However, if you are running your server in a production environment, you should choose Identity or Impersonate, rather than Anonymous.

TABLE 8.2: Default Impersonation Levels

Value	Description
Anonymous	The server application doesn't check the identity of the caller.
Identity	The server application verifies the username associated with the client application.
Impersonate	The server application impersonates the client application by performing tasks as the client application. This option is available only on the computer running the server.
Delegate	The server application performs processing tasks on another computer as the client application. Windows 2000/NT doesn't support this option. It's reserved for future use.

The last option on the Default Properties tab is Provide Additional Security for Reference Tracking. This basically asks the server to count the number of the connected client applications in addition to the normal reference count maintained by the COM object. Checking this check box prevents a programmer from merely resetting the reference count to zero. It also slows down your object and requires more memory. From a Visual Basic perspective, this option has little or no benefit, because Visual Basic doesn't provide an easy way to directly change an object's reference count.

DCOM Default Security for Windows 2000/NT

The Default Security tab, shown in Figure 8.3, is used to specify which users or groups of users may access an object, launch an object, or configure an object's permissions. These values are used only when there isn't a corresponding value for a specific object.

NOTE

In order to add a new object to DCOM, your username or a security group you belong to must be included in the Default Configuration Permissions list.

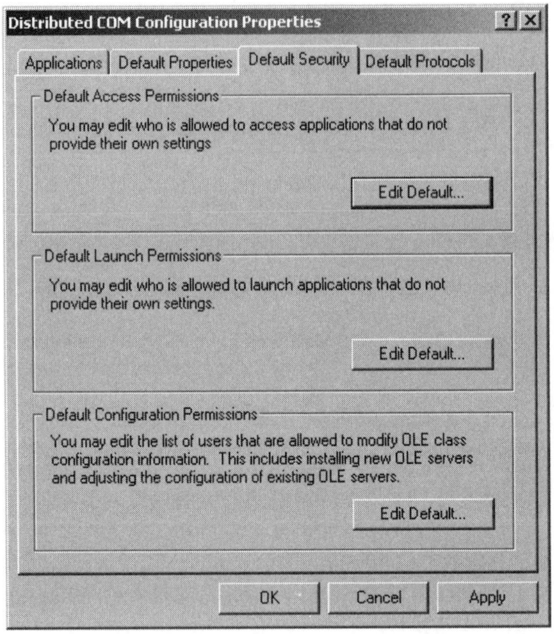

FIGURE 8.3:

The Default Security tab for
Windows 2000/NT

Clicking the Edit Default button for any of the three sets of permissions displays the Registry Value Permissions dialog box. In Figure 8.4, you can see the dialog box for `DefaultAccessPermission` listed as the Registry value. When you choose Default Launch Permissions or Default Configuration Permissions, that key name is listed here.

The Registry Value Permissions dialog box includes the list of users and groups of users and their level of permission. Table 8.3 lists some common security groups found on Windows 2000/NT systems. The Type of Access drop-down box allows you to choose to allow or deny access to a particular user or group of users. If a user or group of users is not listed here, it will be denied access. You can also select a particular user or group of users from this list and change its type of access by changing the value displayed in the Type of Access drop-down box.

The Registry Value Permissions dialog box

TABLE 8.3: Some Common Windows 2000/NT Security Groups

Group	Description
Interactive	The group of users who log on to the Windows 2000/NT Server console directly
Network	The group of users who access Windows 2000/NT resources through a network
Creator/Owner	The group of users who have created or own a Windows 2000/NT sharable resource
Everyone	All users who can access Windows 2000/NT Server
System	The Windows 2000/NT Server operating system itself

If you want to delete a user or group of users from the list of users, click the Remove button.

Clicking the Add button displays the Add Users and Groups dialog box, shown in Figure 8.5. You can use this dialog box to select the names of individual users and groups of users and their type of access. This information is extracted from the server listed in the List Names From drop-down box at the top of the dialog box.

By default, the Add Users and Groups dialog box shows only groups of users. By clicking the Show Users button, you can see all of the users on the server in addition to all of the groups of users. If you select a group of users, clicking the Members button displays the list of users in that group. Clicking the Search button displays a dialog box that will help you find a user or group of users.

FIGURE 8.5:

The Add Users and Groups dialog box

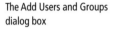

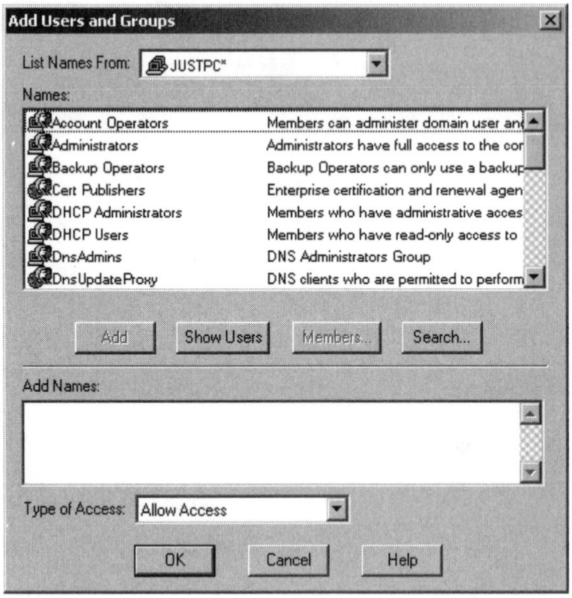

> **TIP**
>
> In general, it's better to manage groups of users than individual users when defining security rules. If none of the groups are appropriate for your DCOM application, you can create a new group in Active Directory. Select Start ➢ Programs ➢ Administrative Tools ➢ Active Directory Users and Computers to access this tool. Then choose the server containing the directory information and click the Create a New Group in the Current Container button to add a new group to the server.

After you've selected one or more users or groups of users, clicking the Add button adds them to the Add Names list box. Once you've added all of the names to the Add Names box, you can choose the type of access they should have in the Type of Access drop-down box. Clicking OK adds all of these users and groups of users with the specified access to the Registry Value Permissions dialog box.

DCOM Default Protocols for Windows 2000/NT

Windows 2000/NT supports a number of networking protocols that work with DCOM. On the Default Protocols tab, shown in Figure 8.6, you can specify the protocols that DCOM can use to communicate with other systems.

FIGURE 8.6:

The Default Protocols tab for Windows 2000/NT

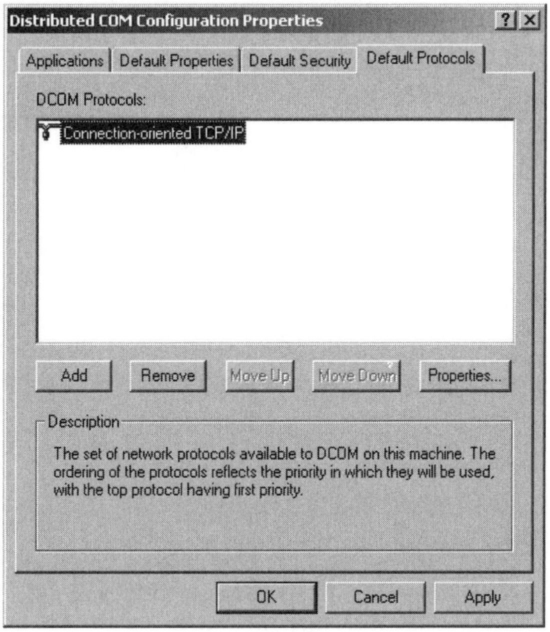

The order of the list is important, because DCOM will attempt to establish a connection to a server system using the protocol listed first. If it can't establish a connection with the first protocol, it will try each of the remaining protocols until it finds one that works. You can use the Move Up and Move Down buttons to rearrange the order of the protocols.

Clicking the Add button displays a dialog box listing each of the protocols available. The protocols available on Windows 2000/NT Server are listed in Table 8.4. Choose the protocol you want to add and click OK.

TABLE 8.4: Networking Protocols Supported by DCOM on Windows 2000/NT

Protocol	Description
Connection-oriented NetBIOS over IPX	A connection-oriented protocol that allows NetBIOS communications over a Novell IPX-based network
Connection-oriented NetBEUI	A connection-oriented protocol that operates over a NetBEUI network
Connection-oriented TCP/IP	A connection-oriented protocol that works over the Internet
Datagram UDP/IP	A connectionless protocol that works over the Internet
Datagram IPX	A connectionless protocol that works over a Novell IPX-based network
Tunneling TCP/IP	A connection-oriented protocol that provides a secure connection over the Internet

NOTE   The only choice for a networking protocol on a Windows 95/98 system is connection-oriented TCP/IP. If you plan to use a mix of Windows 2000/NT and 95/98 systems, you will need to use TCP/IP for your networking protocol.

You can view the properties associated with a protocol by selecting a protocol and clicking the Properties button. Depending on the protocol, you may see a dialog box like the one shown in Figure 8.7. You can enter the appropriate information and click the OK button. Unless you have a special situation, the default values for a protocol's properties are fine.

DCOM Applications for Windows 2000/NT

Now that we've covered all of the default values for DCOM, let's look at how to set values for a specific application. From the Applications tab (see Figure 8.1, shown earlier), scroll down until you find EchoServer.Echo and click the Properties button. You see the application's Properties dialog box, as shown in Figure 8.8. This dialog box has five tabs of its own: General, Location, Security, Identity, and Endpoints.

FIGURE 8.7:

Properties for the connection-oriented TCP/IP protocol

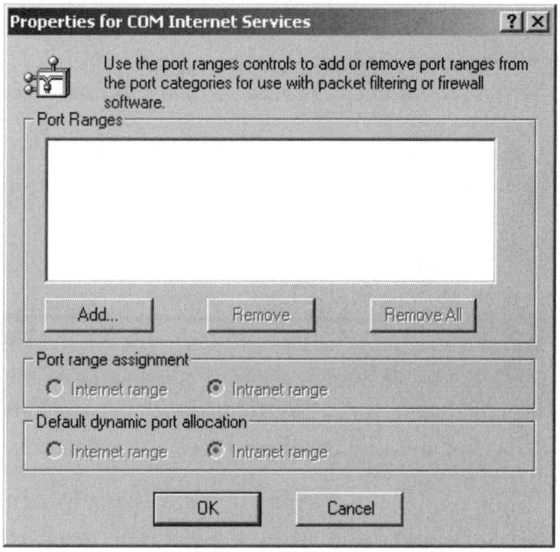

FIGURE 8.8:

An application's Properties dialog box

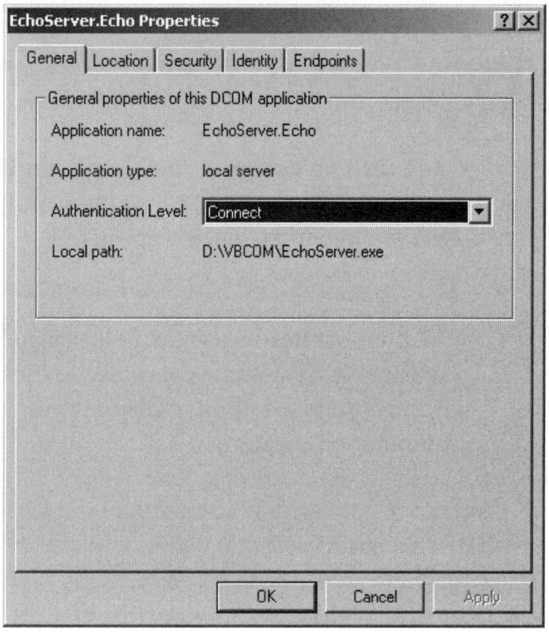

If the DCOM Configuration utility can't identify the name of a DCOM application, it will list its GUID instead.

Any values you enter in the Properties dialog box will override the default values you specified for the system. Thus, you can place additional security on an object that you don't want people to access, or you can remove all security for testing purposes.

General Properties   Figure 8.8 shows the general properties for the Echo-Server.Echo object. You can change only the Authentication Level setting on this tab. (Values for Authentication Level are listed earlier in Table 8.1.) If you haven't specified a value for this object, the default values you set earlier will be assumed.

The rest of the display just confirms information that is set elsewhere. For instance, the application type can be remote server, local server, or remote or local server. This information is controlled by the values you specify on the Location tab. The local path is defined when you register the COM object on the system, and the application name is cast in bits when you build the object in Visual Basic.

Location Properties   Figure 8.9 shows the Location tab for the EchoServer .Echo object. You can see that there are three choices for where the object will run:

- The Run Application on the Computer Where the Data Is Located option works with the GetObject function and chooses which computer to use based on the filename you specify.

- The Run Application on This Computer option runs the object locally.

- The Run Application on the Following Computer option allows you to enter the name of the remote computer in the box immediately below. You can click the Browse button to display a dialog box that helps you locate the computer on the network.

You can choose any combination of the three locations. The first location that works is the location that will be used. Let's assume that you checked all three boxes. If your data is located on a remote system, DCOM will try to load the object on that machine. (This option applies only when you create an object based on a data file such as an Excel worksheet or a Word document.) If the object isn't available on that machine, DCOM will attempt to load the object locally. If the object is available locally, it will attempt to run the application on the specified computer system. If none of these locations works, then DCOM will return an error message.

FIGURE 8.9:

The Location tab for
EchoServer.Echo

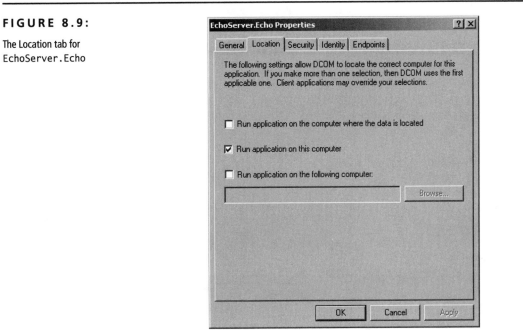

Checking the Run Application on the Following Computer check box is essentially the same as specifying the name of the computer in the CreateObject function. The primary advantage of using DCOM over explicitly specifying the name in the CreateObject function is that you don't need to worry about managing the name in your program. If you choose to move the object from one computer to another, all you need to do is to update the DCOM information. Your program remains unchanged. Of course, you can still specify the name of the computer when you use the CreateObject function. This will override any value you specify in the DCOM Configuration utility.

Security Properties   On the Security tab, shown in Figure 8.10, you see a display similar to the one on the Default Security tab (see Figure 8.3, shown earlier). The primary difference between the two displays is that the object's dialog box has the option to explicitly specify whether you want to use the default permissions or provide a list of users and groups of users who can access the object.

FIGURE 8.10:

The Security tab for
EchoServer.Echo

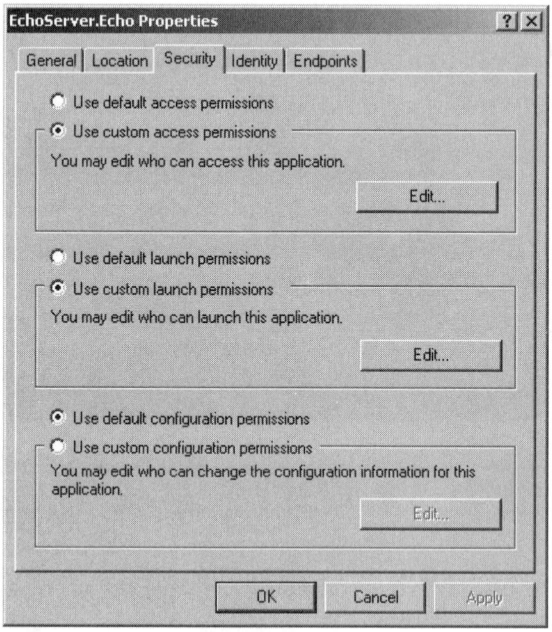

Selecting the custom permission option enables the corresponding Edit button. Clicking the Edit button displays the same Registry Value Permissions dialog box you saw back in Figure 8.4. As described earlier, you can use this dialog box to select the users and groups of users and their level of access to the object. Remember that any value you enter here overrides the corresponding default value.

NOTE   You should set the default security values so that no one can access an object remotely. This prevents someone from using a standard object to gain access to the operating system. Then you can relax the security restrictions on the objects you want to make available on an object-by-object basis.

Identity Properties   The Identity tab, shown in Figure 8.11, allows you to specify which user's security profile should be associated with the DCOM object:

- The Interactive User option selects the username of the person who is creating the instance of the object. Selecting this option means that the user who is logged on to the server's console will be used to determine the security settings. If there isn't a user logged on to the console, an error will be returned to any remote user trying to create the object.

- The Launching User option selects the username of the person who first launched the object. If you select this option, the security profile of the user who launched the COM object will be used.

- The This User option lets you supply an explicit username and password. If you select this option, the specified username will determine the security rights of the COM object. You can click the Browse button to open a dialog box that helps you find the username and its associated security profile. Before you choose this option, realize that using a dedicated username for the COM object can be a real hassle if your system's policies require you to change its password periodically.

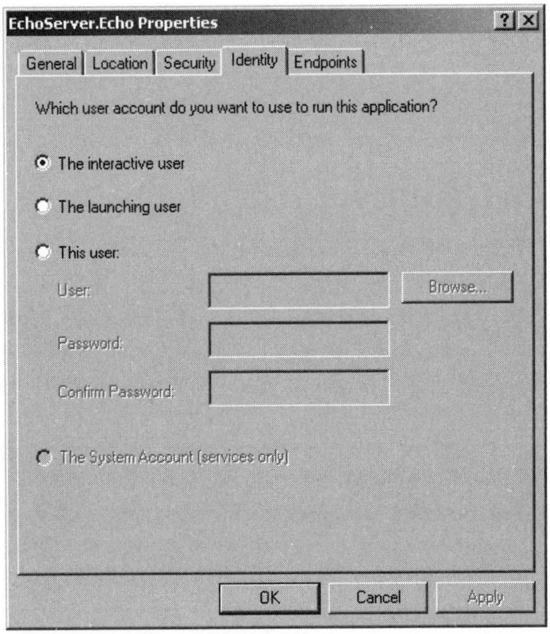

FIGURE 8.11:

The Identity tab for
EchoServer.Echo

Endpoint Properties   The Endpoints tab, shown in Figure 8.12, allows you to list the communications protocols that can be used with your COM application. You also can set specific options for each selected protocol.

FIGURE 8.12:

The Endpoints tab for
EchoServer.Echo

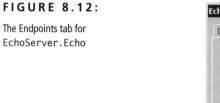

Setting Windows 95/98 Options

Compared with the Windows 2000/NT options, the options in the Windows 95/98 version of the DCOM Configuration utility are rather simple. This is because Windows 95/98 doesn't have a sophisticated security subsystem like its more powerful cousins. However, Microsoft has adapted many of the same capabilities to fit on a Windows 95/98 platform.

> **NOTE**
>
> Windows 98 comes with the software necessary to run DCOM already integrated into the operating system. Windows 95 users need to install DCOM manually. Check Microsoft's web site at www.Microsoft.com/com for more information about how to download the latest version of this software.

DCOM Default Properties for Windows 95/98

The Default Properties tab for Windows 95/98, shown in Figure 8.13, looks almost identical to the one for Windows 2000/NT (see Figure 8.2). The only difference you can see immediately is that the Enable COM Internet Services on This Computer check box is missing from the Windows 95/98 version. However, the really important difference involves fewer choices for the Default Authentication Level and Default Impersonation Level options.

FIGURE 8.13:

The Default Properties tab for Windows 95/98

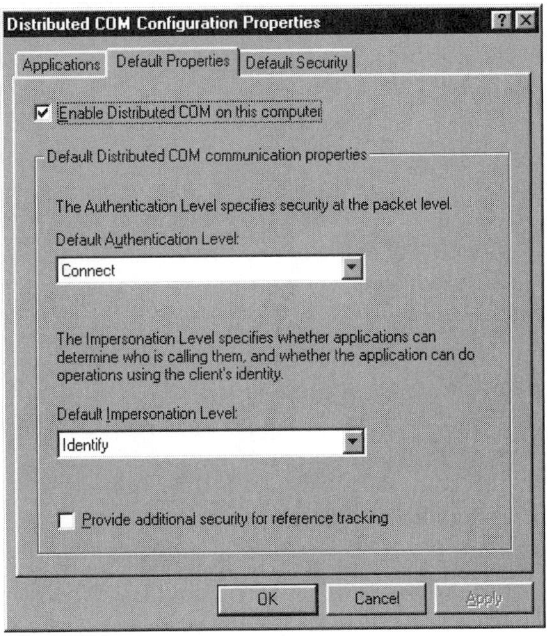

You are limited to only two choices for Default Authentication Level. You can choose to verify security when you initialize the DCOM object by selecting Connect, or you can skip security checking by choosing None.

The Default Impersonation Level setting also has only two choices. The Identify setting instructs the DCOM server to verify the username of the client making the request. If you specify Impersonate, the DCOM server will perform tasks based on the security permissions of the client's username.

DCOM Default Security for Windows 95/98

The Default Security tab, shown in Figure 8.14, allows you to specify who can access DCOM applications. Unlike the Default Security options under Windows 2000/NT, with the Windows 95/98 version, you can control only who can access the DCOM applications. You can't control who can launch or configure the applications.

FIGURE 8.14:

The Default Security tab for Windows 95/98

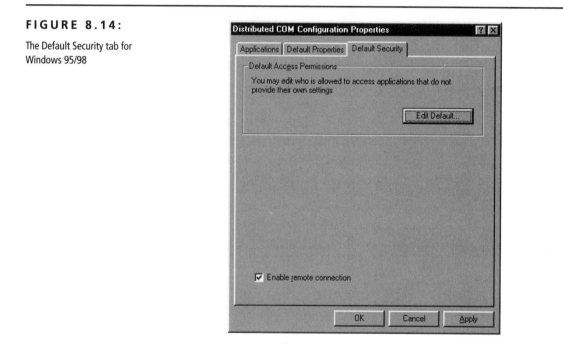

You can grant permission to other systems to access this machine by checking the Enable Remote Connection check box at the bottom of the Default Security tab. Unless your objects use the WithEvents keyword (such as our EchoServer object does), you probably will want to leave this check box unchecked to prevent outside systems from accessing your machine.

NOTE   WithEvents is a relatively inefficient method with which to pass information back to the calling program. It requires five complete round trips to set up and execute a single callback. This extra network overhead may cause problems on a heavily loaded network and will certainly slow down your application if you use a large number of callbacks.

When you click the Edit Default button, the Access Permissions dialog box, shown in Figure 8.15, appears. This dialog box lists the users who can access DCOM objects on your system. I suggest leaving this list empty for end-user machines, because you probably don't want users trying to access objects on your local machine.

FIGURE 8.15:

The Access Permissions dialog box

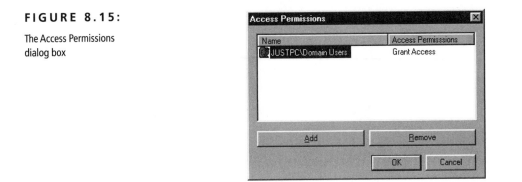

Clicking the Add button in the Access Permissions dialog box displays the Add Access Permissions dialog box, shown in Figure 8.16. The DCOM Configuration utility goes to the domain server (in my case, JUSTPC) to obtain a list of users and groups of users associated with the domain and displays them on the left side of the dialog box. On the right side of the dialog box are two lists of users: those who you want to explicitly grant access and those who you want to deny access. Simply select the user or group of users from the left side and click the Grant Access button or the Deny Access button. Clicking OK merges these changes with the information in the Access Permissions dialog box.

If you're wondering why you might want to explicitly deny access to someone, consider how security groups work. You may want to grant access to everyone in a group except for one or two individuals. So you have three choices:

- You could create a new security group without those individuals and grant access to that group.

- You could grant access to each individual directly.

- You could grant access to the group and then deny access to the specific individuals who shouldn't have access.

The Add Access Permissions
dialog box

The last option probably makes the most sense if you want to make the change for
only a short period of time. The first option makes the most sense in the long run.

DCOM Applications for Windows 95/98

Just like the Windows 2000/NT version of the DCOM Configuration utility, the
Applications tab in the Windows 95/98 version displays all of the objects that are
available for use by DCOM. Figure 8.17 shows this tab, with our EchoServer.Echo
object listed first.

You can choose any object on this list and click the Properties button to display
the list of object-specific properties that override the default DCOM properties.
The object's Properties dialog box has three tabs in this version: General, Location, and Security.

General Properties   The General tab for a specific object lists information
about the object, including its name, its type, where it's located on disk, and the
name of the computer where it should be run. Figure 8.18 shows this tab for the
EchoServer.Echo object.

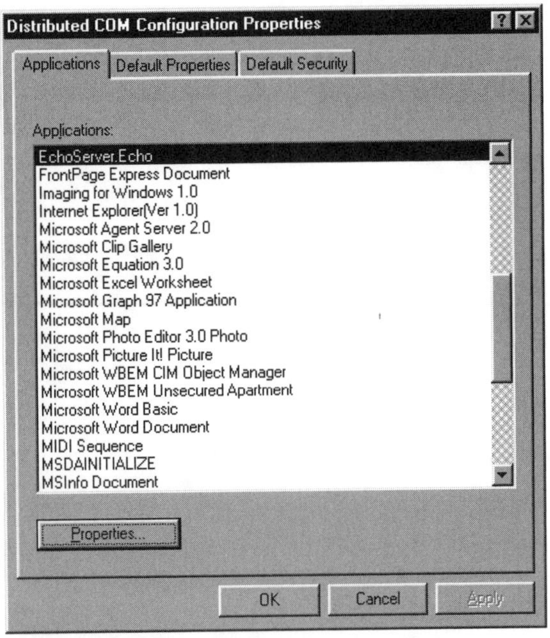

FIGURE 8.17:

The Applications tab for Windows 95/98

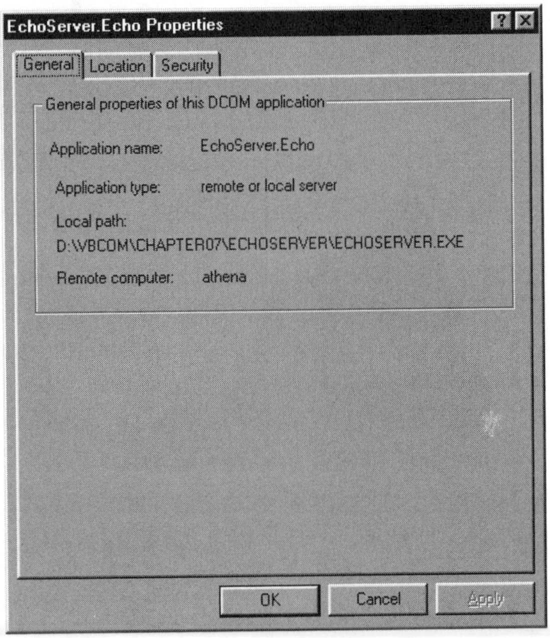

Distributed COM Configuration Properties

Applications | Default Properties | Default Security

Applications:

EchoServer.Echo
FrontPage Express Document
Imaging for Windows 1.0
Internet Explorer(Ver 1.0)
Microsoft Agent Server 2.0
Microsoft Clip Gallery
Microsoft Equation 3.0
Microsoft Excel Worksheet
Microsoft Graph 97 Application
Microsoft Map
Microsoft Photo Editor 3.0 Photo
Microsoft Picture It! Picture
Microsoft WBEM CIM Object Manager
Microsoft WBEM Unsecured Apartment
Microsoft Word Basic
Microsoft Word Document
MIDI Sequence
MSDAINITIALIZE
MSInfo Document

Properties...

OK   Cancel   Apply

FIGURE 8.18:

The General properties tab for Windows 95/98

EchoServer.Echo Properties

General | Location | Security

General properties of this DCOM application

Application name: EchoServer.Echo

Application type: remote or local server

Local path:
D:\VBCOM\CHAPTER07\ECHOSERVER\ECHOSERVER.EXE

Remote computer: athena

OK   Cancel   Apply

Location Properties   Figure 8.19 shows the Location tab for the EchoServer .Echo object. As in the Windows 2000/NT version of the DCOM Configuration utility, your choices are to run the application where the data is located, run the application on the local computer, or run the application on the specified remote computer. If multiple options are checked, the first available one will be the one that is used.

FIGURE 8.19:

The Location properties tab for Windows 95/98

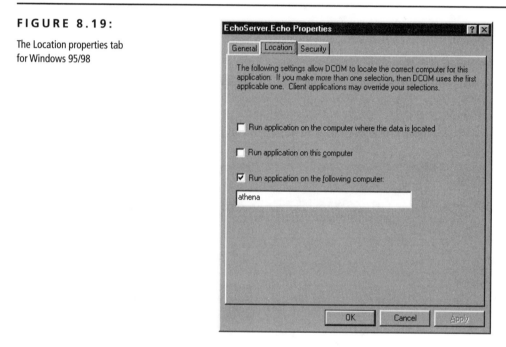

Security Properties   The Security tab, shown in Figure 8.20, allows you to define the users and groups of users who have access to your object. You can choose to use the default access permissions or specify a custom set of access permissions. If you choose to specify custom access permissions (something I highly recommend), you use the same dialog boxes that you used on the Default Security tab to define who can and who can't access the object.

FIGURE 8.20:

The Security properties tab
for Windows 95/98

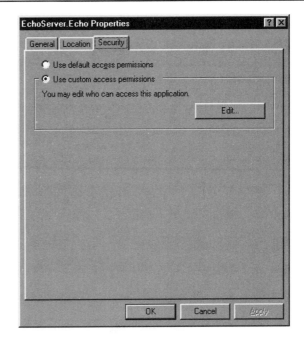

EchoServer and EchoClient Revisited

The EchoServer and EchoClient programs from Chapter 7 included one other feature that is useful when testing your application across the network: the ability to return the name of the computer and the name of the current user. Since you don't know where your COM object is executing, I've added a couple of properties to the Echo object that use Win32 API routines to get the name of the computer and the username of the person running the program. Figure 8.21 shows the Echo Client window.

NOTE   These functions are included in the original programs we built in Chapter 7, so all you need to do is to load the programs for that chapter (available from the book's associated web pages).

FIGURE 8.21:

Getting information from
the remote computer

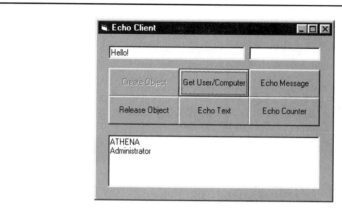

You will find these routines helpful as you try various combinations of security parameters in DCOM. Knowing who is actually running the application and the name of the machine will help you verify that you have successfully switched from running the application on your local machine to running it on the remote machine.

Listing 8.1 shows how to get the name of the computer and return it as a property value in the EchoServer.Echo object.

Listing 8.1   The ComputerName Property Get routine in EchoServer

```
Public Property Get ComputerName() As String

Dim r As Long
Dim s As Long
Dim t As String

t = String(CInt(MAX_COMPUTERNAME_LENGTH + 1), Chr(0))
s = MAX_COMPUTERNAME_LENGTH
r = GetComputerName(t, s)
ComputerName = Left(t, s)

End Property
```

This routine begins by initializing a string with binary zeros. We do this because the Win32 API routine GetComputerName expects a C-style string, which must end with a binary zero. The maximum length of the computer name is specified by the MAX_COMPUTERNAME_LENGTH constant. It also takes the length of the string in bytes as a separate parameter. GetComputerName returns the name of the computer in the first parameter and the length of the name in the second parameter, which we feed into the Left routine to truncate any garbage. We ignore the return value from the GetComputerName routine, because the routine will just return an empty string for the computer name.

The UserName property, shown in Listing 8.2, is similar to the ComputerName property, except that it uses the GetUserName routine rather than the GetComputerName Win32 API routine. The maximum length of the username is stored in the UNLEN constant.

Listing 8.2   **The UserName Property Get routine in EchoServer**

```
Public Property Get UserName() As String

Dim r As Long
Dim s As Long
Dim t As String

t = String(UNLEN + 1, Chr(0))
s = UNLEN
r = GetUserName(t, s)
UserName = Left(t, s)

End Property
```

Calling the routine from EchoClient is merely a matter of calling the two routines and displaying the value in the Text property of the Text2 control, as shown in Listing 8.3.

Listing 8.3   **The Command3_Click event in EchoClient**

```
Private Sub Command3_Click()

Text2.text = MyEcho.ComputerName & vbCrLf & MyEcho.UserName

End Sub
```

Troubleshooting Common DCOM Errors

Most of the errors that you'll encounter while using DCOM relate to security. This is especially true when you are using a Windows 2000/NT server to host the remote object. The best way to deal with a security bug is to find a combination of settings that work. I usually start by removing all security from the object. Next, I put the security settings back in, one item at a time until I encounter the error. After I know what is causing the error, I can try different variations until I understand why the error is happening.

TIP   For more information about Windows 2000 and security, see *Mastering Windows 2000 Server* by Mark Minasi (Sybex, 1999).

The following sections provide some troubleshooting tips for three common DCOM errors.

Error 70: Permission Denied

If you get error 70, try the following steps:

1. Verify that DCOM is enabled on both the client and the server computers.

2. Verify that the username associated with the local computer has permission to access the remote computer and the remote object.

3. Use the DCOM Configuration utility to make the following changes to the DCOM server on the remote computer and try it again.

   a. Select the object from the Applications tab and click the Permissions button.

   b. On the Security tab, modify the settings for Custom Access Permissions and Custom Launch Permissions so that Everyone, System, and Interactive have Allow Access permission.

   c. Also on the Security tab, set the permissions for Custom Configuration for Creator-Owner, System, and Interactive to Full. Set Everyone to Read.

    d. On the Identity tab, select the Interactive user or specify a username for a user who is a member of the Administrators security group. Be sure to include any passwords.

4. If this still doesn't work, use the DCOM Configuration utility to change the Default Authorization Level setting to None and the Default Impersonation setting to Impersonate.

5. On a Windows 95/98 system, try granting access to The World in the Default Security tab of the DCOM Configuration utility.

6. If all else fails, reboot both the client and the remote computers. Some changes you can make with the DCOM Configuration utility won't take effect until after the computer is rebooted. This is especially true for Windows 95/98 systems.

Error 429: ActiveX Component Can't Create Object

If you get error 429, try checking the following items:

- Make sure that DCOM is properly installed and enabled on both the client and server computers.

- Verify that the DCOM server is properly registered on the client computer.

- Verify that the remote object exists on the remote computer and is properly registered. It is possible that the object was registered at one time and all of the proper entries were made in the DCOM Configuration utility, but someone unregistered the DCOM server. This might also happen if the DCOM server was updated and now has a new GUID.

- If the program just sits there and waits for a long time before displaying the message, check the remote computer to see if the CPU utilization is at 100%. This is caused by a security problem where the remote object is trying to write into the Registry, but the username associated with the remote object doesn't have permission to write into the Windows Registry. To fix this problem, update the security permissions for the username associated with the remote object or switch the username to one with the correct permissions.

Error 462: The Remote Server Machine Does Not Exist or Is Unavailable

If you get error 462, check these two items:

- Verify that the name of the remote computer is spelled correctly.

- Verify that you can connect to the remote computer. It is possible that the remote computer is down or that there is a networking problem that involves the two computers.

Final Thoughts

DCOM is a powerful technology that allows you to build distributed applications. You can easily use COM to build application servers, which provide common services for your application. Then you can use the facilities in DCOM to adjust where the application servers are located without impacting your current application.

DCOM brings with it the security tools that can prevent unauthorized use of your COM objects. This is very important when you are connected to the Internet. Without this level of protection, someone could easily access your computer over the Internet and take the opportunity to destroy the data on your computer.

Despite its features, DCOM in itself is not a complete solution to building multiple-tier applications. There are issues of scalability and load balancing. DCOM allows you to specify where an application server is located, but this specification must be made manually. DCOM can't automatically shift a request from a busy application server to one that is not as busy.

While you can develop a solution using DCOM to address these issues, Microsoft has already developed a solution, which is available in COM+. Starting with Chapter 10, I'll cover the COM+ transaction server and the rest of the COM+ tools that address these and other issues related to building distributed applications.

CHAPTER

NINE

9

Programming Databases with COM Objects

- Data sources

- Data consumers

- The DataSpinner control

- The AddressDisplay control

Up until now, I've avoided talking about database issues. I did that for two reasons. One is that ActiveX controls are complicated enough without trying to cover database issues at the same time. The other reason is that the same techniques you use to access a database through an ActiveX control also work with an ActiveX DLL and an ActiveX EXE. Thus, it makes sense to cover databases in a single chapter, after you've learned about the various types of COM objects.

For database programming, you can bind COM objects to a database `Record-set`. You can bind an object to a single database column or multiple columns in a `Recordset` object. Then, as you move through the `Recordset` object, the values will be changed automatically, and your object will be called on to perform various tasks associated with the bound data.

In this chapter, you'll learn about the ActiveX Data Objects (ADO) model. Then we'll build a simple program that demonstrates the techniques for database programming with COM objects.

NOTE This chapter focuses on how to do database programming with COM objects. I assume that you already know how to program a database using ADO. If you need more information, see the *VB Developer's Guide to ADO* by Mike Gunderloy (Sybex, 1999).

Using Data Sources and Consumers

One of the biggest enhancements to Visual Basic was the ability to program using ADO. ADO offers a simpler, yet more powerful, interface to the database. Visual Basic 6 is the first version to ship with ADO. Also new in Visual Basic 6 is the ability to bind a COM object to an ADO data source. This means that you can build ActiveX controls whose values are automatically updated by the database, just like those supplied by Microsoft.

The ADO model breaks the world into two classes of objects: data sources and data consumers. A data source is an object that provides data to data consumers. A data consumer receives data from a data source. A common data source is the

ADO Data Control. A common data consumer is a text box. However, you don't need to use these controls. You can easily build your control using either a class module or a `UserControl` module.

Data Sources

A data source is responsible for generating an ADO `Recordset` object, which can be accessed by a data consumer. All you need to do is populate the `Recordset` with whatever data you want before you release it. Typically, you populate a `Recordset` object directly from a database, such as Microsoft SQL Server. However, the data in the `Recordset` object does not need to come from a database; it can come from any source.

A data source has two key elements: the `DataSourceBehavior` property and the `GetDataMember` event. When the `DataSourceBehavior` property has a value of vbDataSource (or 1), the object becomes a data source. Then the `GetData-Member` event will be triggered whenever the data source needs an object pointer to the `Recordset` object. Whenever the current record in the `Recordset` object changes, the data consumer will be notified and can update its information.

Beyond these properties, your control doesn't need much else to operate as a data source. You may want to include one or more methods to move to other records in the `Recordset`. You also might want to provide other status information from the `Recordset`, such as `RecordCount` and `AbsolutePosition`.

A data source has the option to provide multiple `Recordset` objects to a data consumer. These are identified by a value known as the `DataMember`. This value is passed to the `GetDataMember` event, and it's your job as the builder of the data source to define how to choose the `Recordset` object to be returned. If your data source object returns only one `Recordset` object, this value can be ignored.

Data Consumers

A data consumer receives data generated by a data source. It doesn't deal with the `Recordset` object directly. Instead, it provides a set of one or more properties that will receive data from the data source. As the properties are updated, the data consumer performs whatever activity is needed.

Data consumers come in two flavors: simple and complex. This doesn't reflect the complexity, but identifies whether the object has one data value or multiple data values. You set this via the DataBindingBehavior property. A value of vbSimpleBound (or 1) means that the object has a single data value. A value of vbComplexBound (or 2) means that the object has more than one value.

Each data value that the data consumer wants to bind to a data source must be a separate property value. Then each property must be marked as data bound using the Procedure Attributes dialog box.

Once the object is ready to be used, you must bind it to a data source object, using the DataSource property. If your object has only one data value, you can use the DataField property to bind it to a specific column provided by the data source object. You can specify how the value should be formatted using the DataFormat property. If your data source supports multiple data members, you need to specify a value for the DataMember property to identify which data member you want.

The DataBindings Collection

If there are multiple values to be bound, you need to use the DataBindings collection. This collection allows you to bind multiple values between the multiple data sources and the data consumer. For each property, you can specify values for DataSource, DataField, and several other properties.

The DataBindings collection is just a Visual Basic collection of objects. It has the standard Add method, which can be used to add new bound objects to the collection, and the standard Item method, which can be used to retrieve and modify DataBinding objects inside the collection.

The DataBindings Object

Table 9.1 lists all of the properties associated with the DataBinding object. These properties are used to determine the relationship between the data consumer and the data source. The functions of these properties are fairly straightforward. The exceptions are the IsBindable and IsDataSource properties, which are targeted toward intelligent wizards (who often generate an unintelligible mass of code that almost does what you intended).

TABLE 9.1: DataBinding Object Properties

Property	Description
DataChanged	True when the value in the bound property has changed
DataField	Specifies the name of the database field that is bound to the property
DataFormat	Specifies the format that should be used to display a data value
DataMember	Allows you to request an alternate source of information from the data source
DataSource	Specifies the data source that is bound to the property
IsBindable	True when the property can be bound to a data source
IsDataSource	True when the property is a data source
PropertyName	Contains the name of the bound property

Building Bound Controls

To demonstrate how to use data consumers and data sources, we'll build a pair of ActiveX controls, called DataSpinner and AddressDisplay. These are designed to work with a SQL Server database table called AddressBook. Together, these pieces implement a simple address book, as shown in Figure 9.1.

> **NOTE**   Although we use ActiveX controls in this project, the same concepts and techniques will work for ActiveX DLLs and ActiveX EXEs.

FIGURE 9.1:

The AddressBook program

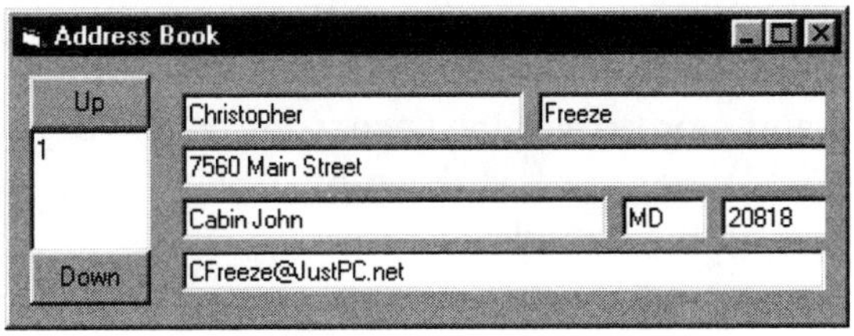

Database Design

The AddressBook table merely contains name and address (both e-mail and snail mail) information. A field called AddressID is included with the table to ensure that each row has a unique key value. Table 9.2 lists the fields in the AddressBook table.

TABLE 9.2: The AddressBook Table

Field	Type	Description
AddressID	Int	An IDENTITY(1,1) value that is unique in the table
FirstName	Varchar(64)	The person's first name
LastName	Varchar(64)	The person's last name
Street	Varchar(64)	The person's street address
City	Varchar(64)	The person's city
State	Char(2)	The person's state
Zip	Int	The person's zip code
EMailAddress	Varchar(64)	The person's e-mail address

NOTE   You can find the AddressBook program, along with the sample data and SQL statements necessary to create the database, on this book's web pages.

The DataSpinner Control

The DataSpinner control has only had two main functions: one scrolls through the Recordset forward, and the other scrolls backward. When we reach the beginning or end of the Recordset, we simply move the cursor to the other end and proceed as if the Recordset had no beginning or end. Although users can't add new records in this control, they can update any of the fields. This design keeps the control simple.

Drawing the Data Source

Unlike the ADO Data Control, the DataSpinner control has buttons that are oriented vertically. This gives us something a bit different from the ADO Data Control and also looks nicer beside the AddressDisplay control. We use regular CommandButton controls at the top and bottom and a multiple-line text box in between. Figure 9.2 shows the elements of the DataSpinner control.

Making Global Definitions

As with most COM objects, we need to define some variables to store copies of the properties and to hold information that we'll use throughout the module. We also include definitions for a Click event and a Scroll event. A Click event will be raised when someone clicks the text box. The Scroll event will happen each time the user moves the cursor to a new record in the Recordset. Listing 9.1 shows the global definitions for DataSpinner.

Listing 9.1   Global definitions in DataSpinner

```
Option Explicit

Private cn As String
Private db As ADODB.Connection
Private ds As String
Private pw As String
Private rs As ADODB.Recordset
Private us As String

Event Click()
Event Scroll()
```

Setting Properties

There are four main properties in this control:

Connection	Contains the connection string to the database
RecordSource	Contains a SQL Select statement to retrieve data from the table
Password	Contains the password associated with UserName
UserName	Contains the name of an authorized user of the database

These properties are implemented with Property Get and Property Let routines. They each follow the same basic structure, so once you see one, you know how the other three work.

In Listing 9.2, you see the UserName Property Get routine. This routine merely returns the value of whatever is in the module variable us.

Listing 9.2   **The UserName Property Get in DataSpinner**

```
Public Property Get UserName() As String

UserName = us

End Property
```

The routine in Listing 9.3 does the exact opposite. It copies the value passed to it in the parameter u into the module variable us. Then it uses the PropertyChanged routine to signal to the UserControl that the property's value has been changed.

Listing 9.3   **The UserName Property Let in DataSpinner**

```
Public Property Let UserName(u As String)

us = u
PropertyChanged "UserName"

End Property
```

The DataSpinner control also includes the typical InitProperties, Read-Properties, and WriteProperties events that will remember the settings for the control's properties. You can refer to the source program to see what these routines look like.

Getting the Data Member

The real key to this control's function is the GetDataMember event, shown in Listing 9.4. This event opens the database and returns the Recordset object to the calling program.

Listing 9.4   **The GetDataMember event in DataSpinner**

```
Private Sub UserControl_GetDataMember _
    (DataMember As String, Data As Object)

If db Is Nothing Then

    If Len(cn) > 0 And Len(us) > 0 Then
        Set db = New ADODB.Connection
        db.Open cn, us, pw

        Set rs = New ADODB.Recordset
        rs.Open ds, db, adOpenDynamic, adLockOptimistic
        rs.MoveFirst

    End If

End If

Set Data = rs

End Sub
```

First, we see if we've already opened the database by checking the db object. If the object doesn't have a valid object reference (the reference is Is Nothing), then we know that we need to open the database.

However, before we open the database, we verify that we have values for both the Connection and UserName properties. If the length of the module-level variables is greater than zero, we try to open the database and the Recordset. We open the connection to the database by creating an instance of the ADODB.Connection object and using the Open method with the connection information, username, and password.

Next, we create a new instance of the ADODB.Recordset object and use the Open method with the RecordSource and the Connection object we just created. We also tell the Open method to use a dynamic cursor and optimistic locking. (Both of these parameters would be nice to have as properties if we planned to use this control in a serious application.)

After we open the Recordset object, we move the cursor to the first record in the Recordset by using the MoveFirst method. Using this method here isn't really necessary, but it does help to ensure that the cursor is at a known location.

At the end of the routine, we assign whatever is in rs to the Data parameter and return the information to the calling program. Note that Data will be set to Nothing if we couldn't open the database for some reason.

Scrolling through the Recordset

Scrolling through the Recordset is fairly easy, as shown in Listing 9.5.

Listing 9.5   The Command2_Click event in DataSpinner

```
Private Sub Command2_Click()

If Not rs Is Nothing Then
    rs.MoveNext
    If rs.EOF Then
        rs.MoveFirst

    End If
    RaiseEvent Scroll

End If

End Sub
```

We begin by verifying that rs contains a valid reference to the Recordset object. Then we use the MoveNext method to move to the next record. If we reach the end of the Recordset (rs.EOF is True), then we reposition the cursor back to the beginning of the Recordset using the MoveFirst method.

Finally, we fire the Scroll event to let the client program know that the current record has changed. Although this isn't necessary, it will let the client program perform any other tasks related to displaying a new record.

Getting the Fields

To make life easier for the programmer using this control, we make all of the fields available in the Recordset available through the control. This is accomplished through the simple Property Get routine shown in Listing 9.6. The only tricky part of this routine is that we must use a Set statement to return the value, because we're returning an object reference.

Listing 9.6   **The Fields Property Get routine in DataSpinner**

```
Public Property Get Fields() As Fields

Set Fields = rs.Fields

End Property
```

Terminating the Object

When the object is no longer needed, we need to make sure that the database connection is closed. We use the UserControl_Terminate event, shown in Listing 9.7, to perform this activity.

Listing 9.7   **The UserControl_Terminate event in DataSpinner**

```
Private Sub UserControl_Terminate()

If Not db Is Nothing Then
   rs.Close
   Set rs = Nothing

   db.Close
```

```
        Set db = Nothing

    End If

End Sub
```

This routine checks to see if the db object has a valid object pointer. If it's valid, then we know that we still have an open connection to the database that should be closed. This also implies that the Recordset object rs is also open. We close the Recordset and set it to Nothing to release its resources. Then we do the same thing for the database Connection object.

The AddressDisplay Control

The AddressDisplay control displays the information from the DataSpinner control. This control is designed to show six pieces of information: the person's first name, last name, street address, city, state, and zip code. Because we have more than one field, we need to use complex binding.

Drawing the AddressDisplay Control

The AddressDisplay control consists of six text box controls that display each of the six fields that can be bound to a data source. Figure 9.3 shows the elements of this control.

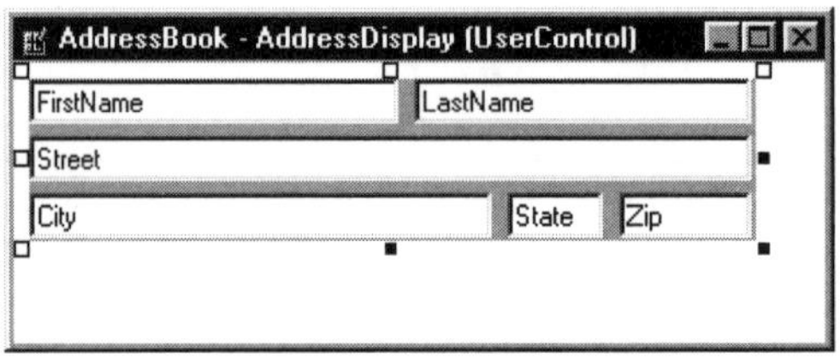

FIGURE 9.3:

Drawing the AddressDisplay control

Defining the Property

Let's see how the FirstName property works. The other properties use similar code. The FirstName Property Get routine is shown in Listing 9.8.

Listing 9.8   **The FirstName Property Get routine in AddressDisplay**

```
Public Property Get FirstName() As String

FirstName = Text1.Text

End Property
```

This routine returns the value stored in the Text1 text box control. We could have created a local variable to keep a local copy of the value, but the slight improvement in performance really isn't worth the effort. However, if you needed to perform some processing (such as formatting a numeric value) before displaying it, you probably will want to keep a local copy of the value also.

The FirstName Property Let routine is shown in Listing 9.9.

Listing 9.9   **The FirstName Property Let routine in AddressDisplay**

```
Public Property Let FirstName(f As String)

If CanPropertyChange("FirstName") Then
   Text1.Text = f
   PropertyChanged "FirstName"

End If

End Property
```

This routine introduces a new function that we haven't used before. This function, called CanPropertyChange, allows you to determine if the property value can be changed. If CanPropertyChange returns True, then it is safe to assign the new value to the text box control and call the PropertyChange routine.

NOTE   The CanPropertyChange routine always returns True in Visual Basic 6, but this will probably change in a future release of Visual Basic. Knowing this, lazy programmers will include the check now, so we don't need to worry about it in the future.

One other situation needs to be handled for each property. In case the user changes the value directly in the text box, the Extender object that provides the binding support needs to be notified of the change. We do this by including another call to PropertyChanged in each text box's Change event, as shown in Listing 9.10.

Listing 9.10   **The Text1_Change event in AddressDisplay**

```
Private Sub Text1_Change()

PropertyChanged "FirstName"

End Sub
```

Unless you include the call to PropertyChanged, the changed information will not be updated in the database.

Marking the Property As Data Bound

Simply creating the properties doesn't make them bindable to a data source. You need to use the Procedure Attributes dialog box (choose Tools ➢ Procedure Attributes from the main menu) to mark each property as data bound.

In Figure 9.4, you can see the information related to the FirstName property. Note the short description of the property in the Description field. This value will be displayed when the user looks at the property in either the Object Browser or the Properties window.

At the bottom of the dialog box is the information about the property's data binding:

> **Property Is Data Bound**   Putting a check mark in this check box marks the property as being bindable. It also enables the rest of the fields beneath it.

> **This Property Binds to DataField**   Checking this option means that the property will be automatically updated using the field name specified in the DataField property. You can check this field if you have a complex binding object, but then you will have one field that is treated differently from the rest, which might confuse some programmers who use your control.

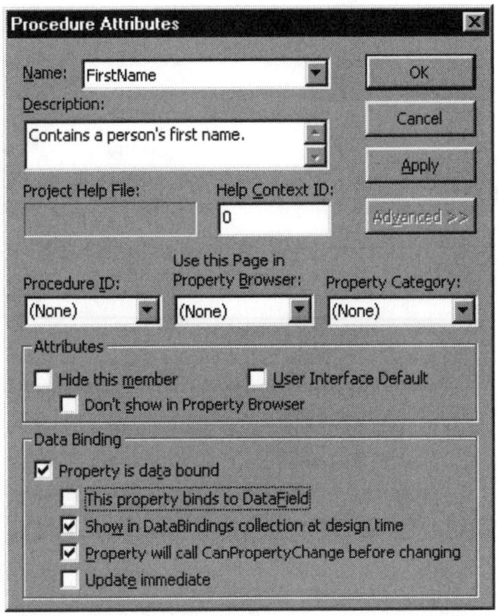

FIGURE 9.4:

Marking a property as data bound

Show in DataBindings Collection at Design Time   Checking this check box allows programmers who use your control to bind the property at design time. Unless you have a good reason not to do this, you should. Most of the power of a bound control comes from establishing the binding information at design time. This eliminates much of the code you need to write, which is the main reason for using bound controls in the first place.

Property Will Call CanPropertyChange Before Changing   Checking this check box means that your code includes a call to the CanPropertyChange function and will respect the value it returns.

Update Immediate   Checking this check box indicates that the Extender object should perform an update immediately instead of waiting for the cursor to move to another record in the Recordset. Because the standard controls don't support this feature, I suggest not checking this option.

Our goal is to make other programmers' lives easier by building controls that take much of the drudgery out of programming and leave them free to focus on issues of design and user interface. I suggest that you avoid using options that create a control that works differently from the rest of the controls, such as the This Property Binds to DataField and Update Immediate options in the Procedure Attributes dialog box. Otherwise, you open the door for confusion and problems somewhere down the road.

The AddressBook Program

After building these controls, we need a program to try them out. The goal of the AddressBook program is to show you how you can build a meaningful program using data-bound ActiveX controls.

NOTE   The DataSpinner control assumes it will access a SQL Server database located on athena, using an initial database of VBCOM, with a user ID of sa and no password. It also assumes that you created the AddressBook table, as defined in the supplied SQL script file. You should change this information to fit your circumstances. For example, by changing the Connection property, you can point to any database server you wish. If you change the name of the table or the database containing the table, you should modify the RecordSource property. You can also change the UserName and Password properties to fit your environment.

Painting the Form

The AddressBook form contains three controls: DataSpinner, AddressDisplay, and a text box control. Figure 9.5 shows the elements of this form. I decided to include the text box control to show how you can easily bind multiple objects to a single data source, including objects that have a complex binding relationship with the data source.

FIGURE 9.5:

The AddressBook form

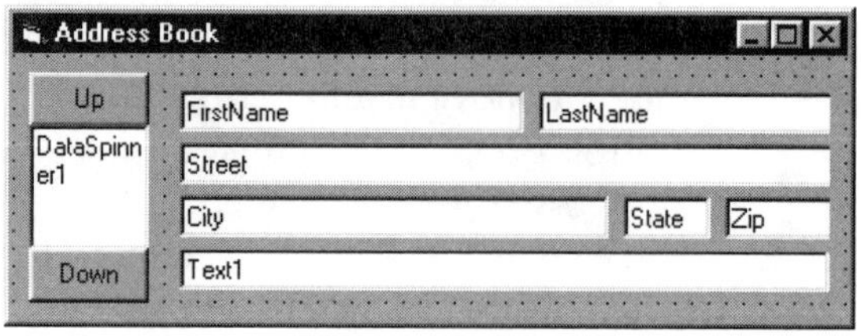

Binding Controls

Binding the text box to the `DataSpinner` control involves setting the `DataSource` property to `DataSpinner1` and the `DataField` property to `EMailAddress`. This is possible because the text box control supports only simple binding.

However, the `AddressDisplay` control is another story. Because you can bind multiple fields using a single property like `DataField`, you need to perform the binding using the `DataBindings` property. You can do this through the Data Bindings dialog box, shown in Figure 9.6. To open this dialog box, click the button at the end of the `DataBindings` property listing in the Properties window.

FIGURE 9.6:

The Data Bindings dialog box

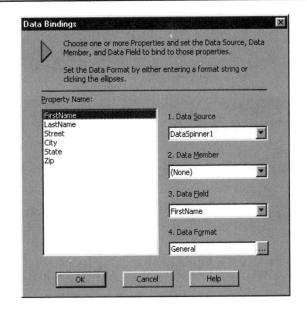

To bind a property, select one of the properties listed on the left side of the Data Bindings dialog box and then choose the appropriate values from the Data Source, Data Member, Data Field, and Data Format drop-down lists. Repeat this process to set up the proper relationships with all of the bindable properties in the control.

Scrolling

We could have an interesting program without any more code than what is in the two controls, but I decided that we needed to do one more thing to make the program aesthetically pleasing—display some information in the DataSpinner control's text box.

We haven't yet used the AddressID value from the table anywhere in the program. I thought it would be natural to use the Scroll event to set this value. This routine is shown in Listing 9.11.

Listing 9.11   The DataSpinner1_Scroll event

```
Private Sub DataSpinner1_Scroll()

DataSpinner1.Text = DataSpinner1.Fields("AddressID")

End Sub
```

This routine takes advantage of the Fields collection object (see Listing 9.6), using it to set the DataSpinner control's Text property. This, in turn, sets the value in the text box in between the two buttons. Each time the record moves to another position in the Recordset, the Scroll event will be fired, and the current value of AddressID will displayed.

Final Thoughts

When building complex database applications, you usually have a group of people working together. These include people like your friendly database administrator (often called the DBA) who maintains the database, the systems analyst who designs the application, and multiple programmers who create the code. I like to include a fourth type of person who is responsible for designing the objects and the core business logic. This person's role is to create useful COM components that make the programmers' jobs easier by letting them focus on functionality and usability issues rather than the details of building the business logic. The AddressDisplay control we created in this chapter is a good example of such a COM component.

The controls we built in this chapter may seem simple, but the concepts behind them aren't. With a little work (less than 50 lines of additional code), the `Data-Spinner` control can easily duplicate the functions found in the ADO Data Control. All you would need to do is to add another pair of buttons to move the cursor to the beginning and end of the `Recordset`, and modify what happens when the Move Next and Move Previous buttons reach the end and the beginning of the `Recordset`, respectively. You could even improve upon it by adding the ability to open and close `Recordset`s on the fly.

Although the `AddressDisplay` control itself meets a very specific need, the techniques used to build it are employed in many different places. For instance, Microsoft's `DataRepeater` control uses the same techniques to display multiple records in a single container, which addresses the need for handling a variable number of records on a fixed-sized form. The `DataRepeater` control is especially useful in applications such as order-entry systems, where you have one header record from one table with the information about a customer, and multiple detail records from another table containing information about the customer's order. You no longer need to resort to tricks such as providing a fixed number of detail lines and awkward scrolling buttons that show only part of the order. The `DataRepeater` control allows you to scroll through all of the selected records quickly and easily, and requires minimal programming effort.

Even though I choose to illustrate data binding using ActiveX controls, it is important to remember that you can use the same techniques to build ActiveX DLLs and ActiveX EXEs. These tools are useful if you don't need a visible presence on your `Form` object. In fact, ActiveX EXEs, when coupled with DCOM, allow you to create specialized application servers that can be used to perform common business logic functions, such as checking for data consistency and performing complex database updates. Since the application server can run separately from both the database server and the end user's workstation, you've built yourself a three-tier application system with very little effort.

The biggest drawback to building three-tier applications using ActiveX EXEs is that they don't scale up very well. Although you may be able to run a few dozen users against a single application server, you may not be able to support hundreds or thousands. But don't despair, Microsoft has already recognized this problem and had addressed it with the latest version of COM called COM+. In the next chapter, I'll begin discussing how COM+ can make your life much easier.

PART III

Programming COM+ with Visual Basic

CHAPTER

TEN

Introducing COM+

- Transaction processing

- COM+ transactions

- Message queues

- Transaction server communications

Just as COM was developed to a standard for building object-oriented programs in a Windows environment, COM+ was developed as a standard for designing distributed *n*-tier application systems. COM+ builds on standard COM, and it incorporates new versions of tools, like Microsoft Transaction Server (MTS) and Microsoft Message Queues (MSMQ), plus brand-new tools like the Microsoft In-Memory Database system (IMDB).

COM+ is built using C++, and some of the features can be accessed only from C++. However, this doesn't mean that you can't use COM+ from Visual Basic. In fact, many of the features are actually easy to use in Visual Basic, once you understand how. Because this is a book for Visual Basic programmers, I'll focus on those COM+ features that work well with Visual Basic and leave the rest for the C++ programmers.

NOTE   At the time this book was going to press, Microsoft decided to delete some of the features from COM+ that had been included in the widely distributed Windows 2000 Beta 3. These features include the In-Memory Database, component load balancing, and the Transaction Shared Property Manager. While the technology behind them is not going away, it is unclear how these features will be packaged and licensed. Because I think that the In-Memory Database facility is particularly useful, I decided to leave information about it in the book, hoping that Microsoft will release it so that you can take advantage of it in the future.

Transaction Processing

In the business world, you often encounter the term *transaction*. A transaction may be a purchase transaction, where you buy a series of goods and pay for them. It might be a deposit to your savings account. A transaction also can be when you register for a college class. It could even be something as simple as participating in an Internet-based survey.

Basically, a transaction is the fundamental unit of work in an application system. A transaction must complete its work without intervention from a user. Everything from the user that is needed to process the transaction has already been collected and is available for processing.

In Windows, transactions are built using COM+ components and are executed on a special server called an application server or a transaction server. It's the server's responsibility to run the transactions based on requests from the users, to provide adequate security for the transactions, and to take the appropriate actions if the transactions or any systems fail.

Each transaction must meet a specified set of criteria known as the ACID test. Each letter in ACID stands for a different criterion: Atomicity, Consistency, Isolation, and Durability. You may recall that I mentioned these in Chapter 1. Now that we've gotten to the part about COM+ programming, let's take a closer look at these transaction criteria.

Atomicity

Atomicity means that either all or none of a transaction is completed. A transaction is a fundamental unit of work and can't be subdivided. If the transaction completes successfully, all of the changes it makes will remain. If the transaction aborts, then all of its changes are undone.

Consider an airline reservations system. When you make a reservation, you specify a number of parameters, such as first class or economy class, aisle seat or window seat, and so on. You want the reservation to succeed only if all of these parameters are met. Otherwise, you want the reservation to fail, so you can try again. It's an all-or-nothing proposition. This is the same concept behind an atomic transaction. Either everything in the transaction succeeds or nothing does.

Consistency

Another aspect of a transaction is that it must always leave the system in a consistent state. Consider what happens if you transfer money from your savings account to your checking account. This translates into two database updates. The first update deducts the amount of money you're moving from your savings account. The second update adds the amount of money to your checking account.

Now consider what happens if the process fails between the two updates. The database will ensure that any completed updates will be saved, but it will not save any uncompleted updates. In this case, it means that the update that deducted the money from your savings account wouldn't be lost, but the update that credited the money to your checking account would be lost. In other words, you lost the money. If the two updates were reversed, you would be getting money from nowhere (but we know that banks don't work that way).

By incorporating the two updates into a transaction, you can ensure that the database is left in a consistent state. Either both updates are completed or both are not completed. In our banking example, this means that there wouldn't be any lost money. The database would recognize that the transaction never finished, so none of the database updates should be kept.

Isolation

While not as obvious as the previous characteristics of a transaction, isolation is also very important. Each transaction lives in its own world where it can't see the processing that is going on with any other active transactions. To put it another way, each transaction sees only a consistent view of system.

This concept is important because it allows the system to recover from failures. While the system is actively processing transactions, you may have dozens or even hundreds of active transactions at any point in time. However, with transaction isolation, this can appear as a single stream of transactions, where one transaction is completed before the next begins. This process allows recovery programs to work and makes it possible to implement distributed database systems.

Durability

The last characteristic of a transaction is its ability to survive system failures. Once a transaction has been completed, it is critical that the changes it made aren't lost.

For this reason, it's important that the system keep logs and backups of all the transactions that were processed. These files make it possible for work to be recovered in case of a catastrophic system failure.

Message Queues

Message queues provide the ability to perform asynchronous tasks in COM+. Your client application creates a message containing a request for service and puts it in the server's input queue. The server processes incoming messages from the queue and returns the results in an outgoing queue. The client application periodically checks the server's outgoing queue for a response. When the client application sees the response, it receives it and continues processing.

For an analogy, consider Jill, who spends her day receiving e-mail from people asking about the weather. As requests come into the inbox, Jill selects the oldest message, looks out the window, and sends a reply. If there are no messages in the inbox, Jill waits until one shows up. When one does, the requester receives an immediate response. On the other hand, if there are many messages in the inbox, the person with the most recent request will need to wait while Jill answers the requests that were received ahead of that one.

Now let's return to this process implemented in a computer. By not requiring a synchronous connection to the server, the client is freed to do other tasks. This is especially useful in situations where the client is a laptop and doesn't have a continuous connection to the server.

Likewise, the server benefits, because it is free to process the request on its own schedule. The server will process the requests in the order in which they were received. If the server is heavily loaded, the requests will wait in the queue until the server is ready to process them, taking a little longer to process than when the server is lightly loaded.

This approach is also great for long-running tasks. The client application can request the server to run a task that will take a while to process. Then the application can check back periodically to see if it is finished. You may be thinking that this isn't really such a new concept. In fact, submitting long-running tasks to a server for processing is exactly what batch processing on a mainframe is all about.

Chapter 11 describes how COM+ works with message queues.

The In-Memory Database System

The In-Memory Database system (IMDB) is designed to provide high-performance access to transient information. It's not designed to replace a regular database, but rather to supplement that database by providing a place to cache frequently accessed information.

IMDB works best in read-only or read-mostly situations, where the database is located on a different machine from the application server. IMDB allows you to keep a copy of data from a database server locally. This means that the data is copied once from the database server into IMDB memory. In an application in which you're constantly reading information from that table, you can significantly reduce the time it takes to get the data, and thus reduce the amount of time it takes to execute the transaction.

IMDB data is typically loaded from a table residing in a SQL Server or an Oracle database. Updates made to IMDB can be passed back, so that the back-end database server can make the appropriate updates.

You also can create temporary tables in IMDB. These tables will live only while the application is running. When the application finishes, the tables will go away. This is useful for holding intermediate results of a database query or other data that may span multiple transactions. IMDB also lives in the same process as the component accessing the in-memory data, which is another reason why is provides better performance than a database cache.

WARNING IMDB doesn't support SQL because the extra overhead of implementing SQL would have a major impact on performance. This means that you can't create objects using SQL statements or run SQL queries on your tables.

Chapter 12 is all about IMDB and how you can use it to improve the performance of your database applications.

Other COM+ Features

Along with transactions, message queues, and IMDB, COM+ includes several other features that are important to its proper operation:

Administrative tools   COM+ comes with a comprehensive set of administrative tools called Component Services. The tools allow you to define new transactions, set security, and perform general housekeeping.

COM+ security   The security included with COM+ permits you to authenticate users, perform work on their behalf using a privileged username, or impersonate users and perform tasks based on their security permissions. Security has been much improved over what existed in MTS and DCOM.

You now can specify role-based security for your transactions and include programmatic security within your transactions. I'll talk more about security in Chapter 13.

Queued components   This facility provides an easy way to execute a COM object asynchronously. It transparently places a set of message queues between your program and the component. Neither your application nor the COM object can tell that there is something in the middle that queues the requests and responses. Unfortunately, until Visual Basic 7 is released, there isn't direct Visual Basic support for queued components.

Component load balancing   One of the problems with DCOM was its inability to easily shift work from one computer to another depending on the server's workload at the time. COM+ incorporates a dynamic load-balancing algorithm based on response time. New instances of objects are created on the server with the best response time in order to spread the workload around. This is a rather complex facility that is mainly of interest to VC++ programmers.

Object pooling   This feature allows an application to create objects that are assigned to a pool and used as needed. Because the objects don't need to be loaded and created each time they are used, you can improve your transaction's performance significantly. Unfortunately, Visual Basic 6 does not support this feature.

COM+ and Visual Basic

Writing the code for a COM+ transaction using Visual Basic isn't much more complicated than creating an ActiveX DLL. There are a few special objects that you need to use to take advantage of the transaction facilities, but writing the code is fairly straightforward.

However, there is more to building a transaction than just writing the code. You need to define your transaction through the Component Services utility and set a number of options that relate to how the transaction executes and who can access it. While this isn't difficult either, it is more complicated than using the DCOM Configuration utility to configure a DCOM-based application server.

NOTE
As I write this part of the book, only the latest beta versions of Windows 2000 Professional and Server support COM+. At this time, COM+ does not run on Windows 95/98 or any other version of Windows, including Windows NT 4. Be sure to check whether the platform you're writing for supports COM+ before you build your application.

COM+ Applications

A COM+ application is a collection of one or more COM objects. These COM objects are constructed in Visual Basic using an ActiveX DLL project. All of the features of the class module can be used within a COM+ object. The biggest difference between a regular COM object and a COM+ application is that a COM+ application can take advantage of some special objects associated with the COM+ transaction server, the COM+ queued components, and the COM+ IMDB.

There are four basic types of COM+ applications:

Server applications   A server application is the most common form of a COM+ application. It runs under control of the transaction server. The application can interact with the transaction server through the objects associated with the transaction's context.

Library applications   A library application is a specialized form of a COM+ application that runs locally on the client computer. It runs in the same address space as the client program that created it. This means less overhead to the client program, because several COM+ applications can use the same components. However, because this object isn't running under control of the transaction server, it can't take advantage of load balancing, remote access, or queued components.

Application proxies   An application proxy contains the registration information necessary for an application to remotely access a server application. If you run it on the client computer, all of the information necessary to access a specific remote server application will be installed on the client computer.

COM+ preinstalled applications   COM+ comes with a set of applications that a help you configure and administer your COM+ system. These applications include COM+ System Administration, COM+ Utilities, and IIS System Applications.

Transaction Types

Each COM object has a transaction property that determines how it works under the transaction server. Table 10.1 lists the possible transaction values.

TABLE 10.1: COM+ Transaction Values

MTSTransactionMode Property Value	COM+ Transaction Support Value	Numeric Value
NotAnMtsObject	Disabled	0
NoTransactions	Not Supported	1
RequiresTransaction	Required	2
UsesTransaction	Supported	3
RequiresNewTransaction	Requires New	4

You can set this value by setting the class object's MTSTransactionMode property value in Visual Basic or by setting the object's Transaction Support property value in the Component Services utility. The value set in Visual Basic will be used as the initial value of the Transaction Support property in the Component Services utility; however, you can override this value simply by choosing a new value in the Component Services utility.

- NotAnMTSObject implies that the object isn't supported under the COM+ transaction server.

- Disabled means that the object doesn't support transactions. When a new instance of the object is created, its object context is created without a transaction.

- RequiresTransaction means that the component's objects must execute within the scope of a transaction. When a new instance of the object is created, its object context is inherited from the object context of the client. It the client doesn't have a transaction, a new transaction is created for the object. If the client is a COM+ transaction, then a new transaction will not be started, because one is already active.

- `UsesTransaction` means that the component's objects can execute within the scope of a transaction. When a new instance of the object is created, its object context is inherited from the object context of the client. If the client doesn't have a transaction, the new object will run without a transaction.

- `RequiresNewTransaction` means that the component's objects must execute within their own transactions. When a new instance of the object is created, a new transaction will automatically be created for the object, even if the calling object is already executing within a transaction.

Transaction Context

Every COM object that is run under control of the COM+ transaction server is provided with a set of objects known as a *context*. A context represents the smallest unit of execution for a component. Each instance of a COM object is assigned to a context. Multiple objects can use the same context, depending on how they were defined and created.

COM+ uses the context objects as a way to provide runtime services. The properties and methods both show and set how the object will be handled. The root object of a context is the `ObjectContext` object. You can get a copy of this object in your application by using the `GetObjectContext` function, as shown below:

```
Dim MyContext As ObjectContext
MyContext = GetObjectContext()
```

All of the other objects in the context can be referenced from this object, either directly or indirectly.

The ObjectContext Object

Probably the most important object is `ObjectContext`, which is the primary object for communicating with the transaction server. You can get a copy of this object by calling the `GetObjectContext` function. Table 10.2 lists the various properties of the `ObjectContext` object.

TABLE 10.2: Properties of the ObjectContext Object

Property	Description
ContextInfo	Returns an object reference for the ContextInfo object
Count	Returns the number of property objects
Item	Returns an object reference to a specific property object
Security	Returns an object reference to the SecurityProperty object

Table 10.3 lists the ObjectContext object's methods. Of the methods available for the ObjectContext object, the most important are SetAbort and SetComplete. The SetAbort method communicates to the transaction server that the transaction should be aborted and all of its updates should be undone. The SetComplete method lets the transaction server know that the transaction completed its work satisfactorily and that it is safe to commit all of its updates.

TABLE 10.3: Methods of the ObjectContext Object

Method	Description
CreateInstance	Creates a new instance of the specified using the current object's context
DisableCommit	Specifies that the object's work is incomplete and has left the system in an inconsistent state
EnableCommit	Specifies that the object's work may not be complete, but the system is in a consistent state
IsCallerInRole	True when the object's direct caller is in the specified role, either as an individual or as part of a group
IsInTransaction	True when the object is executing inside a transaction
IsSecurityEnabled	True when security is enabled
SetAbort	Instructs the transaction server to undo any of the transaction's actions, perhaps because an unrecoverable error has occurred or the system is in an inconsistent state
SetComplete	Instructs the transaction server to commit all updates to the system because the transaction has completed its work successfully

The CreateInstance method should be used to create new objects under COM+. This method will pass along the current context for its execution. If the object isn't registered with COM+, the object is merely created and no context will be assigned. Otherwise, the object will be created based on the Transaction Support value:

- If this value is set to Does Not Support Transactions, the object will be created without any transaction support.

- If this value is set to Requires a Transaction or Supports Transactions, the new object will inherit the current transaction.

- If this value is set to Requires a New Transaction, a new transaction is created for the object.

The ContextInfo Object

The ContextInfo object contains information about the current context. You can get a reference to this object from ObjectContext.ContextInfo. Table 10.4 lists the methods of the ContextInfo object.

TABLE 10.4: Methods of the ContextInfo Object

Method	Description
GetActivityId	Returns the identifier of the current activity
GetContextId	Returns the identifier of the current context
GetTransaction	Returns an object pointer to the transaction object
GetTransactionId	Returns the identifier of the current transaction
IsInTransaction	True when the object is executing inside a transaction

The SecurityProperty Object

The SecurityPropertyObject allows your object to determine the username associated with either the base program that is using the object or with the program or object that directly created the object. Table 10.5 lists the methods of the SecurityProperty object. This object may be referenced directly by using the ObjectContext.Security property.

NOTE   The GetDirectCreatorName and GetOriginalCreatorName were originally used in MTS version 2. They shouldn't be used with COM+, because they return unpredictable results.

TABLE 10.5: Methods of the SecurityProperty Object

Method	Description
GetDirectCallerName	Returns the username associated with the program or object that created this object directly
GetDirectCreatorName	Used in MTS 2 and unsupported in COM+
GetOriginalCallerName	Returns the username associated with the base program that created this object
GetOriginalCreatorName	Used in MTS 2 and unsupported in COM+

A Simple COM+ Application

Building a COM+ application begins the same way as creating a COM object. The first step is to design the interface for your application. This includes defining the objects you will need to build, plus their properties, methods, and events. Then you can go on to build your application in Visual Basic and install it on the COM+ transaction server.

Unlike the previous examples in this book, the example we'll start here spans multiple chapters to demonstrate the concepts behind COM+. The Contact Manager application allows someone to track contacts made with various people. The information includes notes about the contact, action items that result from the contact, and a date and time to follow up the contact. For instance, suppose that a sales organization periodically contacts potential customers. When the salespeople make telephone calls, they can make notes directly into the computer application. If the customers have any specific requests, such as for more information, these requests and their handling can be tracked.

The Database Tables

The Contact List sample COM+ application uses a database with three tables, named Contacts, ContactInfo, and ActionItems.

The Contacts table contains items to describe the person contacted. Thus, most of its information relates to ways to contact the person, including their address, telephone number, fax number, and e-mail address. Each contact is assigned a unique integer value called ContactId. This value will be used to tie records in the other tables to the information contained in this table. Table 10.6 lists the fields in the Contacts table.

TABLE 10.6: The Contacts Table

Field	Type	Description
ContactId	Int	A number that uniquely identifies a contact
FirstName	Varchar(64)	The contact's first name
MiddleName	Varchar(64)	The contact's middle name (may be blank)
LastName	Varchar(64)	The contact's last name
Prefix	Varchar(64)	The contact's name prefix, such as Mr., Mrs., Miss, or Dr. (may be blank)
Title	Varchar(64)	The contact's title
Organization	Varchar(64)	The organization that employs the contact
Street	Varchar(64)	The street address where the contact receives mail
City	Varchar(64)	The city where the contact receives mail
State	Varchar(64)	The state where the contact receives mail
Zip	Varchar(16)	The zip code where the contact receives mail (extended zip codes are acceptable)
Telephone	Varchar(32)	The contact's telephone number
FAX	Varchar(32)	The contact's fax number
Email	Varchar(64)	The contact's e-mail address

The `ContactInfo` table contains information about a single contact. This information includes the date and time the person was contacted, the name of the person making the contact, and how the person was contacted (via phone, fax, or another method). It also includes the date when the next contact should be made (for example, the customer told the salesperson, "I'm busy now, so please call back next year."). The combination of `ContactId` and `DateContacted` are used to provide a unique key to this table. Table 10.7 lists the fields in the `ContactInfo` table.

TABLE 10.7: The ContactInfo Table

Field	Type	Description
ContactId	Int	Reference to a contact in the `Contacts` table
DateContacted	Datetime	The date and time of this contact
UserName	Varchar(64)	Reference to staff member making the contact
HowContacted	Int	Contains values that describe how the person was contacted: 0=unknown, 1=phone, 2=in person, 3=mail, or 4=e-mail note
FollupDate	Datetime	The date and time of the next contact; should be greater than the current date and time (if this field is `Null`, no follow-up contact was requested)
ActionRequired	Bit	`True` when there are action items from this contact

The `ActionItems` table contains specific items that need to be completed following the contact. This could be a customer's request for information or scheduling a meeting to discuss more details about a product. The `ContactId`, `DateContacted`, and `ActionItemNumber` values are used to uniquely identify a record in this table. Because someone other than the person who made the original contact may be assigned the job, another `UserName` field is included to record who actually completed the action item. Table 10.8 lists the fields in the `Action-Items` table.

TABLE 10.8: The ActionItems Table

Field	Type	Description
ContactId	Int	Reference to a contact in the Contacts table
DateContacted	Datetime	The date and time of the contact
ActionItemNumber	Int	Uniquely identifies the action item for a specific value of ContactId and DateContacted
ActionItem	Varchar(64)	The description of the action item
UserName	Varchar(64)	The username of the person who completed the action item
DateCompleted	Datetime	The date and time the action was completed (a Null value means that the action item has yet to be completed)

The COM+ Application's Properties

When you first create the empty COM+ application, the Visual Basic wizard attempts to pick good values for the application's properties. However, it's your job to review those properties and change them to reflect the specific needs of your applications.

General Properties

The General tab of the application Properties dialog box contains the name of the application and a description of the application. The description can be any set of text you desire, up to 500 characters long. Also shown on this tab is the GUID of the application itself. Figure 10.1 shows the general properties of the Contact Manager application.

Security Properties

The Security tab of the application Properties dialog box controls how much or little security is used at the application level. Figure 10.2 shows the security properties of the Contact Manager application.

FIGURE 10.1:

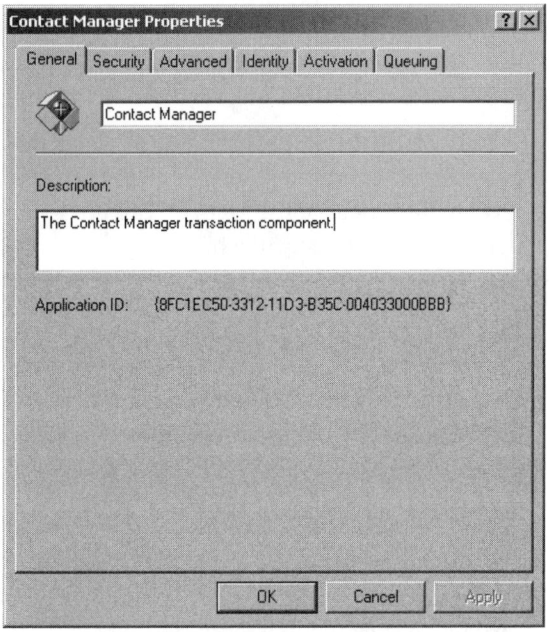

General properties of the
Contact Manager application

FIGURE 10.2:

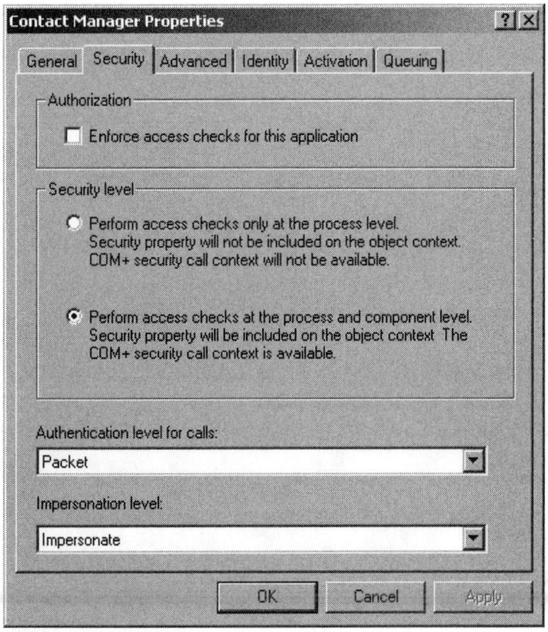

Security properties of the
Contact Manager application

For the sample application, we disable all security for this application by unchecking the Enforce Access Checks for This Application check box. This means that the username must be either explicitly authorized to use this application or that it is a member of a security group that is authorized to use the application.

You can choose to perform access checks only at the process level or at the process and component level. For the sample application, we choose the lower level to also include the security call context, which will allow our application to perform its own security checking.

The last two fields on this form are directly from the DCOM Configuration utility. You can choose to authenticate the user at the Connect, Call, Packet, Packet Integrity, Packet Privacy level, or none of the above. You can also choose an impersonation level as Anonymous, Identify, Impersonate, or Delegate. Our sample application is set to Packet and Impersonate.

Advanced Properties

The Advanced tab of the application Properties dialog box, shown in Figure 10.3, allows you to fine-tune how the component operates within the transaction server. You can choose to shut down the application if it is idle after a specified number of minutes. The Contact Manager application will shut down after 3 minutes of no activity.

FIGURE 10.3:

Advanced properties of the Contact Manager application

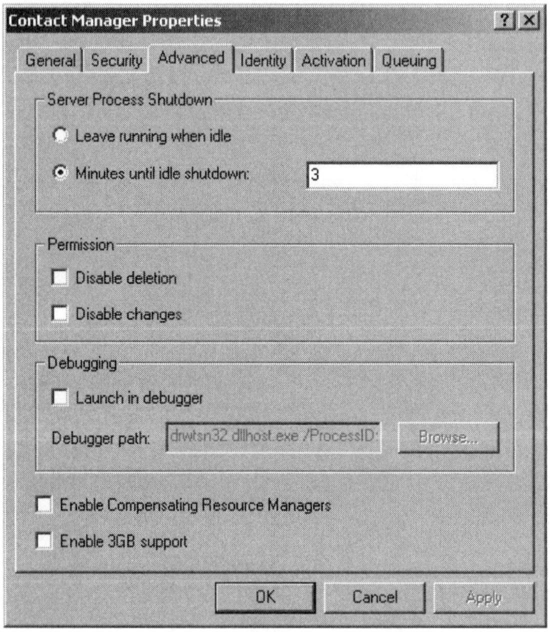

You can specify that your application can't be deleted by checking the Disable Deletion check box or that it can't be changed by checking the Disable Changes check box. Unfortunately, the option for running the application in a debugger is one of those C++-only features. Although it's true that you can debug Visual Basic code from C++, this requires a detailed knowledge of how Visual Basic creates object code, because the C++ debugger works only on object code.

You can enable the Compensating Resource Manager to assist with resource sharing. The Enable 3GB Support setting works only on Windows 2000 Advanced Server, which has been configured to handle 3GB of memory. (Address spaces in the normal version of Windows 2000 Server are limited to 2GB.)

Identity Properties

The Identity tab of the application Properties dialog box allows you to specify the username, which will be used to run the application. You can choose the interactive user who is signed onto the console (the default), or you can specify a username and password. Figure 10.4 shows the identity properties for the Contact Manager application.

FIGURE 10.4:

Identity properties of the Contact Manager application

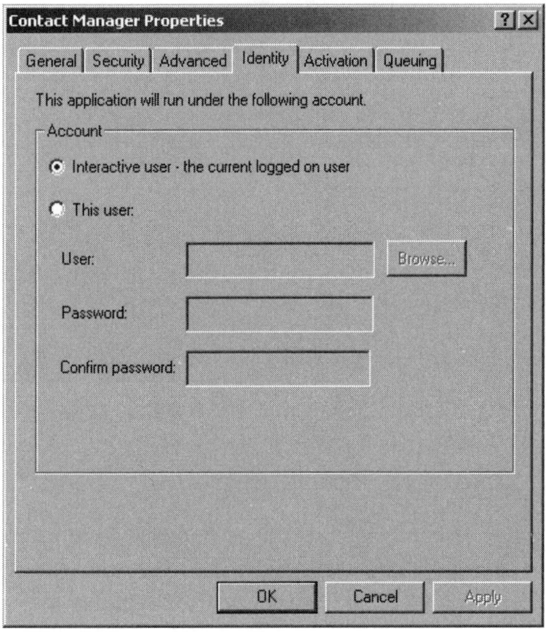

Activation Properties

The Activation tab of the application Properties dialog box, shown in Figure 10.5, allows you to specify how the application will be loaded. You can choose from two options:

- Library Application, which will run in the client's address space

- Server Application, which will run under control of the COM+ transaction server

Contact Manager will run as a server application.

FIGURE 10.5:

Activation properties of the
Contact Manager application

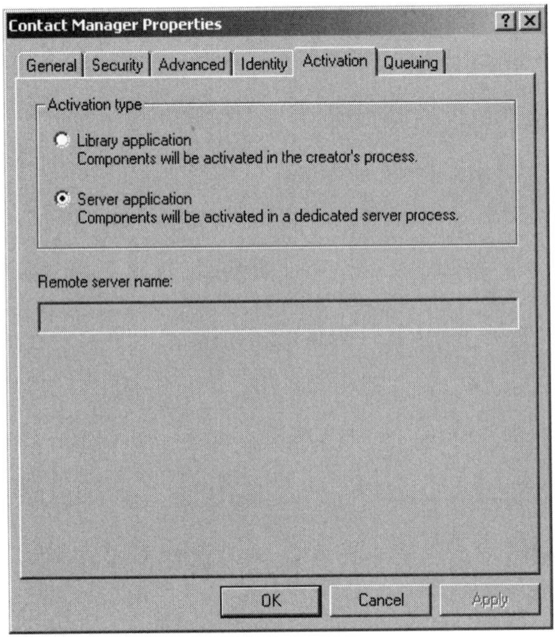

Queuing Properties

The Queuing tab of the application Properties dialog box allows you to specify that your application uses COM+ queued services (MSMQ). It also allows you to specify whether the application functions as a listener and will be activated when a message arrives in the queue. Because this program doesn't use message queues, both boxes are unchecked. Figure 10.6 shows the queuing properties of the Contact Manager application.

Queuing properties of the Contact Manager application

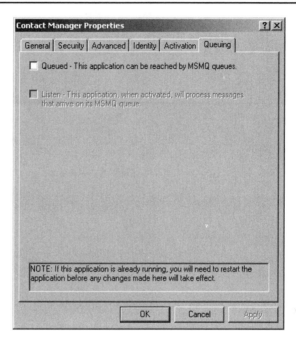

The COM+ Component's Properties

After you've created the COM+ application, you can easily review and change the settings for each component using the component's Property dialog box. Right-click the component you wish to review and select Properties. A tabbed dialog box will appear, allowing you to review settings in the following categories: General, Transactions, Security, Activation, Concurrency, and Advanced.

General Properties

The General tab of the component's Property dialog box displays a description of the application that can be up to 500 characters long. It also displays the path and filename of the DLL file and the GUIDs for the COM object and the application. Figure 10.7 shows this dialog box.

Transactions Properties

The Transactions tab, shown in Figure 10.8, allows you to specify the level of transaction support the component needs. See the "Transaction Types" section earlier in this chapter and Table 10.1 for a discussion of these properties.

Security Properties

The Security tab, shown in Figure 10.9, displays the roles that have been created for this component. These are defined through the application's Properties dialog box. You can optionally disable all of the security checking at the component level by unchecking the Enforce Component Level Access Checks check box.

FIGURE 10.8:

The Transactions tab of the ContactMgr.Contact Properties dialog box

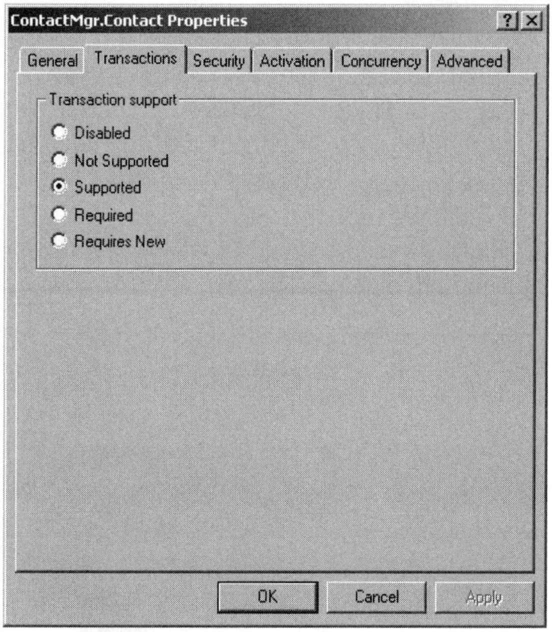

FIGURE 10.9:

The Security tab of the ContactMgr.Contact Properties dialog box

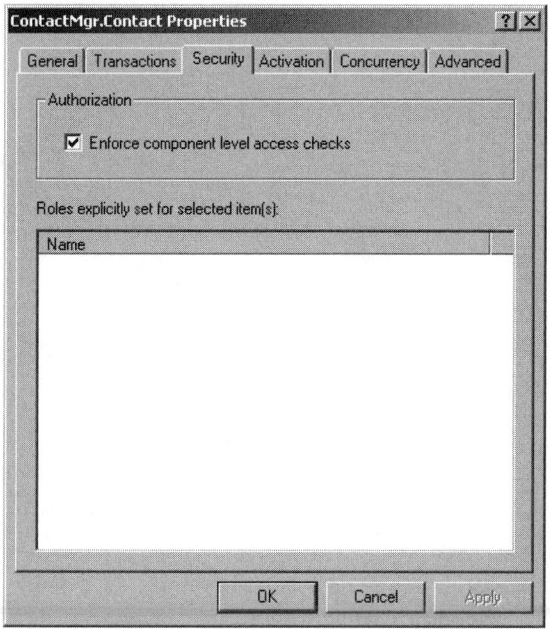

Activation Properties

The Activation tab, shown in Figure 10.10, defines how the component will be started. Unfortunately, Visual Basic 6 does not support object pooling, so that part of the dialog box is disabled. This is due to Visual Basic's lack of support for multiple threads. The Enable Object Construction check box allows you to pass a string to the object when it is created. This parameter can be safely ignored by the Visual Basic programmer. Similarly, Visual Basic doesn't offer native support for the facilities represented by the remaining options, and they should be left with their default values.

FIGURE 10.10:

The Activation tab of the ContactMgr.Contact Properties dialog box

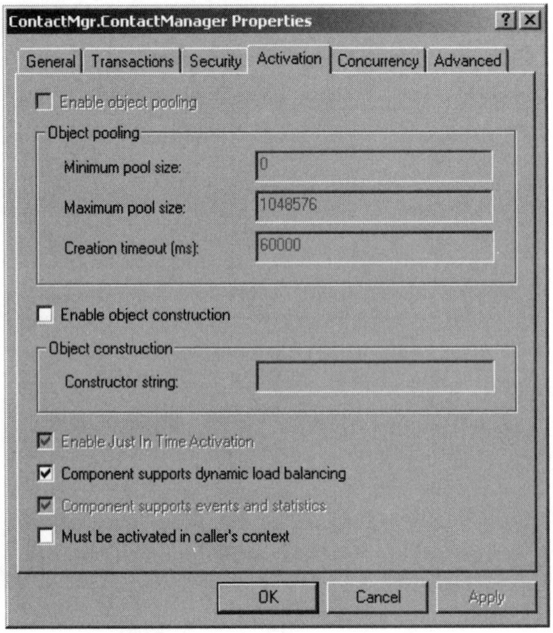

Concurrency Properties

The Concurrency tab, shown in Figure 10.11, specifies the level of synchronization support that is required between transactions. These values depend on the transaction support specified on the Transaction tab. This tab also shows the threading model used by the component.

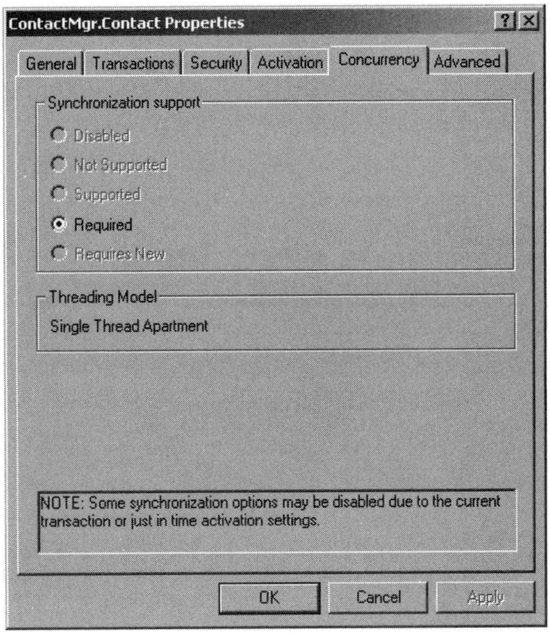

FIGURE 10.11:

The Concurrency tab of the
ContactMgr.Contact Prop-
erties dialog box

Advanced Properties

The Advanced tab, shown in Figure 10.12, allows you to define an alternate component that will be used in place of the dead-letter queue. I'll cover this issue in
detail in Chapter 11 when I talk about message queues.

COM+ Object Construction

In order to demonstrate the differences between a regular COM object and one
designed to be part of a transaction, I've created a simple class called Contact.
This class has two methods:

- The GetName method returns a contact's name in individual pieces (first
  name, last name, and so on).

- The GetFullName method returns a single value with all of the pieces of the
  name put together.

FIGURE 10.12:

FIGURE 10.12:

The Advanced tab of the ContactMgr.Contact Properties dialog box

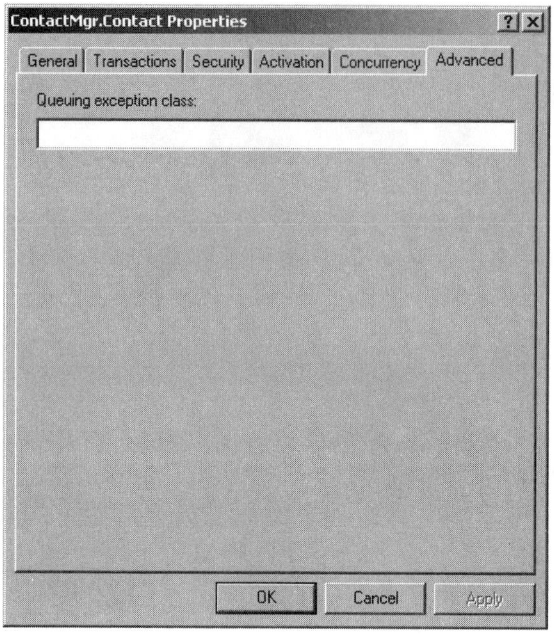

NOTE   The GetFullName and GetName routines are similar. The GetName routine is discussed here. For details about the GetFullName routine, go to www.Sybex.com or www.JustPC.com and follow the links to download the sample program.

The GetName routine, shown in Listing 10.1, returns information about the specified ContactId. The information about the current contact is stored in a series of module-level variables that use the database field name preceded by an x. This allows me to use the real database field names as parameters, which is less confusing to the programmers who will use this object.

Listing 10.1   The GetName routine in Contact

```
Public Sub GetName(ByVal ContactId As Long, _
    Prefix As String, FirstName As String, _
    MiddleName As String, LastName As String)
```

```
Dim o As ObjectContext

Set o = GetObjectContext()

App.LogEvent "ContactMgr.Contact.FullName:" & _
    "Original caller=" & o.Security.GetOriginalCallerName

If FindContact(ContactId) Then
    Prefix = xPrefix
    FirstName = xFirstName
    MiddleName = xMiddleName
    LastName = xLastName

Else
    Prefix = ""
    FirstName = ""
    MiddleName = ""
    LastName = ""

End If

o.SetComplete

End Sub
```

The routine begins by declaring the variable o to hold the ObjectContext and then calling the GetObjectContext function to get the context for this transaction. Once we have the context, we use the object to get the username of the original caller and write it to the application log using the App.LogEvent method.

TIP   Since a COM+ transaction runs under control of a server, it doesn't have a visual component with which you can display errors. However, there is a tool called the **App.LogEvent** that will write a string to the application log file. You can view this file in Windows 2000 Server through the Component Services utility (select the Event Viewer and the Application Log). But use this facility with caution, since it is easy to overflow the application log.

Next, we use the `FindContact` function to search for the specified contact. If the contact is found, we return the information from the appropriate module-level variables; otherwise, we return empty strings. Once we've set the return values, we use the `SetComplete` method to inform the COM+ transaction server that the transaction ran properly.

The last step is to create the actual DLL file that will be used by the COM+ transaction server. You can do this by selecting File ➢ Make Project.DLL from the main menu.

COM+ Component Definition

After you've created the COM object, you need to define it in the Component Services utility. This is a two-part process:

- Create an empty application that will hold the information about the COM+ application.
- Import the application into COM+.

An Empty Application in COM+

To create an empty application in COM+, follow these steps.

1. Choose Start ➢ Programs ➢ Administrative Tools ➢ Component Services.

2. Under Console Root, open COM+ Applications by selecting Component Services, then Computers, and then the name of the computer on which you want to create the service. Figure 10.13 shows an example of a COM+ Application listing.

3. Right-click Component Services and choose New ➢ Application. This starts the COM Application Install Wizard. Click Next to begin defining your application.

4. Click the Create an Empty Application button to move to the next window.

5. Enter the name of your new application and choose Server Application, as shown in Figure 10.14. Then click Next.

FIGURE 10.13:

Listing the COM+ Applications on My Computer

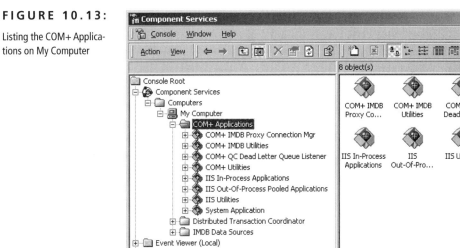

FIGURE 10.14:

Enter the name and type of your new COM+ application.

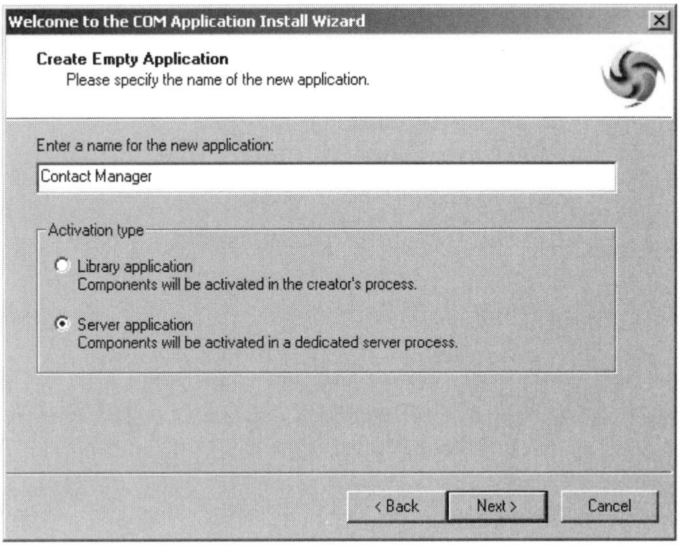

6. Choose the user account that the application will run under. You can choose to use the security of the username who is logged onto the server's console (the interactive user) when the application is run, as shown in Figure 10.15. Alternatively, you may enter the name and password of a specific user. Click Next to go to the final step in the process.

NOTE   For testing purposes, I suggest that you use the username of the interactive user logged on to the server's console. Then you should sign on as Administrator (or use a username with the same privileges as Administrator). This will remove most of the security restrictions on your transactions. Once you're satisfied that the transaction is working properly, you can create a username for that particular transaction and use that instead of the interactive user. Grant this username only the privileges the transaction needs to run. This approach will help prevent security problems in the long run.

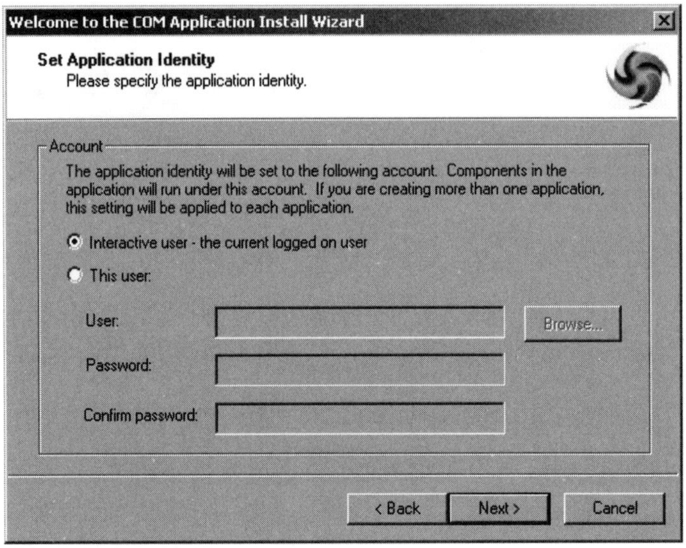

FIGURE 10.15:

Choose the identity that the COM+ application will use.

7. Click Finish to complete the process and build the empty application.

Application Importing

Within the Component Services utility, you need to perform these steps to import your application.

1. Expand the application you just created to display the Components and Roles folders that are underneath it, as shown in Figure 10.16.

2. Right-click the Components folder and select New ➢ Component from the pop-up menu. This starts the COM Component Install Wizard.

3. Click Next to move to the Import or Install a Component step, as shown in Figure 10.17. Click the Install New Component(s) button.

4. In the file-open dialog box that appears, choose the name of your DLL file and click Open. The Install New Components dialog box appears, as shown in Figure 10.18.

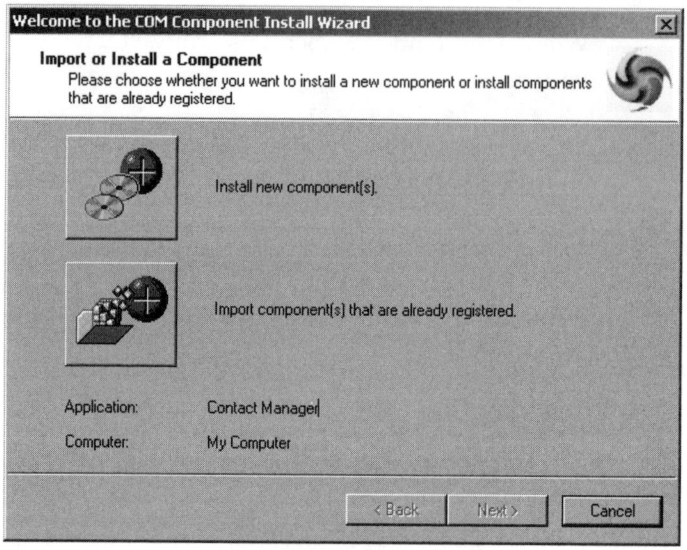

FIGURE 10.17:

Choose the Install New Component(s) button.

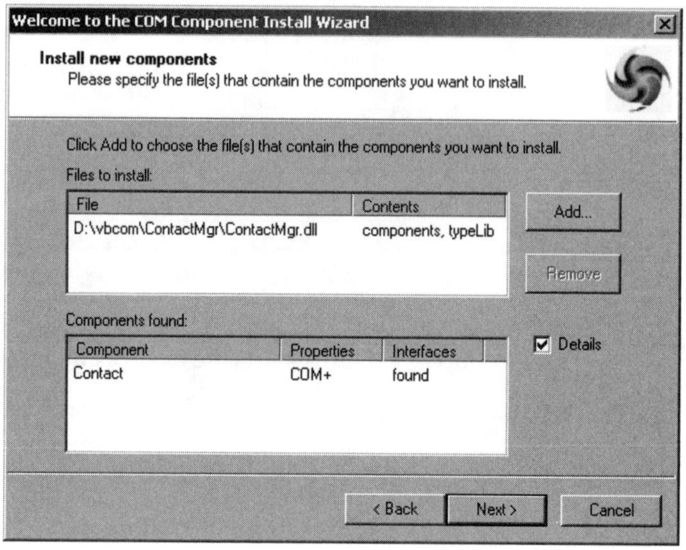

FIGURE 10.18:

Review the information about your component.

5. If you need to install more than one DLL file, click the Add button to display the file-open dialog box again. Click Next when you have selected all of the DLL files that make up your application.

6. In the final step of the wizard, click Finish to add the component to the application.

NOTE   You can also use drag-and-drop to import a DLL. Dragging the DLL into the component pane of the COM+ application in Component Services will import the DLL and register all of its components.

Client Program Construction

Having a COM+ application is meaningless unless you have a client program that will use it. Listing 10.2 shows The Command1_Click event in ContactClient.

Listing 10.2   The Command1_Click event of ContactClient

```
Private Sub Command1_Click()

Dim p As String
Dim f As String
Dim m As String
Dim l As String

Set Contact = CreateObject("ContactMgr.Contact")

Contact.GetName 1, p, f, m, l

Text1.Text = p
Text2.Text = f
Text3.Text = m
Text4.Text = l

Set Contact = Nothing

End Sub
```

This routine begins by reserving space for the return values from the `GetName` method. Then we use the `CreateObject` function to create an instance of the `ContactMgr.Contact` object.

After we create an instance of the object, we call the `GetName` method using a `ContactId` value of 1 to retrieve the person's first, middle, and last names and the name prefix. Then we display this information is a series of text boxes. Finally, we destroy the object by setting `Contact` equal to `Nothing`.

Final Thoughts

Using a transaction server can offer big benefits to someone building a complex distributed application. However, many of the features don't come into play until you start building database applications. Transactions allow you to build relatively complex update processes with the knowledge that either all of the updates will succeed or none of them will get through. This makes it easier to ensure that your database is intact.

One of the most common problems encountered by a database administrator is that an application left the database in an inconsistent state. Although it's relatively easy to find a physically corrupted database, detecting an inconsistent database can be a real challenge. You need to examine a database for subtle problems, such as a row in one table that requires a row in a different table, or a total in a summary record that doesn't agree with the values in the detail records. In some cases, you may never be able to find the problem. Consider the transfer of funds from your savings account to your checking account. If the second update was never done, how could you verify that the database was inconsistent? (Hint: you need a table to keep track of the raw transactions as well as the accounts.) The more effort you put into preventing problems, the more time you will save down the road when you need to fix problems.

COM+ works with Visual Basic 6, but there are a number of features that work only with Visual C++. These include object pooling and various threading models that require using the C++ interface. For the most part, these features are needed only in really large-scale applications, so the lack of these features won't adversely impact the majority of Visual Basic programmers. For a complete discussion of COM+ and its related technologies, see *Mastering COM and COM+* by Ash Rofail and Yasser Shohoud (Sybex, 2000).

CHAPTER
ELEVEN

Understanding
Message Queues

- Message queue processing

- Types of queues

- Advantages of message queues

- The message queue object model

- COM+ queued components

In Chapter 7, I showed you a way to trick an ActiveX EXE program into running asynchronously from your application. At that time, I suggested that you might want to use message queues to perform asynchronous processing. This chapter explains how and when to use message queues in your Visual Basic programs.

Understanding How Message Queues Work

Although they are not strictly part of the COM+ architecture, message queues can be extremely useful when developing COM-based applications. They allow a program or a COM component to communicate with another COM component without waiting for that component to complete its task. In fact, the COM component may not even begin its task before the originating program resumes processing. This permits the calling program to continue processing as normal while it waits for the results from the COM component.

Synchronous versus Asynchronous Processing

Normally, when you are using a COM component and you issue a method or request a property, your program is blocked until the method or property returns to your program. This is known as *synchronous processing*. The client program needs to send a request to the server to perform a function. Figure 11.1 shows how a request is handled using synchronous processing. The client computer issues a request to the server and waits until the server completes the request.

FIGURE 11.1:

Processing a synchronous request

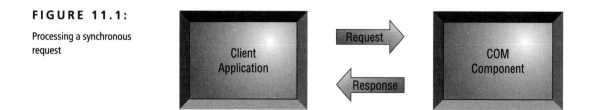

Asynchronous processing occurs when your program requests a server to perform a function, and then continues to process its local code while waiting for the function to be completed. Message queues allow you to place your request on the server's incoming queue. Then, rather than spend your time waiting for the task to be completed, you can check for a response. Figure 11.2 shows how a request is handled using message queues.

FIGURE 11.2:

Processing an asynchronous request

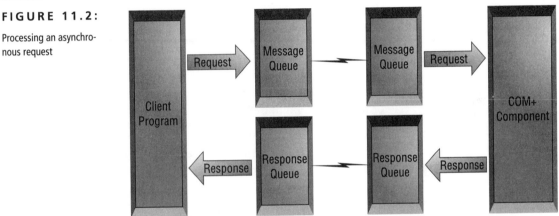

The best way to think about how message queues work relative to normal components is to compare sending a request via e-mail to calling over the phone and making the same request. When using the phone, the client explains the request to the server. The server processes the request while the client waits, then the server provides a response to the client. This wastes a lot of time, because the client is idle while the server is processing the request. Also, other clients can't reach the server for processing.

When the server processes requests via e-mail, the client doesn't need to wait until it can get a call through to the server, then wait again while the server is processing the request. The client merely prepares the request as an e-mail note and periodically checks the inbox for a response from the server. This may take a little longer than waiting on the phone, but it leaves the client free to pursue other tasks while waiting for a response.

Result Return

The results generated by the request can be returned to the client in several different ways:

- No response is necessary. For example, suppose that the client requested a report. When the server completes the report, the report can be printed or sent back to the user via e-mail. There is no need for the application to explicitly communicate with the client program.

- Raise an event in the client application. Since we're dealing with an ActiveX DLL, you can define the object `WithEvents` and simply have the server fire an event when the request has been completed. The event definition could include parameters containing the results, or the client program could use a property or method to obtain the results from the object.

- Check on the status via a synchronous request. You could include a way for the user to check on the current status of the request by explicitly checking a property or using a method that would return the status of the request. When the status indicates that the request has been processed, the client program could get the results by accessing a property or using a method.

- Use message queues to receive the response. Consider the case of a salesperson working at remote sites with a laptop. There isn't a full-time connection to the server. The salesperson could collect a series of requests while on site and place them into the message queues for submittal when the laptop is connected to the server. After transmitting the requests, the return queues would be checked for the results of previous requests. If the laptop were connected for a long enough period of time, the current batch of requests might be processed during that connection, and those results would also arrive via the reverse queue.

Which way you choose to get results depends on a number of factors, such as how long it will take to process the request and whether there is a full-time connection to the server.

Types of Queues

There are six different types of queues, as listed in Table 11.1. The underlying technology used to implement the various types of queues is the same. The only difference is how they are used.

TABLE 11.1: Message Queue Types

Queue Type	Description
Message	Used for normal application processing. Client applications can send messages to the queue, while server applications retrieve messages from the queue.
Administration	Used by an application to retrieve status information about messages in a message queue. For example, an acknowledgment message indicates that a message was received or retrieved from the application at the queue's destination.
Response	Used by client applications to receive responses from the server application.
Report	Used to track the progress of messages as they move through the system.
Journal	Used to store messages that have been retrieved from their destination.
Dead-letter	Used to store application messages that can't be delivered.

Queues can also be labeled as public or private. Public queues are registered in the Active Directory and can be located by anyone with access to the Active Directory. Private queues are registered on an individual computer and can be found by anyone knowing the names of the computer and the queue. Of course, security rules may apply to both public and private queues—just because you can find a queue doesn't mean that you will have access to that queue.

There is also one other classification for queues. A normal message queue can be a transactional queue. All messages sent or read from a transactional queue must be done as part of a transaction.

Benefits of Message Queues

It's true that using message queues can increase the complexity of your application, and not all applications benefit from the use of message queues. However, the advantages of using this feature may outweigh the additional effort that is required to build and maintain the application. Furthermore, message queues have very little overhead. The following sections describe the main benefits of using message queues.

Component Availability

Just because you have a full-time connection to the server doesn't mean that the server will always be available. If the server crashes or there is a network problem between the client and the server, your users won't be able to do any work if you use normal synchronous processing. However, if you use message queues, your users can continue to enter data that will be buffered locally until the server can be accessed again. When the server becomes available, the information that was buffered locally is automatically transmitted to the server for processing.

Component Performance

By queuing the requests for processing, the user need not wait for the server to finish processing one request before starting on the next request. Thus, you can create your application to prioritize how the processing is done. This is important when a server becomes overloaded. Those tasks that need an immediate response, such as checking inventory levels, can be handled as a normal COM+ object. Those tasks that are not as time-sensitive, such as printing an invoice, can be deferred until the server is less busy by using message queues.

Component Lifetimes

Delays caused by transmitting information over the network and interacting with the user extend the amount of time that an object actually exists inside the transaction server. By using message queues, the exchange of information is handled outside the transaction server. This means that the object exists for far less time than it would without using message queues. This translates into better performance in the transaction server, because fewer system resources are needed to process the actual transaction.

Disconnected Applications

By using reverse queues (as described earlier in the "Result Return" section), a full-time connection to the server isn't necessary. Requests can be queued up until a connection to the server is established. Then the requests are transmitted to the server for processing. At the same time, the reverse queues are downloaded to the client containing the results of previous requests. If the connection remains up long enough, the server might be able to complete the new requests and return the results through the reverse queue.

Message Reliability

Message queues rely on a database to store the requests. This ensures that the requests are protected from system failures. If and when the database needs to be recovered, the requests in the queues also will be recovered. Since the time to transmit and add the request to a queue is much less than the time a normal object exists, it is less likely that the failure would occur in the middle of a specific request. Or, looking at it another way, a system failure is far more likely to impact many more synchronous transactions than those transactions stored in a queue.

Server Scheduling

Another advantage of message queues is the ability to shift the work sitting in a queue to a time when the server is less busy. Thus, message queues have the ability to duplicate the batch-processing features of the mainframe world. Shifting work to a less busy time means that there are more server resources to process critical tasks in real time, which translates to better response time for the tasks that need it the most.

Using Message Queues from Visual Basic

Message queues are easy to use from Visual Basic. You can use them outside the COM+ transaction server, but it usually makes sense to use them together. Let's explore how you can make message queues a valuable part of an application.

Public and Private Queues

As mentioned earlier in the chapter, message queues come in two flavors: public and private. You can find information about public queues by using an Active Directory server. You can search for various properties of a queue so that you can locate the right one. To use a private queue, you must know the name of the queue and the machine on which it is located.

The PathName property holds the name of a queue. The name of a queue takes the form of *machinename\queuename*. The following queue names represent two different public queues on two different machines (Athena and Mycroft).

```
Athena\myQueue
Mycroft\myQueue
```

By default, all queues are public. However, if you include the \Private$ keyword between *machinename* and *queuename*, the queue won't be included in the Active Directory. Here are two examples:

```
Athena\Private$\myQueue2
Mycroft\Private$\myQueue2
```

Note that if you don't have access to an Active Directory, every queue you create will be private.

Message Queue Objects

The message queue objects available to the Visual Basic programmer are illustrated in Figure 11.3.

FIGURE 11.3:

The message queue object model

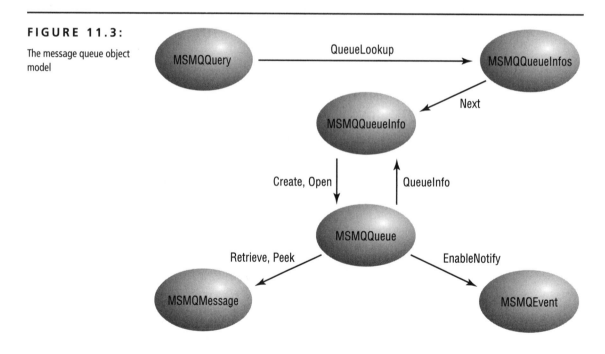

The basic object is MSMQQueue, which contains a way to access the messages contained in a queue. The actual messages are returned in MSMQMessage objects. You can tell the queue server to trigger an event in your program each time a new message arrives in a particular queue. These events are defined through the MSMQEvent object.

Information about a queue is stored in the MSMQQueueInfo object. You use this object to create and open queues, as well as to get details about a particular queue. The MSMQQuery object is used to search an Active Directory server for one or more queues that meet the specified criteria. It will return an MSMQQueueInfos object, which contains one or more MSMQQueueInfo objects.

Let's take a closer look at these objects and their properties and methods.

The MSMQQueue Object

MSMQQueue is the fundamental object in the message queues. It provides the necessary properties and methods to access the information in the queue. Of the properties listed in Table 11.2, the most useful is QueueInfo. This property returns the MSMQQueueInfo object, which contains many of the details about the queue.

TABLE 11.2: Properties of the MSMQQueue Object

Property	Description
Access	Indicates whether you can send messages, peek at messages, or receive messages from the queue
Handle	Returns the handle of the open queue
IsOpen	Returns True if the queue is open
QueueInfo	Returns a MSMQQueueInfo object containing additional information about the queue
ShareMode	Indicates whether the queue is available to everyone for sending, peeking, and receiving data or whether messages can be received by only this process

Once the queue has been opened, you use the methods listed in Table 11.3 to access the information in the queue.

TABLE 11.3: Methods of the MSMQQueue Object

Method	Description
Close	Closes the queue
EnableNotification	Starts the event-notification process
Peek	Returns the first message in the queue, without receiving the message from the queue; if the queue is empty, it will wait for a message to arrive
PeekCurrent	Returns the current message in the queue, without receiving it
PeekNext	Returns the next message in the queue, without receiving it
Receive	Returns the first message in the queue and removes it from the queue
ReceiveCurrent	Returns the current message in the queue and removes it from the queue
Reset	Moves the cursor to the start of the queue

There are two basic ways to access the information in the queue: receiving and peeking. The Receive method returns the first message from the queue and then deletes it from the queue. This is probably the most common way to retrieve messages from the queue.

The Peek... methods allow you to look at the messages inside the queue without removing them. The Peek method returns the first message in the queue. The PeekNext method returns the next message in the queue. Using these methods, you can scan through all of the messages in the queue, looking for the message you want to process. Then you can use the ReceiveCurrent method to return that message and remove it from the queue.

The EnableNotification method instructs the message queues to trigger events using the MSMQEvent object. Note that this object needs to be declared with the WithEvents keyword in order to receive the events. You can specify that the event will be fired when there is a message in the queue, the event will be fired when a message is at the queue's current location, or the event will be fired when a message is at the queue's next location. Remember that an aborted transaction will remain in the queue, so it is possible that multiple messages may be in front of the current message in the queue.

The MSMQMessage Object

The MSMQMessage object contains the message that is sent and received. As you can see in Table 11.4, there are many properties associated with each message.

T A B L E   1 1 . 4 : Properties of the MSMQMessage Object

Property	Description
Ack	Specifies the type of acknowledgment message that is returned
AdminQueueInfo	Returns an object reference to an MSMQQueueInfo object used for acknowledgment messages
AppApecific	Contains application-specific information
ArrivedTime	Contains the date and time the message arrived at the queue
AuthLevel	Specifies whether or not the message should be authenticated when received
Body	Contains the body of the message (the length of the message must be less than 4MB)
BodyLength	Contains the size of **Body** in bytes.
Class	Specifies the type of message (see Table 11.5)
CorrelationId	Contains a 20-byte application-defined value that can be used to link messages together
Delivery	Specifies how the message is delivered: normal delivery (where it may be possible to lose the message in the case of system failure) or more reliable delivery (which may take more time and resources to deliver)
DestinationQueueInfo	Returns a reference to an MSMQQueueInfo object for the destination queue
EncryptAlgorithm	Specifies the encryption algorithm used to encrypt the body of the message
HashAlgorithm	Specifies the hash algorithm used to authenticate a message
Id	Returns the identifier for the message (this value is automatically generated by the message queues)
IsAuthenticated	Specifies whether the local queue manager authenticated the message

Continued on next page

TABLE 11.4 CONTINUED: Properties of the MSMQMessage Object

Property	Description
Journal	Specifies whether a copy of the message was stored in the journal queue
Label	Contains an application-specific value describing the message
MaxTimeToReachQueue	Specifies how many seconds the message has to reach the destination queue before the message will be canceled and an error message will be returned to the sender
MaxTimeToReceive	Specifies how many seconds the message has to be received from the destination queue before the message will be canceled and an error message will be returned to the sender
Priority	Specifies the priority of the message in the range from 0 (low priority) to 7 (high priority), used to order the messages in the queue (this value is ignored by transactional messages)
PrivLevel	Specifies how the message is encrypted: none, 40-bit encryption, or 128-bit encryption
ResponseQueueInfo	Returns an object reference to an MSMQQueueInfo object, which will be used to send any response information
SenderCertificate	Specifies the length of the sender certificate buffer
SenderId	Specifies the name of the user who sent the message
SenderIdType	Specifies whether the SenderId value was included with the message
SendTime	Returns the date and time the message was sent
SourceMachineGuid	Returns the GUID associated with the sending computer
Trace	Specifies where a message will be returned to the sender in the report queue for each hop taken by the message in the delivery process

The most important property is the **Body** of the message. This value has a type of **Variant**, so you can assign it a value from any Visual Basic data type. You can even assign objects to **Body**; however, you must not use the **Set** statement to do so, since you want to send a copy of the object, not a copy of the object reference. You can transmit as much as 4MB of data in the **Body** property, though you should always try to minimize the amount of data you send using message queues.

The **Class** property can have any of the values listed in Table 11.5.

TABLE 11.5: Values for the Class Property

Constant	Description
MQMSG_CLASS_NORMAL	Normal message
MQMSG_CLASS_ACK_REACH_QUEUE	Positive acknowledgment message meaning that the message reached the destination queue
MQMSG_CLASS_ACK_RECEIVE	Positive acknowledgment message meaning that the message was received by the application
MQMSG_CLASS_NACK_ACCESS_DENIED	Negative acknowledgment message meaning that the sending application doesn't have access rights to the destination queue
MQMSG_CLASS_NACK_BAD_DST_Q	Negative arrival acknowledgment message meaning that the destination queue isn't available to the sending application
MQMSG_CLASS_NACK_BAD_ENCRYPTION	Negative arrival acknowledgment message meaning that an encrypted message couldn't be decrypted
MQMSG_CLASS_NACK_BAD_SIGNATURE	Negative arrival acknowledgment message meaning that the message couldn't be authenticated because the digital signature was invalid
MQMSG_CLASS_NACK_COUND_NOT_ENCRYPT	Negative arrival acknowledgment message meaning that the message couldn't be encrypted
MQMSG_CLASS_NACK_HOP_COUNT_EXCEEDED	Negative arrival acknowledgment message meaning that the hop count was exceeded
MQMSG_CLASS_NACK_Q_EXCEED_QUOTA	Negative arrival acknowledgment message meaning that the destination queue was full
MQMSG_CLASS_NACK_REACH_QUEUE_TIMEOUT	Negative arrival acknowledgment message meaning that either the Max-TimeToReachQueue value or the MaxTime-ToReceive value was reached before the message got to the destination queue

Continued on next page

TABLE 11.5 CONTINUED: Values for the Class Property

Constant	Description
MQMSG_CLASS_NACK_PURGED	Negative arrival acknowledgment message meaning that the message was purged before reaching the destination queue
MQMSG_CLASS_NACK_NOT_TRANSACTIONAL_Q	Negative arrival acknowledgment message meaning that a transactional message was sent to a nontransactional queue
MQMSG_CLASS_NACK_NOT_TRANSACTIONAL_MSG	Negative arrival acknowledgment message meaning that a nontransactional message was sent to a transactional queue
MQMSG_CLASS_NACK_UNSUPPORTED_CRYPTO_PROVIDER	Negative arrival acknowledgment message meaning that the destination queue doesn't have the enhanced (128-bit) cryptographic provider installed
MQMSG_CLASS_NACK_Q_DELETED	Negative read acknowledgment message meaning that the message was deleted before it could be received from the queue
MQMSG_CLASS_NACK_Q_PURGED	Negative read acknowledgment message meaning that the queue was purged and the message doesn't exist
MQMSG_CLASS_NACK_RECEIVE_TIMEOUT	Negative read acknowledgment message meaning that the message was not received before the MaxTimeToReceive value was reached
MQMSG_CLASS_NACK_RECEIVE_TIMEOUT_AT_SENDER	Negative read acknowledgment message for a transactional message meaning that the message was not received before its time to be received timer expired (this value is set by the local queue manager)
MQMSG_CLASS_NACK_REPORT	Message sent each time a message enters or leaves a queue server

You can set the CorrelationId property of a message being returned to the sender to the ID value of the received message. This allows the original sender to link the two messages together.

If you need to know for certain whether a message was successfully delivered, you should set the Ack property to MQMSG_ACKNOWLEDGE_FULL_REACH_QUEUE or MQMSG_ACKNOWLEDGE_FULL_RECEIVE. By ORing these values together, you will receive every possible positive or negative error message (listed in Table 11.4) in the administrative queue in the sending application.

WARNING   Do not use the Set statement to assign an object to the Body property. The Body property must hold a copy of the object's contents, not merely a reference to the object. This ensures that when the message is received, the contents of the object are available for processing.

The MSMQMessage object has two methods. The AttachCurrentSecurityContext method attaches a certificate to the message. This certificate contains security information that will be used by the receiver to authenticate a message.

The key method is Send. After defining all of the properties associated with your message, the Send method is used to send the message to the specified MSMQQueue object. The MSMQQueue object needs to be opened prior to sending the message, but it can be closed once the message has been sent. If you set ResponseQueueInfo to a valid MSMQQueueInfo object, any responses generated by sending the message will be directed to that queue.

The MSMQQueueInfo Object

The MSMQQueueInfo object sets or provides information about a queue. This information is used to create a new queue or to discover the characteristics of an existing queue. Table 11.6 lists the properties of MSMQQueueInfo.

TABLE 11.6: Properties of the MSMQQueueInfo Object

Property	Description
Authenticate	Specifies that the queue accepts only authenticated messages
BasePriority	Specifies a base priority for all messages sent to a public queue
CreateTime	Returns the date and time the public queue as created
FormatName	Specifies the format name of the queue

Continued on next page

TABLE 11.6 CONTINUED: Properties of the MSMQQueueInfo Object

Property	Description
IsTransactional	Specifies that only messages from transactions will be accepted
IsWorldReadable	Indicates whether everyone or only the owner of the queue can read the messages
Journal	Specifies whether the messages retrieved from the message queue are saved in the journal queue
JournalQuota	Specifies the maximum size of the journal queue in kilobytes
Label	Describes the queue
ModifyTime	Returns the date and time the public queue was last modified
PathName	Specifies the path and name of the queue
PathNameDNS	Returns the DNS path name of the queue
PrivLevel	Specifies the privacy level of the queue
QueueGuid	Returns the GUID of the queue
Quota	Specifies the maximum size of the queue in kilobytes
ServiceTypeGuid	Specifies the type of service provided by the queue

The MSMQQueueInfo object also is used to create or open a message queue. You set the name of the queue in the PathName property and then use the Create or Open method. The other methods are Delete, Refresh, and Update, as listed in Table 11.7.

TABLE 11.7: Methods of the MSMQQueueInfo Object

Method	Description
Create	Creates a new queue based on the properties set in this object and returns an MSMQQueue object to the calling program
Delete	Deletes the queue associated with this object
Open	Returns the MSMQQueue object specified by PathName
Refresh	Refreshes the property values for this queue
Update	Updates the Active Directory for a public queue or the local computer with the current property values for this queue

MSMQQuery Object

The MSMQQuery object is used to search the Active Directory for public queues. The LookupQueue method allows you to search for a queue as follows:

- By a specific value for a queue's GUID

- By the type of service

- By the label

- By the date and time the queue was created

- By the date and time the queue was modified

You can also search for these values using an expression that includes relational operators.

LookupQueue returns an MSMQQueueInfos object containing a collection of MSMQQueueInfo objects that meet the specified search criteria.

NOTE   The LookupQueue method works only with public queues, since it searches the Active Directory for information. This method will not help you find a private queue that is defined on a single computer.

The MSMQQueueInfos Object

The MSMQQueueInfos object contains a collection of MSMQQueueInfo objects that were returned by the MSMQQuery.LookupQueue method. It contains only two methods, Next and Reset, which can be used to iterate through the collection of MSMQQueueInfo objects.

Next returns an object pointer to the next MSMQQueueInfo object in the collection. If the current object is the last object in the collection, the Next method will return Nothing. Reset resets the current queue pointer to the first MSMQQueue-Info object in the collection.

The MSMQEvent Object

The MSMQEvent object is used to define queuing events in your application. There are only two events: Arrived, which occurs when a new message arrives in the queue, and ArrivedError, which occurs when there is an error.

In order to use these events, you must create a new instance of the MSMQEvent object using the WithEvents keyword. Then you can call the MSMQQueue.Enable-Notification method, specifying the MSMQEvent object you just created.

MSMQEvents can be shared among multiple MSMQQueue objects. When the event is fired, the queue containing the new message will be one of the parameters to the event. The other parameter indicates how the event was triggered and should be included when you reenable the event. Be sure to reenable the MSMQEvent object using the MSMQQueue.EnableNotification method each time the Arrived event is fired; otherwise, the event will be triggered only once.

NOTE   Just because an Arrived event was triggered doesn't mean that there is a message to be processed. Since multiple applications (and multiple instances of a single application) can share the same queue, it is possible that one of the other applications has already received and processed the message that triggered the event.

Message Queues and COM+ Transactions

COM+ transactions using message queues work automatically with the COM+ transaction server and the ObjectContext object. Getting the ObjectContext object and performing the SetComplete or SetAbort method automatically commits or rolls back any operations you made to the queues. In other words, no messages are removed from the queues or physically sent until the transaction is either committed or rolled back.

There is one big issue about using message queues and transactions. While inside a transaction, you can only send messages to transactional queues—queues that were created with the IsTransactional parameter of the MSMQQueueInfo.Create method equal to True. Also, any messages that are sent automatically have their MSMQMessage.Priority value set to zero. This ensures that the messages are processed in the order in which they were received.

The message queues also include their own implementation of transactions in case you don't want to use the COM+ transaction server or want to work outside its control. You need to use the MSMQCoordinatedTransactionDispenser to begin a transaction while under control of the COM+ transaction server. Use the MSMQ-TransactionDispenser object if you're not under control of the COM+ transaction server. These objects allow you to create a new transaction for your message queues. Then use the MSMQTransaction object to either commit the transaction or to abort the transaction.

The MSMQTransactionDispenser Object

The MSMQTransactionDispenser object is used when you're not running under the COM+ transaction server's control. It has only one method, BeginTransaction, which is used to begin a transaction. It returns an MSMQTransaction object, which you use to mark the end of the transaction.

The MSMQCoordinatedTransactionDispenser Object

The MSMQCoordinatedTransactionDispenser object interacts with the COM+ transaction server to ensure that the activities performed in the message queues are coordinated with those performed by the transaction server. Like the MSMQ-TransactionDispenser object, MSMQCoordinatedTransactionDispenser has only one method, BeginTransaction, which is used to mark the beginning of a transaction. It returns an MSMQTransaction object that you use when the transaction is completed.

The MSMQTransaction Object

The MSMQTransaction object is created by the MSMQCoordinatedTransactionDispenser.BeginTransaction method. This object has the Transaction property, which returns the "magic cookie" used by the transaction dispenser.

MSMQTransaction has three methods. The Abort method terminates the transaction and rolls back all of the actions taken on the queue, including deleting sent messages and restoring any messages that were removed from the queue. The Commit method is used to post the changes to the queue as complete, so that any messages that were sent while the transaction was active are released. The InitNew method is used to associate the MSMQ transaction with a non-MSMQ transaction that is already active.

Building COM+ Message Queues

To demonstrate how to build COM+ message queues, we'll continue working with the Contact Manager application we started in Chapter 10. In this chapter, we'll add a pair of queues—one to send requests and one to send responses. We'll also create a utility library that is designed to hold code and definitions on both the client and the server. This will help minimize the number of times the server must be accessed.

Design Approach

The sending queue will be used to send a request to the ContactManager object for processing. In this example, the only request will be to return a particular contact ID. The ContactManager will process the request and return the information in the response queue.

The CMRequest Object

The CMRequest object is shown in Listing 11.1. This object is designed to package the information that will be used to send a request for information to the server as the body of the message.

Listing 11.1   **The CMRequest object**

```
Public Enum CMRequestType
    CMUnknown = 0
    CMFindAContact = 1

End Enum


Public Request As CMRequestType
Public ContactId As Long
```

NOTE   When you create an object that you want to send in the Body of a message queue, be sure to set the Persistable property of the object to Persistable. Otherwise, the values in the object will be lost.

As you can see, this object currently contains only two properties:

- `Request` is an enumerated type. Currently, it has the two values `CMUnknown` and `CMFindAContact`.

- `ContactId` holds a `ContactId` value.

You may be wondering why we're going to all this trouble when all we really need to send is the `ContactId` value. It basically boils down to a personal preference. The method I've outlined here is easily expandable to handle many different requests, while still using only a single request queue. Simply passing the `ContactId` value would work fine in this situation, but if I wanted to expand the types of requests the transaction supported, I would need to add a new queue for each request type.

The Contact Object

Also in this library is a slightly revised `Contact` object, as shown in Listing 11.2. In the previous version, we used the `Contact` object to perform various operations using a contact's information. Now we're using the `Contact` object to return the complete information to the requester.

Listing 11.2   The Contact object

```
Public ContactId As Long
Public FirstName As String
Public MiddleName As String
Public LastName As String
Public Prefix As String
Public Title As String
Public Organization As String
Public Street As String
Public City As String
Public State As String
Public Zip As String
Public Telephone As String
Public FAX As String
```

This doesn't mean that we're abandoning the other functions, such as `GetFull-Name`. They still exist in the object, but they have been modified to work on the information stored in the object.

Request Processing

Processing a request involves three main steps:

- Initializing the environment where the requests will be sent
- Sending the request to the server
- Receiving the request and displaying the information to the user

Let's look at the code for accomplishing each of these steps.

Initializing the Environment

When we start the ContactClient program, we create and open a queue to receive responses from the server. Listing 11.3 shows the Form_Load event.

> **NOTE** The queue used in this example is tied to a single machine. If you have multiple users who use the computer, consider including the username as part of the queue name to ensure that the message is delivered to the right person.

Listing 11.3   **The Form_Load event in ContactClient**

```
Private Sub Form_Load()

Set RespInfo = New MSMQQueueInfo
RespInfo.PathName = ".\Private$\ContactClient"
RespInfo.Create

Set RespQueue = RespInfo.Open(MQ_RECEIVE_ACCESS, _
    MQ_DENY_NONE)
Set RespEvent = New MSMQEvent
RespQueue.EnableNotification RespEvent, , 0

End Sub
```

Here, we create a new MSMQQueueInfo object, define the path name for the queue, and execute the Create method. Then we create a new MSMQEvent object and set it so that it will be triggered whenever a response message is received.

NOTE Generally, I like to use private queues for responses from the server. This is because while there is only one queue for the server to receive requests, there will be one queue for each user to receive responses. Since only the server will be sending messages to these queues, there's no reason to make these queues public.

Sending a Request

To get information from the ContactManager, you need to prepare a request and put it into the ContactManager's request queue. This is done in the client program by accepting a value for ContactId and clicking the Find a Client button, which triggers the Command1_Click event, shown in Listing 11.4.

Listing 11.4   The Command1_Click event in ContactClient

```
Private Sub Command1_Click()

Dim ri As MSMQQueueInfo
Dim rq As MSMQQueue
Dim rm As MSMQMessage

Dim cm As Request

If IsNumeric(Text1.Text) Then
   Set cm = New CMRequest
   cm.ContactId = CLng(Text1.Text)
   cm.Request = CMFindAContact

   Set rm = New MSMQMessage
   rm.Label = "FindAContact"
   Set rm.ResponseQueueInfo = RespQueue.QueueInfo
   rm.Body = cm

   Set ri = New MSMQQueueInfo
   ri.PathName = "Athena\ContactManager"
   Set rq = ri.Open(MQ_SEND_ACCESS, MQ_DENY_NONE)

   rm.Send rq
```

```
    rq.Close

    Set cm = Nothing
    Set ri = Nothing
    Set rm = Nothing
    Set rq = Nothing

End If

End Sub
```

This routine begins by verifying that the value for ContactId is numeric. Then we create a new CMRequest object called cm to send to the ContactManager's request queue and save the values for ContactId and Request.

Next, we create a new MSMQMessage object to hold the request. We set the message's Label property to a descriptive value of the request. We don't specifically use this property in either the client side or the server side, but it doesn't hurt to include this information. It could prove useful in debugging the application. Another way to differentiate between types of requests would be to use the Label property to hold the type of request.

After setting the Label property, we set the ResponseQueueInfo object to the RespQueue.QueueInfo object so that the server can send the message back to this client. Finally, we copy the contents of cm into the Body property of the message. Notice that we didn't use the Set statement, because we want a copy of the object, not merely a pointer to the current instance of the object.

The next step is to open the ContactManager's request queue and use the message's Send method to send it to the newly opened message queue. Once the message is on its way, we close the queue and destroy the objects we created in this routine.

Waiting for a Response

After sending the request to the server, nothing is going to happen in the client program until the RespEvent_Arrived event occurs. This event, shown in Listing 11.5, is triggered when a message arrives in the response queue.

Listing 11.5   **The RespEvent_Arrived event in ContactClient**

```
Private Sub RespEvent_Arrived(ByVal Queue As Object, _
   ByVal Cursor As Long)

Dim c As Contact
Dim m As MSMQMessage

Set m = Queue.Receive(, , , 1000)
If Not (m Is Nothing) Then
   Set c = m.Body

   Text2.Text = c.GetFullName
   Text3.Text = c.Title
   Text4.Text = c.Organization
   Text5.Text = c.Telephone

End If

RespQueue.EnableNotification RespEvent, , 0

End Sub
```

We use the `Receive` method to retrieve the message from the queue. Then we check whether the message actually contains something by seeing if the object is not `Nothing`.

Now that we have a valid message, we can get the `Contact` object from the message's `Body` property and set the individual text box fields with the message's contents. Then we need to reset the event using the `RespQueue.EnableNotification` method. Otherwise, the next message will not trigger the `Arrived` event.

Realize that, in some cases, when the `Arrived` event fires, there may not be a message to receive. If you have multiple programs that receive messages from the same queue, the `Arrived` event in all of them will be triggered. The first one to `Receive` the message will get it, so the others won't have a message to receive. Also, if your system is processing a very high volume of messages, the message that triggered the `Arrived` event may not be the message you receive if you have multiple programs receiving messages.

Introducing Queued Components

Now that you've seen what it takes to use message queues in your application, let's take a look at a new way to build asynchronous applications. Queued components are really just COM components that include a transparent message queue between the client program and the server component. The requests from your program are sent via the message queue to the COM object for execution, while your program continues to run without waiting for the call to be completed.

Unfortunately, Visual Basic 6 doesn't provide direct support for queued components. You could create an ActiveX DLL in Visual Basic and define it as a COM+ application using the Component Services utility, but you wouldn't be able to use the Visual Basic IDE to debug it.

How Queued Components Work

Queued components rely on the regular message queues for its infrastructure. As illustrated in Figure 11.4, Microsoft implemented three tools that work with message queues to automatically deliver the messages.

FIGURE 11.4:

Queued components are handled by a recorder, listener, and player.

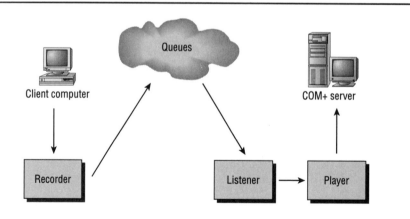

When the client program calls a queued component, it really calls a special piece of code called the *recorder*. The recorder intercepts the request from the client program and puts together a message that is sent on to the server using a message queue. On the server, a *listener* receives the message and sends it to the *player*, which unpacks the message and calls the method requested by the client.

Limitations of Queued Components

As Robert A. Heinlein said, "TANSTAAFL" (There Ain't No Such Thing As A Free Lunch). In this case, it means that while you gain the ability to use message queues without explicit support in your program, you don't have the full range of capabilities provided by COM when using queued components.

You must pass all parameters to a queued component by value. Because there isn't a return path, your program will never see the updated values. Actually, this isn't a big limitation, and it also applies to message queues. In order to use a message queue, you must do the same thing, since a message queue is a one-way street.

Any objects passed to a queued component must be persistable using IPersist-Stream. Otherwise, the information will be lost.

The total size of the entire message must be less than the maximum size of a message queue message. I doubt that many people want to use a 4MB parameter, but you may want to ship a complex object with a lot of data, such as a rather large Recordset or image.

Speaking of Recordset objects, only Recordsets created using client-side cursors can be sent to a queued component. This is because server-side cursors can't be marshaled using IPersistStream.

Creating an instance of the queued component is not as simple as creating a new instance of a regular COM or COM+ object. You need to include a series of parameters along with the object name. These are known as *queue moniker* parameters. These parameters include the name of the server computer, the name of the queue, and other information that affects how the message is constructed. This information must be included as part of the object name in the CreateObject and GetObject functions.

Final Thoughts

Message queues have many more uses than may be apparent at first. Obviously, they are useful for long-running tasks and frequently disconnected users. Additionally, message queues are handy in many high-volume transaction systems, especially where the transaction rate fluctuates over time.

Consider the situation of an ATM network, where the transaction rate peaks during lunchtime. Conventional wisdom says that you should buy a server with sufficient capacity to handle this peak traffic. This is because if you can't handle the transactions as fast as they come in, the transactions start to compete with each other for system resources. This competition results in more system overhead, as the system tries to accommodate the workload. This extra overhead can force an already overloaded system into failure.

By using messaging queues, you can attempt to equalize the workload so that your server processes transactions only up to its capacity. The transactions that it can't process remain in the queue until the currently executing transactions finish. So, rather than overloading your server, the length of the queue will grow and shrink as needed. This leaves your server free to run at its peak level of performance.

You may be thinking that this type of processing will dramatically increase the time it takes for responses to requests. I've seen many situations where reducing the number of concurrently executing tasks actually provided better response time. Remember that forcing the system to try to find resources that don't exist wastes resources that would have been better used to perform useful work.

Support for queued components will be added to Visual Basic 7. Then you will be able to easily build message queues into your applications. But this doesn't mean that programming message queues will become obsolete. Message queues are far more functional and flexible than queued components. This flexibility will be useful in many enterprise applications, where the model offered by queued components isn't adequate.

CHAPTER
TWELVE

Understanding the In-Memory Database System

- How the In-Memory Database system works

- Considerations for using IMDB

- IMDB configuration

- IMDB programming

The In-Memory Database (IMDB) system is a new feature in Windows 2000. This feature can improve database performance or provide a high-performance shared data cache. It works by keeping its data in memory rather than using disk storage. Of course, using memory as a storage medium means that your data can be lost due to system crashes or power failures. However, for many applications, like temporary storage for a transaction or a read-only translation table, IMDB is ideal.

This chapter discusses how to use the IMDB system with a Visual Basic COM+ application. The database system can be used in two ways: as a stand-alone system or as a cache for an underlying database.

NOTE   At the time this book was going to press, Microsoft decided not to include the In-Memory Database (IMDB) feature in the final version of Windows 2000 Server. However, this feature was in the widely distributed Windows 2000 Beta 3. I decided to leave information about this very useful facility in the book, because I believe that Microsoft will release it soon. The IMDB feature may not be exactly as presented here—it may be packaged and licensed differently—but the technology behind IMDB is not going away. This chapter explains how IMDB works so that you can understand the basics and be able to take advantage of the technology whenever it becomes available.

Understanding How IMDB Works

IMDB is basically a limited-function, memory-based database management system. It can be accessed in Visual Basic by using the ActiveX Data Objects (ADO). It is not a general-purpose database system. It does not support SQL queries. But it is fast.

When a client program reads data, IMDB uses a memory-mapping technique to make the desired data available. When the client program writes data, it is sent to the IMDB server for processing. The server updates the information in memory, and it will update an external back-end database, depending on how the table was defined.

IMDB supports both SQL Server databases and Oracle databases. You can choose to load an entire table into memory directly from a back-end database when the IMDB service is started (static loading), or you can load records into memory when requested by the client program (dynamic loading).

Note that you need not couple an IMDB database to a back-end database server. The IMDB is a great tool for creating temporary database tables. These tables are useful for storing the intermediate results of a transaction. Note that there is no protection against data loss in these tables. If the IMDB server stops for any reason, all the data in these tables is lost and can't be recovered.

Deciding If IMDB Is for You

The fact that IMDB provides quick access to your data doesn't necessarily mean that your applications will run faster. In some cases, they could even run slower. There are five major factors you need to consider before you choose to use IMDB:

- The amount of data you want to keep
- Whether you want to use static loading or dynamic loading
- How often you need to update data
- The amount of disk I/O operations involved
- Whether you want to share the data

These issues are discussed below.

Volume of Data

IMDB is limited by the amount of real memory available in a computer. Just because IMDB can use 2GB of memory in a Windows 2000 Server machine doesn't mean you want it to.

The reason that the IMDB is so fast is because it keeps everything in memory. If you can't keep the data in memory, you're defeating the purpose of an in-memory database. In other words, don't expect to create a 2GB IMDB on your 128MB server and see an improvement in performance.

Ideally, the total size of your IMDB should be less than the amount of main memory you have available, minus the memory already used by Windows and the rest of the applications running on that server. However, that doesn't mean that you won't see improvements on systems with less memory than the amount of data you want to keep in the cache. It just means that you may not receive the full benefit of using the IMDB.

> **NOTE**
> When designing applications, you need to keep in mind that memory is cheap, relative to other parts of a computer. Adding memory to a server will often improve performance better than adding another CPU.

Static versus Dynamic Loading

There are two basic ways to initialize your IMDB tables:

- Static loading, in which you load the entire table whenever you start the database

- Dynamic loading, in which you load records as they are requested by the client

With static loading, you pay a big price when the system is first started. However, once the data is loaded, you don't need to load the data again. This approach is great when you access most of the records in the table.

If most of the records aren't going to be accessed, you might want to consider dynamic loading. Then you pay the penalty for loading the first record.

The Read-to-Write Ratio

The main advantage of caching data comes from the fact that most applications read the same information many times. By keeping a copy of the data in a place where it can be quickly accessed, you can significantly improve the performance of an application.

This advantage goes away if you need to update this data frequently. In this case, not only do you need to update the data in the cache, but you also must update the data in primary storage. This extra overhead often offsets the performance gains that you may get from caching.

The Total I/O Rate

By storing tables in memory, you avoid performing disk I/O (input/output) operations. However, if you're not doing many disk I/O operations, then you might not get any real benefit from keeping tables in memory. In other words, why bother trying to eliminate disk I/O activity that you don't have?

You also need to consider who is doing the I/O. For instance, if your application is reading an external flat file, there isn't much benefit to using IMDB, unless you convert the flat file to a database table. However, you can use IMDB to significantly reduce the number of I/O operations done by your database system.

Shared Data

When you need to store temporary data inside a transaction, you have a couple of options:

- You can store it in memory as part of an instance of an object.

- You can store it in a database table.

If you want to share this information among multiple transactions, then you usually save the data in a database table. Storing the data in an instance of an object can lead to situations where you can't easily access the data.

Preparing to Use IMDB

You need to perform a few steps before you can use IMDB on your system. The exact set of steps depends on how you plan to use it:

- If you want to create temporary tables, you need to configure IMDB and then set up security and start the IMDB service.

- If you want to connect to a back-end database system, you need to configure IMDB, set up security, establish the data source name, set up access to the back-end database, add the tables to be used, and start the service.

IMDB Configuration

You enable and configure IMDB from the Component Services utility (select Start ➤ Programs ➤ Administrative Tools ➤ Component Services). Expand the Component Services icon to display the computers that can be managed from this location. Right-click the computer on which you want to configure IMDB and select Properties from the pop-up menu. Choose the Options tab to see the dialog box shown in Figure 12.1.

FIGURE 12.1:

The Options tab of the computer's Properties

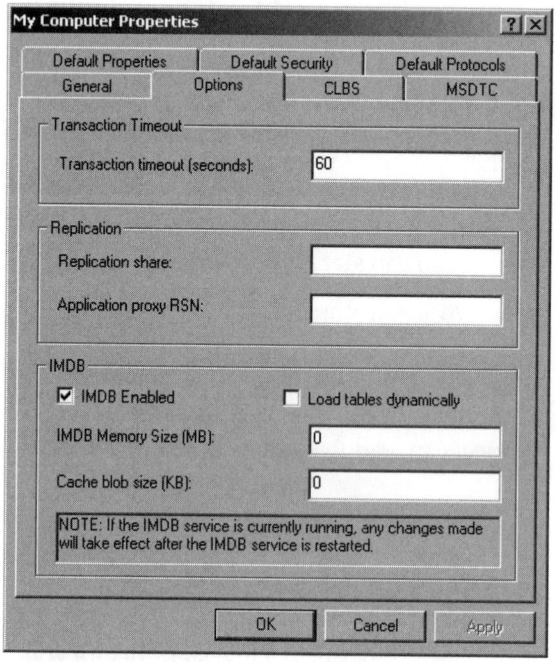

Set the following options in the IMDB section of the dialog box:

- Check the IMDB Enabled box to enable IMDB.

- Check the Load Tables Dynamically box if you want the data loaded into the cache the first time it's requested by the user.

- Choose the number of megabytes of memory you wish to allocate to IMDB. A zero in this field means to use the default, which is computed as the maximum of 16MB, the total virtual memory minus 256MB or the amount of physical RAM minus 32MB. If possible, specify the amount of memory you actually need for the IMDB, so you don't waste memory that could benefit other applications.

- Choose the maximum size in kilobytes for a blob field. Blobs smaller than this size will be cached. Larger fields will be loaded only when requested.

NOTE   If IMDB is already enabled, any changes you make here will not take effect until IMDB is shut down and restarted.

IMDB Security Settings

Configuring IMDB security involves setting two values: the username with which the IMDB service will run and the users who can access the IMDB. You need to use the Active Directory Users and Computers utility to create the username and define the security groups. You use the Component Services utility to associate the username with the appropriate function.

Setting the IMDB Service Username

By default, IMDB runs under LocalSystem, which is fine if you use it only to hold temporary tables. However, if you plan to cache a back-end database or access networked resources, you should change this value to a username that has permissions to access back-end database or networked resources.

You change the IMDB service username through Component Services utility. Expand the Services icon to show all of the services running on this server. Then right-click on Imdb Server and select Properties from the pop-up menu. Choose the Log On tab to specify the user that the service will run under. This tab is shown in Figure 12.2.

Select the This Account button to specify a username. Click the Choose User button to pick the username from a list, or enter the name directly into the text box. Enter the password associated with the username twice, then click OK to accept the new username.

FIGURE 12.2:

Select a username for IMDB
to run under.

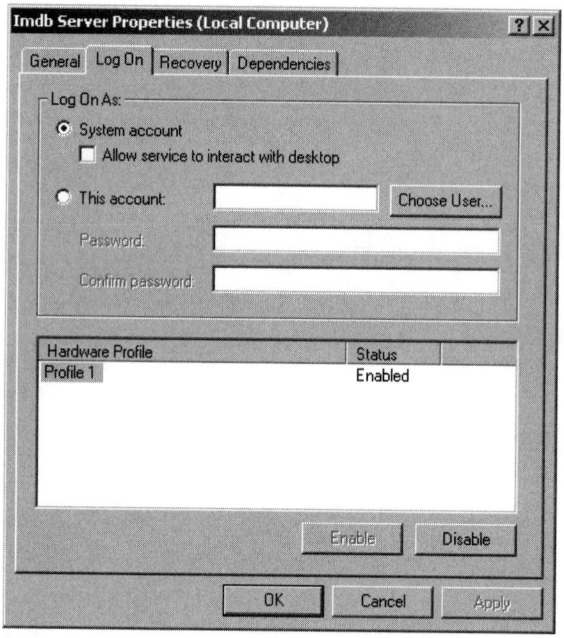

Setting Trusted Users

A user who has access to the IMDB is known as a *trusted user*. As with the other settings, you use the Component Services utility to add a trusted user or group to IMDB. To get to the Users icon, expand the icons in the following order:

- The COM+ Applications icon under the computer you wish to modify
- The System Application icon to show Components and Roles
- The Roles icon to show a series of icons, including IMDB Trusted User
- The IMDB Trusted User icon to show the Users icon

Right-click the Users icon and choose New ➢ User from the pop-up menu. The Select Users or Groups dialog box appears with a list of users and groups (you may need to wait a bit for the system to display this information), as shown in Figure 12.3.

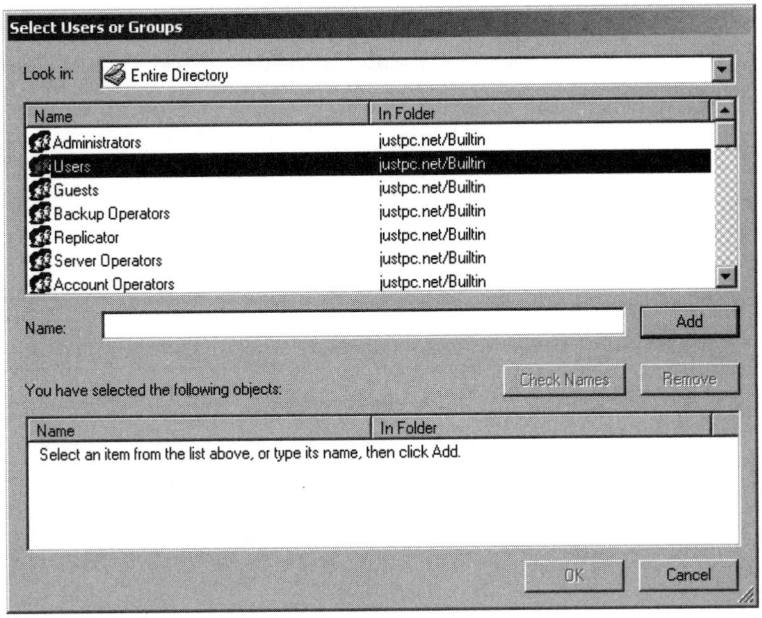

FIGURE 12.3:

Select users and groups to be added to the IMDB trusted user list.

Select the user or group you want to add to the list of trusted users and click the Add button. Continue until you have identified all of the users and groups you want to add. Then click OK to add them to the list of trusted users.

Defining a Back-end Data Source

In order to access a back-end database, you need to provide the OLE DB connection information. To do this, in the Component Services utility, expand the COM+ Applications icon to display the IMDB Data Sources icon. Right-click the IMDB Data Sources icon and choose New ➤ Data Source from the pop-up menu. This displays the New IMDB Data Source dialog box, shown in Figure 12.4.

Fill in the dialog box as follows:

- In the Name field, enter the text name that describes this data source.

- In the OLE DB Provider Name field, enter **SQLOLEDB** if you are accessing an SQL Server database, **MSDASQL** if you are accessing the database using ODBC 3, or **MSDAORA** if you are accessing an Oracle database.

- In the Provider Data Source field, enter the name of the server if you are using SQLOLEDB, the ODBC data source name if you are using MSDASQL, or the database alias if you are using MSDAORA.

- In the IMDB Catalog Name field, enter the name of the database you wish to use.

- Optionally, in the Provider Properties field, enter a provider-specific string containing information that will be used by the OLE DB driver. Note that this information is stored unencrypted, so you may not want to supply user ID and password information.

FIGURE 12.4:

Adding an IMDB data source

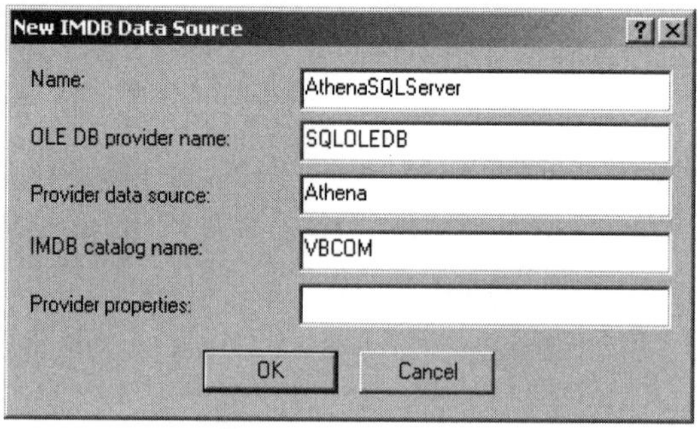

These steps will define the data source, which will be listed under the IMDB Data Sources icon. If you want to modify any of these properties (except for the name, of course), simply right-click the data source you wish to change and select Properties from the pop-up menu. You can also delete the data source by choosing Delete from the pop-up menu and selecting Yes in the confirmation dialog box.

Adding and Removing Tables

Just because you have a link to a database server doesn't mean that you have immediate access to every table in the database through the IMDB server. You must explicitly choose which tables you want to access.

To add a table to IMDB, expand the data source you want to add a table to, right-click the Tables icon, and choose New ➢ Table. This opens the IMDB Data Source Table dialog box, shown in Figure 12.5.

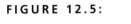

FIGURE 12.5:

Adding a table to IMDB

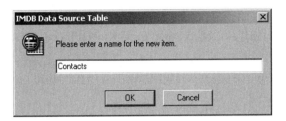

To remove a table, right-click the table, choose Delete from the pop-up menu, and click Yes in the confirmation dialog box.

Starting the IMDB Service

After you've defined all of the items necessary for the way you plan to use IMDB, the next step is to start the service. However, first you should take a moment to review the general properties of the Imdb Server service. You can display this information by right-clicking the Imdb Server icon and selecting Properties. Figure 12.6 shows the General tab of the Imdb Server Properties dialog box.

FIGURE 12.6:

General server properties
for IMDB

Through this dialog box, you can start, stop, pause, and resume the server by clicking the appropriate button. Only the appropriate buttons will be enabled (if the server isn't running, only the Start button is enabled, if the server is running only the Stop and Pause buttons will be enabled, and so on).

In the Startup section of the dialog box, you have three choices:

- Automatic, to automatically start the server when the system is booted

- Manual, to wait for someone to explicitly start the server

- Disabled, to leave the server disabled

Unless you have a specific reason to manually start the server, I suggest leaving this field set to Automatic. Then you won't need to worry about starting the server each time you start the system it runs under.

NOTE   Changing any of the parameters, except for the data sources and tables, requires that you explicitly stop and start the server for them to take effect. If you're not sure that the change has taken effect, try stopping and starting the server to see if that makes a difference.

You also can start the service directly by expanding the Services icon, right-clicking Imdb Server, and choosing Start from the pop-up menu.

Using IMDB in an Application

Once you understand how to define your database, using IMDB is merely a matter of using standard ADO programming techniques to access the database. ADO is designed to be a general-purpose database-access technique. However, IMDB is not a true general-purpose database. This means that there are some restrictions on what you can and can't do with ADO. For the most part, these restrictions aren't hard to live with, especially if you need the performance benefits that IMDB offers.

Programming Considerations

The main points you need to consider when using IMDB in your application are the design of your database, the cursor type, and filtering and sorting of data.

Database Design

You must have a unique primary key for each row in the table. The primary key is also restricted to being a single column. IMDB uses this information to retrieve records from the back-end database.

IMDB allows you to access blob data. But why would you want to? If the blob field is greater than the configured size, it won't be cached in memory. It will be loaded on demand and freed as soon as you're done with it. Blobs tend to take up a lot of space, and you can always access them directly, rather than through the IMDB.

Cursors

IMDB supports only two types of cursors: none and server side. You can't use client or client-batch cursors. Given the choice of none and server side, you should use none. When you specify a server-side cursor, ADO automatically includes a rowset helper that provides `Variant` binding and find and filter functions. Since these features are a standard part of IMDB, you don't need the rowset helper. Thus, specifying none as the type of cursor is the most efficient method, and you don't lose any functionality.

Filtering and Sorting Data

IMDB doesn't support SQL statements, so you are forced to use the `Filter` property of the `Recordset` object if you want to find a single object. The `Filter` property can support rather complex expressions, but IMDB places some strong limits on them.

First you can access only the fields that are indexed in the table or the field that is the primary key. Accessing any other field will cause the `Filter` request to fail.

Second, your filter must return a contiguous block of data. This means that a filter such as the one below will fail, because the resulting `Recordset` will not consist of contiguous rows of data.

```
LastName = 'Freeze' Or LastName = 'Heyer'
```

However, the following statement will work, although it may retrieve more rows than you want.

```
LastName >= 'Freeze' And LastName <= 'Heyer'
```

Even though IMDB doesn't support SQL statements, you can sort your data in the order of the primary key or index. Simply use the Sort method of the Recordset object and specify the desired fields.

NOTE   Transaction programming is not supported in the Recordset object. This is because IMDB is designed to run under control of the COM+ transaction server.

A New Collection Object

One of the goals of interacting with the transaction server is to minimize the number of times data is transmitted between the client and the server. Therefore, it is desirable to pass information back and forth in the form of collections of objects.

For the sample application, we will create the Contacts object, which contains a collection of Contact objects. This object is basically just an interface to the Collection object, which simplifies the programming required.

In Listing 12.1, we declare a new instance of the Collection object. Whenever this object is created, a new collection will be available to hold instances of the Contact object.

Listing 12.1   **The module-level declarations of the Contacts object**

```
Option Explicit

Private c As New Collection
```

The Add method of the Contacts collection simply calls the Add method of the Collection object, as shown in Listing 12.2.

Listing 12.2   The Add method of the Contacts object

```
Public Sub Add(Item As Contact)

c.Add Item, FormatNumber(Item.ContactId, 0)

End Sub
```

This method is typical of most of the other methods in this object. We assume that the object we're dealing with is of type Contact and modify the standard routine to take advantage of this fact. In this routine, we know that we can extract the ContactId value to get a unique value for the Key parameter of the Add method for the Collection object.

The rest of the routines—Item, Remove, and Count—follow the definitions used by the Collection object. (You can see this for yourself in the source code.) However, there is one problem with using the Collection object. We don't have a way for Visual Basic to use the For Each statement to iterate through each object in the collection. Fortunately, there is a little trick we can use to get around this problem. The code in Listing 12.3 will work for any object you create using the Collection object. It takes advantage of a hidden member of the Collection object called _NewEnum. This method is called by Visual Basic when it executes the For Each statement to get the next item in the collection. In order to include the leading underscore, you need to include the square brackets around it, like this:

```
[_NewEnum]
```

Listing 12.3   The NewEnum method of the Contacts object

```
Public Function NewEnum() As IUnknown

Set NewEnum = c.[_NewEnum]

End Function
```

The other part of this trick is to use the Procedure Attributes tool (select Tools ➤ Procedure Attributes and click the Advanced button) to make two changes to the routine. You need to set the Procedure ID to –4, and you need to make the routine hidden. These settings are shown in Figure 12.7.

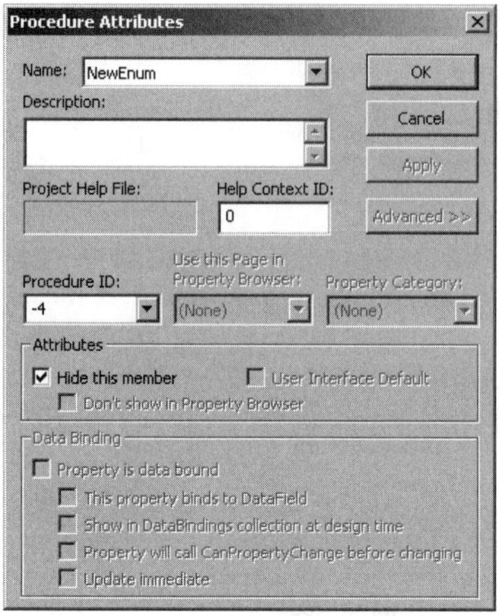

FIGURE 12.7:

Using the Procedure
Attributes tool to tweak
NewEnum

ContactManager Object Enhancements

The ContactManager object operates under control of the COM+ transaction server. We've used this object to provide various functions in earlier examples. Now we'll add a few new routines to support the IMDB function. Specifically, we'll add code to establish a connection to the database and a routine called Get-Contacts, which is used to return a Contacts collection object containing the desired list of contacts.

Module-Level Declarations

The module-level declarations for the ContactManager are shown in Listing 12.4. These are used to hold a database Connection object and a Recordset object while the ContactManager object exists. This simplifies database access and improves performance because we don't need to reestablish these objects each time we need them.

| Listing 12.4 | **Module-level database declarations for the ContactManager object** |

```
Dim db As ADODB.Connection
Dim rs As ADODB.Recordset
```

The OpenDB Routine

The OpenDB routine, shown in Listing 12.5, opens a connection to the IMDB server using MSIMDB as the provider and AthenaSQLServer as the connection string. (This was the value we gave as the name when we defined the data source, as explained in the "Defining a Back-end Data Source" section earlier in this chapter.)

| Listing 12.5 | **The OpenDB routine in the ContactManager object** |

```
Private Sub OpenDB()

Set db = New ADODB.Connection
db.Provider = "MSIMDB"
db.ConnectionString = "AthenaSQLServer"
db.CursorLocation = adUseNone
db.Open

Set rs = New ADODB.Recordset
rs.Open "VBCOM.dbo.Contacts", db, adOpenDynamic, _
    adLockOptimistic

End Sub
```

Selecting adUseNone for the CursorLocation property is a wise idea. IMDB provides the same functions as the adUseServer cursor, but with less overhead.

Once the connection to IMDB is opened, we can access a table by opening a Recordset object. Notice that we specify the fully qualified name for the database table to prevent confusion, and we use a dynamic cursor with optimistic locking. This will allow updates to the database.

The CloseDB Routine

The CloseDB routine, shown in Listing 12.6, simply closes the currently open Recordset and Connection objects. Then it destroys the objects by setting them to Nothing.

Listing 12.6   **The CloseDB routine in the ContactManager object**

```
Private Sub CloseDB()

rs.Close
db.Close

Set rs = Nothing
Set db = Nothing

End Sub
```

The GetContacts Routine

Now that you have gotten through the simple stuff, let's look at the GetContacts routine in Listing 12.7. The goal of this routine is to extract the desired set of contacts from the database. Rather than returning all of the contacts, we use the Recordset.Filter property to restrict the records we need to return.

Listing 12.7   **The GetContacts routine in the ContactManager object**

```
Public Function GetContacts(RecFilter As String) _
   As Contacts

On Error Resume Next

Dim o As ObjectContext
Dim c As Contact
Dim cc As Contacts
Dim i As Long

Set o = GetObjectContext()
```

```
Err.Clear
rs.Filter = RecFilter
If Err.Number <> 0 Then
    App.LogEvent "ContactManager: Can't apply filter (" & _
        RecFilter & ") - " & _
        Err.Description & "-" & _
        Hex(Err.Number)

    Set cc = Nothing

Else
    Set cc = New Contacts

    rs.MoveFirst
    Do While Not rs.EOF
        Set c = New Contact
        c.ContactId = rs.Fields("ContactId")
        c.FirstName = rs.Fields("FirstName")
        c.LastName = rs.Fields("LastName")
        c.MiddleName = rs.Fields("MiddleName")
        c.Prefix = rs.Fields("Prefix")
        c.Title = rs.Fields("Title")
        c.Organization = rs.Fields("Organization")
        c.Street = rs.Fields("Street")
        c.City = rs.Fields("City")
        c.State = rs.Fields("State")
        c.Zip = rs.Fields("Zip")
        c.Telephone = rs.Fields("Telephone")
        c.FAX = rs.Fields("FAX")
        c.EMail = rs.Fields("EMail")

        cc.Add c
        rs.MoveNext

    Loop

End If

rs.Filter = 0
Set GetContacts = cc
Set c = Nothing
```

```
Set cc = Nothing
o.SetComplete

Set o = Nothing

End Function
```

This routine begins by getting an object context, which is necessary because this routine will be executed as a transaction. Then we apply the specified filter (RecFilter) to the current Recordset object (rs). If we get an error, we log an application error and set the Contacts object to Nothing to indicate the error. Remember that setting Contacts to Nothing is not the same thing as having no Contact objects in the collection.

WARNING   The Filter property is greatly restricted under IMDB. You can filter only on columns that have an index or the column that is part of the primary key. Even then, you can only use the filter to return a contiguous set of data. If you make a mistake in the filter criteria, an error will occur and the filter will not be applied.

If the filter works, then we loop through the Recordset object and create a new Contact object for each entry. Then we use the Add method of the Contacts object (cc) to add it to the return value of the function.

Notice that we need to copy each value over one object at a time. A more efficient way to handle this situation would be to create a method in the Contact object that would have a parameter for each of the fields and perform the assignment for us. However, that technique is not as straightforward as the approach we used in this example.

When we reach the end of the Recordset (rs.EOF), we reset the Filter property to 0, which removes the filter. Then we return the cc object as the value of the function, destroy the unused objects, and end the transaction successfully.

The User Program

Using the GetContacts object is fairly straightforward, as you can see in Listing 12.8. Basically, we collect the filter the user wants to use in the Text1 text box and wait until the user clicks the Get Contacts button. Then we process the results and display it in the Text2 text box. Figure 12.8 shows the IMDB Demo Program window.

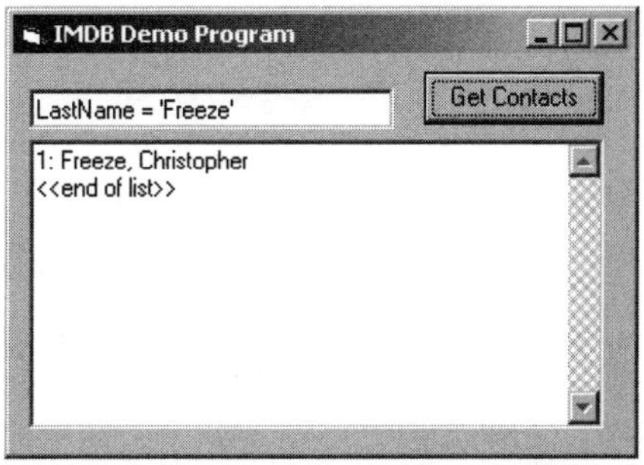

FIGURE 12.8:

The IMDB Demo Program
window

Listing 12.8   **The Client program**

```
Private Sub Command1_Click()

Dim cm As New ContactManager
Dim cc As Contacts
Dim c As Contact

Set cc = cm.GetContacts(Text1.Text)

If cc Is Nothing Then
   Text2.Text = "<<Error in the filter criteria>>"

Else
   Text2.Text = ""
   For Each c In cc
      Text2.Text = Text2.Text & _
      FormatNumber(c.ContactId, 0) & _
      ": " & c.LastName & ", " & _
      c.FirstName & vbCrLf

   Next
   Text2.Text = Text2.Text & "<<end of list>>"

End If

Set cc = Nothing
Set c = Nothing
Set cm = Nothing

End Sub
```

After creating a new instance of the `ContactManager` object, we use the `Get-Contacts` method to return a `Contacts` object called `cc` containing the `Contact` objects that meet the filter criteria. Next, we check if there was an error in the filter criteria by seeing if the return value is `Nothing`. If so, we display the error message.

If the filter worked properly, then we use a `For Each` statement to loop through each object in `cc` and append it to the end of the `Text2` text box. Then we append an end-of-list marker to clearly indicate the end of the contact list. Finally, we destroy all of the objects we used during this session.

Final Thoughts

IMDB is a powerful tool that can make a big difference in your application. However, like many tools that improve your application's performance, you need to understand the trade-offs before you use it. If your server is performing badly because it's low on memory, using IMDB is probably the last thing you want to use. On the other hand, if your database server is swamped with disk I/O activity, then using IMDB could make a big difference.

Having spent many years tuning systems for optimal performance, I found that before you make any changes to your system, you should understand how it currently runs. You need to capture two basic kinds of statistics:

- You need to know how much work your system is doing. This includes measurements such as the number of transactions per second, the number of database requests, and response time. These workload statistics need to be recorded over time to understand when the peak load on the system occurs.

- You need to measure system statistics. This includes such statistics as CPU utilization, memory utilization, paging rate, and disk I/O activity. These statistics also need to be tracked over time and correlated with the workload statistics.

Once you have the statistics, when you make a change that is targeted at improving performance, you'll have some idea what impact the change had on the system.

You can compare what happened after the change with what happened before the change.

Quite often, you'll find that a change that reduces disk I/O activity will increase memory usage, paging rate, or even CPU utilization. Making a system perform optimally is a balancing act, trading CPU utilization for memory utilization, memory utilization for disk I/O activity, and disk I/O activity for CPU utilization. If your system were overloaded in all of these categories, you would be better off directing your efforts toward finding a bigger system. However if you have extra memory and you're running tight on disk I/Os, consider using IMDB to shift the balance a bit.

CHAPTER
THIRTEEN

Understanding Security in COM+

- COM+ security types

- Security configuration

- Security role definition

- Security programming

One important aspect of using COM+ is your application's security. Your COM+ components are available over a network and need to be protected from unauthorized access. In addition to protecting your objects from unauthorized access, you may want to select which functions are available on a user-by-user basis.

This chapter discusses how to include security into your COM+ application. You'll learn about the types of security, and then how to configure security settings and define roles.

Types of Security under COM+

COM+ is tightly integrated with the normal Windows 2000/NT security subsystem. You use the facilities in the Active Directory to create the definitions that are used in COM+. Then, depending on the type of security you're implementing, you use the Component Services utility to specify security options or you build the security into your program.

Under COM+ there are four basic types of security:

- Authentication services establish the identity of a user.

- Impersonation and delegation services provide ways for a user to perform tasks using the permissions of another user.

- Declarative role-based security provides a static way to protect application resources by grouping users into security roles.

- Programmatic role-based security allows your program to dynamically check to see if a user is a member of particular security role.

Each of these is described in more detail in the following sections.

Authentication

The most fundamental part of any security check is verifying the identity of the caller. On a single system, this is relatively easy—a username and a password are usually required to access the system. After the user has been granted access to the system, it is a simple matter to determine what resources the user can access.

However, authenticating a user across a network is far more complex. Each program running on each machine may be required to provide a valid username. Thus, in a typical COM+ transaction environment, you need to worry about the client program, the transaction server, and the database server. Fortunately, Windows 2000/NT includes facilities to authenticate users in this environment.

NOTE   Authenticating users over the Internet is a much different story. Although Windows has the ability to authenticate users running Internet Explorer, you can't assume that all web browsers will have that ability. You should try to design the application in such a way that authenticating the end user isn't as important as authenticating the special users.

Impersonation and Delegation

In some cases, you may want to allow the user to run a program with a number of special privileges. Occasionally, you want the program to perform a function based on the user. For instance, you may have an application that backs up a file on demand. The program needs access to a secure area that the user can't get to, but you want to limit the program to only those files that the user can access. One way to set up this type of access is through impersonation.

When an application impersonates a user, it effectively switches it normal username to that of the end user. Then it performs the tasks it needs using the end user's security profile. After it completes these tasks, the application switches back to its normal username with its security profile. In technical terms, this is the ability of a thread to execute using a security context different from the security context of the process that owns the thread.

Delegation is the ability to impersonate a client over a network. Because of the sensitive nature of this ability, it is necessary to explicitly enable delegation on the user's Active Directory entry (by unchecking the Account Is Sensitive and Cannot be Delegated check box). Then it is up to the application to switch to the user's username.

Role-Based Security

With declarative role-based security, you can define a list of roles for each COM+ application. In each of the roles, you specify a list of usernames and groups that are associated with the role. Then you associate each role with one or more components in the application. With this type of security, in order to use the component, your username (or a security group containing your username) must be a member of a role that is permitted access to the component.

Programmatic role-based security uses the same roles that you create for declarative role-based security, but the security access is determined by the code in your program. By calling functions, you can determine if the user is a member of a particular role. Then, based on the result, you can permit the access to continue or return a security violation.

Configuring Security

Configuring security for a COM+ application involves understanding how COM+ security works, how your application works, and how the people will use it. It also requires an understanding of how people shouldn't use it.

Once you know what kind of security your application needs, you should develop a security plan. Then, based on that plan, you can create the necessary security definitions.

Planning Security

When implementing security in COM+, you need to separate users into multiple groups based on the type of work they do. You should identify whether it is possible to authenticate each group of users. Then you need to identify the various features of your application. With this information, you should be able to create a security matrix similar to the one shown in Table 13.1.

NOTE   You shouldn't expect your table to be as small as the one in Table 13.1. However, this table does give you a simplified idea of the type of information you'll need in order to develop your security plan.

TABLE 13.1: A Security Matrix for the Contact Information System

User Type	View Limited Contact Information	View Full Contact Information	Update Contact Information
External/ unauthenticated	Yes	No	No
Clerical/ authenticated	Yes	No	No
Sales/ authenticated	Yes	Yes	Yes
Managerial/ authenticated	Yes	Yes	No

In this simple example, there are four different classes of users: external, clerical, sales, and managerial. External and clerical users access the same functions. The primary difference between them is that external users are not authenticated, while clerical users are authenticated.

There are also three different features in the application. The first two provide a read-only view of the information in the database. The last feature allows the user to update the information.

Five Rules of Security

Security is a subject that is near and dear to my heart. I've been responsible for planning and implementing systems for complex computer systems for many years. Over the years, I've developed a series of rules that help me design security systems. I hope they can help you as well.

My first rule of security is that having too much security is always better than having too little. No matter how much security you implement, the users will always complain. Thus, I found it's better to start with a very secure system and then relax the security over time if you find that it's too restrictive. If you start with too little security and try to add more over time, the users may rebel and make it difficult, if not impossible, to tighten security.

My second rule of security is that the best security is not disclosing how security is implemented. Keeping a low profile on these details makes it more difficult for someone to gain access to the system.

Continued on next page

My third rule of security is that it should be relatively easy to use. If you make it too difficult, users will paste notes to their computers with detailed instructions on how to access the system. These instructions usually include usernames and passwords that should be kept secret. This is the last thing you want, since that information will make it easy for unauthorized users to get into the system.

My fourth rule of security is that nothing beats a good log file. You should log events such as when a user logs on to the system, when a user logs off the system, each application the user runs, and, if possible, each transaction the user executes. In some cases, the only way to track this information is by adding code to your application to explicitly capture this information. However, once you do have a security breach, the first question everyone is going to ask is what did the interloper do. With a good set of logs, you can answer this question. Sometimes it may take a little effort to cross-reference information between various logs, but in the long run, you'll find that having the information is definitely worth the trouble of collecting it.

My last rule of security is that people on the inside cause most security breaches. In other words, you are more likely to have a security problem with someone who already has access to the system than someone on the outside. I worked in the administrative computer center at a major university for nearly 20 years and had far more security-related problems with people who already had access to the computers than the student population at large.

Remember that sooner or later, you are going to have a security problem. No security system is foolproof. Even the most well-designed system is vulnerable to a current employee who uses his or her authority to do something malicious. The best you can do is take reasonable precautions. When a security problem arises, solving that problem can show you how to improve your security so it doesn't happen again.

Defining Security Roles

The first step in the process of implementing security on a COM+ application is to define the roles. The roles are defined using the Component Services utility at the COM+ application level.

To define a new role in a COM+ application, expand the tree to display the icon associated with your COM+ application. Then expand that icon to show the Components and Roles icons below it. Right-click the Roles icon and select New ➢ Role from the pop-up menu. In the Role dialog box, shown in Figure 13.1, enter the name of the new role.

FIGURE 13.1:

Enter the name of the new role.

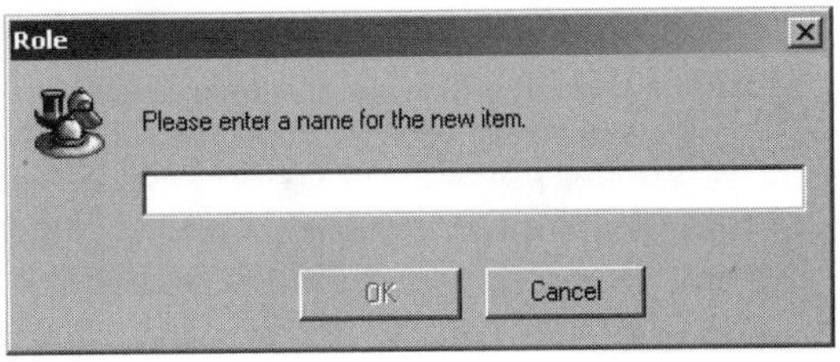

The system creates the new role and places it under the Roles icon. Right-click the new role and select Properties from the pop-up menu. Here, you can supply a description of the role. Figure 13.2 shows the Properties dialog box for the sample External role.

FIGURE 13.2:

Enter a description for the role.

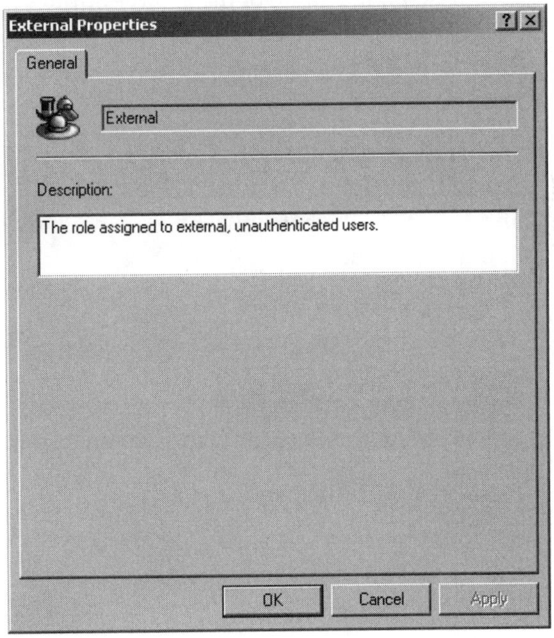

You repeat this process for each of the roles you've defined in your security plan.

Adding Users to a Role

After you've created your roles, you need to add users to those roles. One way to do this is to add each individual username to the role. This approach is time-consuming and difficult to maintain, but it does have the advantage of clearly identifying the users who have this role.

The other approach is to create a security group using the Active Directory Users and Computers utility (Start ➤ Programs ➤ Administrative Tools ➤ Active Directory Users and Computers). This is the same utility that you use to create new users. Once you've created a security group, you can add usernames to that group using the same utility. The main advantage of this approach is that you can use your security groups across multiple COM+ applications. Then you can use the Active Directory Users and Computers utility to add each new user and provide that user with the proper authorization to access your applications.

To add a user or group to a role, in the Component Services utility, expand the icons starting with the computer where the application resides, the COM+ Applications icon, the name of the COM+ application, the Roles icon, and the name of the role that you want to modify. Right-click the Users icon and select New ➤ User from the pop-up menu. This displays the Select Users or Groups dialog box, shown in Figure 13.3.

The list of usernames and security groups is displayed in the top list box. Select one or more users and groups and click the Add button to add the selected users and groups to the bottom list box. When you click OK, these users and groups are added to the role.

Associating Roles with Components

Now that you have created a set of roles for the application, you need to associate these roles with the various components inside the application. This is a two-step process:

- You must enable access checking at the component level; otherwise, anyone who is allowed to access the application will be allowed to access this component.

- Then you must select which roles are permitted to use this application. If the user isn't a member of one of these roles, that user will be denied access to the component.

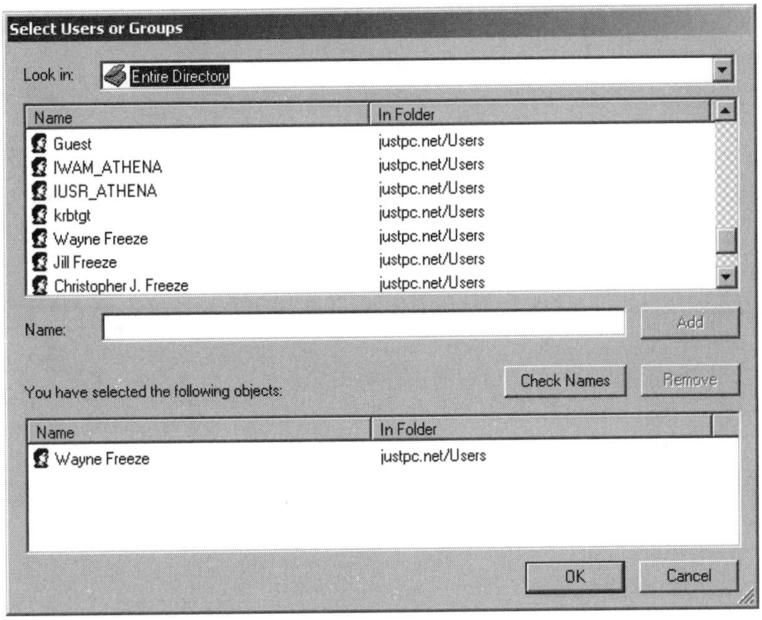

FIGURE 13.3:

Choose a set of users and groups.

To associate a role with a component, in the Component Services utility, expand the icons starting with the computer where the application resides, the COM+ Applications icon, the name of the COM+ application, the Components icon, and the name of the component that you want to modify. Right-click the name of the component and select Properties from the pop-up menu. Then select the Security tab to see the Properties dialog box shown in Figure 13.4.

Check the Enforce Component Level Access Checks check box. Selecting this option requires COM+ to verify that the authenticated user has proper access to this component. Also put a check mark next to each of the roles that you want to grant access to this particular component. The user must be associated with at least one of these roles in order to use any of the routines in this component.

Associating Roles with Interfaces

Even though it is easy to divide an application into multiple components, sometimes you need to apply security at a slightly lower level. COM+ allows you to associate roles with the various interfaces within a COM+ component.

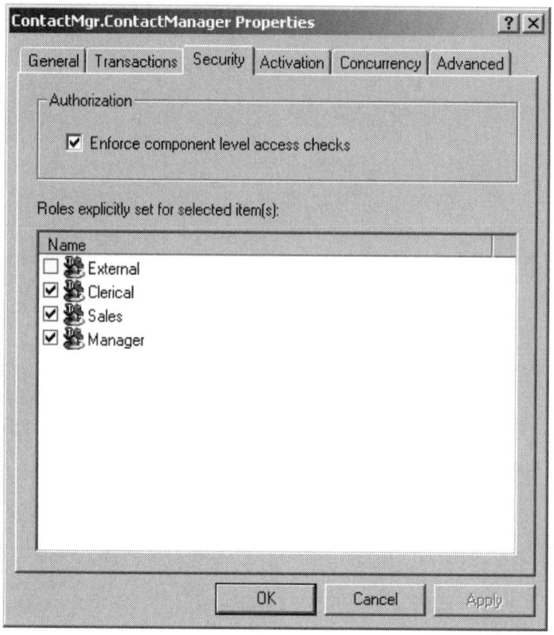

FIGURE 13.4:

Security properties for a component

To associate a role with an interface, in the Component Services utility, expand the icons starting with the computer where the application resides, the COM+ Applications icon, the name of the COM+ application, the Components icon, the name of the component containing the interface that you want to modify, the Interfaces icon, and finally the name of the interface you want to secure. Right-click the name of the interface you want to secure and select Properties from the pop-up menu. Choose the Security tab, as shown in Figure 13.5.

The first thing you notice about this interface is that the roles you set at the component level will automatically be inherited by the interface. Anyone listed in these roles is allowed to access the interface. At the bottom of the property page, you see all of the roles available in the application. By checking any of these roles, you add the role to the list of inherited roles that are allowed to access the interface.

FIGURE 13.5:

Setting security on an interface

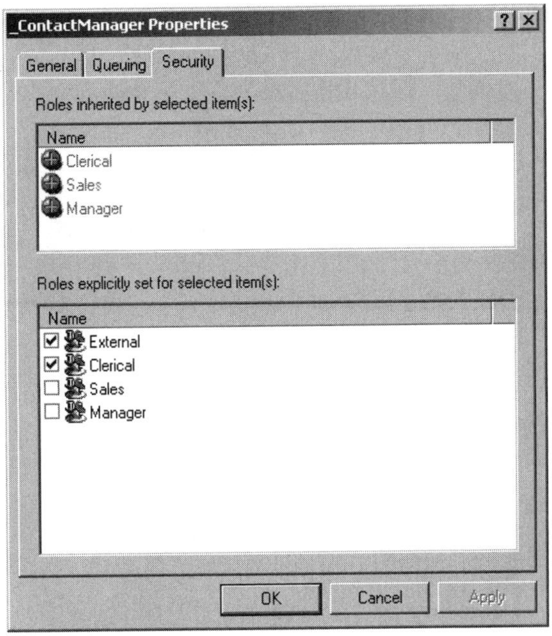

Enabling Security on an Application

After you've defined all of roles, you still have one final task to perform to enable the security. This involves setting the property to enable access checks for the entire application and setting the security level so that security checking is performed at the process and component level.

To enable security, in the Component Services utility, expand the icons starting with the computer where the application resides, the COM+ Applications icon, and the name of the COM+ application that you want to modify. Right-click the application and select Properties from the pop-up menu. Then click the Security tab to display the Properties dialog box shown in Figure 13.6.

Check the Enforce Access Checks for This Application check box at the top of the dialog box to use role-based security in the application. In the Security Level section, select the Perform Access Checks at the Process and Component Level option to enable security checking at the component level.

FIGURE 13.6:

Enable security on the application.

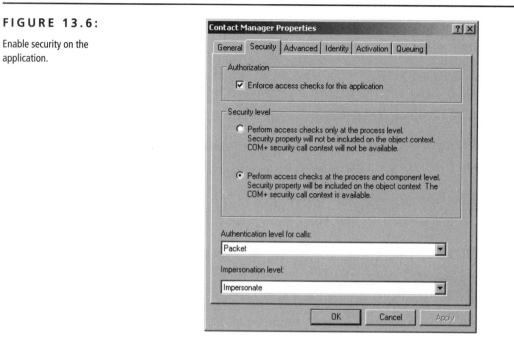

NOTE   Security authorization and impersonation in COM+ applications can be very complex. For additional information on this subject, take a look at *Mastering COM and COM+* by Ash Rofail and Yasser Shohoud (Sybex, 2000).

Programming Security

At this point, we've implemented the security for an application, as outlined in the security plan. But what happens if, as usual, our users change their minds at the last minute? In this case, let's assume that the users added a new requirement that the managers and clerical users be allowed to update their own information. This would be difficult (or maybe impossible) to implement as a set of static rules. However, it's a snap to implement if we write a little code to handle the situation.

Gathering Information

Since security is generally tightly integrated with the application, we will build a routine that gathers the various pieces of security information and returns it as a formatted string. Because the routines to get the security information need to run under the control of the COM+ transaction server, we add the routine shown in Listing 13.1 to the ContactMgr object.

Listing 13.1   The ReturnSecurityInfo routine in ContactMgr

```
Public Function ReturnSecurityInfo() As String

Dim o As ObjectContext
Dim s As SecurityCallContext
Dim t As String

Set o = GetObjectContext()

Set s = GetSecurityCallContext()

t = IIf(s.IsSecurityEnabled, _
    "Security is enabled.", _
    "Security is not enabled.") & vbCrLf

t = t & IIf(s.IsCallerInRole("External"), _
    "Caller is external.", _
    "Caller is not external.") & vbCrLf

t = t & IIf(s.IsCallerInRole("Clerical"), _
    "Caller is clerical.", _
    "Caller is not clerical.") & vbCrLf

t = t & IIf(s.IsCallerInRole("Sales"), _
    "Caller is sales.", _
    "Caller is not sales.") & vbCrLf

t = t & IIf(s.IsCallerInRole("Manager"), _
    "Caller is manager.", _
    "Caller is not manager.") & vbCrLf
```

```
t = t & "Direct caller: " & _
    s.Item("DirectCaller").Item("AccountName") & vbCrLf

t = t & "Original caller: " & _
    s.Item("OriginalCaller").Item("AccountName") & vbCrLf

t = t & "Minimum Authentication Level: " & _
    FormatNumber(s.Item("MinAuthenticationLevel"), 0) & _
    vbCrLf

t = t & "Number of callers: " & _
    FormatNumber(s.Item("NumCallers"), 0) & vbCrLf

ReturnSecurityInfo = t

Set s = Nothing
o.SetComplete
Set o = Nothing

End Function
```

This routine begins like most COM+ transactions by getting the current context with the GetObjectContext function. Then we call the GetSecurityCallContext function to get a pointer to the SecurityCallContext object. Once we have access to the security object, we get the global security status using the IsSecurity-Enabled property and save it in a temporary string called t.

Then we use the IsCallerInRole to check the four roles listed earlier in Table 13.1. If security is enabled, you see different results depending on how the username you're using is assigned to the roles. If security isn't enabled at the component level, the IsCallerInRole will always return True.

We then use the collection of information included with the SecurityCall-Context object to get information about the DirectCaller and the Original-Caller. The direct caller is the username associated with the process that started this transaction. Because of impersonation and delegation capabilities, the username that started this transaction can be different from the original username associated with the base program. That username can be retrieved by using the OriginalCaller key. Also from this collection, we can find the minimum authentication level (MinAuthenticationLevel) and the number of callers (NumCallers).

After we've finished getting the security information, we return the value in t as the value of the function and destroy the SecurityCallContext object. Then we finish the transaction as usual, by using the SetComplete method and destroying the ObjectContext object.

Displaying the Information

This information is displayed using the simple-looking program shown in Figure 13.7. Clicking the Get Security Info button triggers the routine in Listing 13.2.

FIGURE 13.7:

Displaying security
information

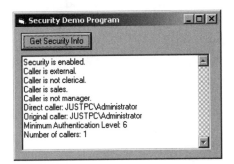

Listing 13.2   **The Command1_Click event in ContactClient**

```
Private Sub Command1_Click()

Dim cm As Object

Set cm = CreateObject("ContactMgr.ContactManager")

Text2.Text = cm.ReturnSecurityInfo

Set cm = Nothing

End Sub
```

This routine creates the ContactManager object and then calls the Return-SecurityInfo method to get the security information. After displaying in the text box, we destroy the object and end the routine.

Final Thoughts

You can determine a lot of information about the person who is using your application, while your application runs under its own unique username. However, when you build transaction-processing systems, you are responsible for building your own security into your application. This can be more difficult than you think.

The security you build into your application must ensure that users can access only the functions that they are entitled to and will be denied access to all others. This isn't difficult to handle for a couple of users, but it can be a nightmare if you support hundreds or thousands of users. If this doesn't scare you, then consider what might happen if an auditor wishes you to prove your security implementation is correct by reviewing your code.

While there are many different ways to implement security, here are three that I've used in the past:

- Separate the application into general-purpose functions and secure functions. Anyone who has access to the application automatically has access to the general-purpose functions. Membership in a specific role is required for each of the secure functions. By limiting the number of special cases you need to handle, you can simplify your code considerably, yet still have a secure application.

- Build your application around a security structure that ensures that each user can access only the functions that user has been authorized to access. Then implement a general-purpose dispatch routine that examines the username and the function requested before invoking the desired function. By using a single point to dispatch your code, it is easy to show that your application is secure.

- Use a table in your database to control access to data in other tables. This table contains a username and a piece of information that is secured, such as an account number. If the user has access to multiple accounts, then include a row in the table relating the username to each account number. Then use a Select statement, such as the one shown below, each time you open a Recordset:

```
Select * From Info, Security Where Info.Account =
Security.Account and Security.Account = "username"
```

Security is something you need to take seriously no matter what your situation. It needs to be planned at the start, just like any other part of your application.

PART IV

Developing COM+ Transactions

CHAPTER

FOURTEEN

14

Developing COM+ Transactions for SQL Server

- The Contact Manager database and application design

- The Contact Manager object design

- Contact information retrieval

- Contact information updates

- Contact searches

Using COM+ without using a database is a little like owning a Porsche without an engine—it looks interesting but isn't very useful. In this chapter, I'll show you how you can build a series of COM+ transactions that are integrated with a SQL Server database. To make the transactions functional, you'll learn how to build a three-tier, client/server-based program that accesses them.

Designing the Contact Manager Application

In Part 3, each of the sample programs deal with a database table called Contacts. Chapter 10 introduced the sample application called Contact Manager, which allows someone to track contacts made with various people. We've used that application to explore various COM+ features, Now we'll continue working with that application, enhancing it so that it works with SQL Server.

The Contact Manager database uses three tables: the Contacts table, the ContactInfo table, and the ActionItems table. These tables are stored in the VBCOM database. In Chapter 10, Tables 10.6, 10.7, and 10.8 list the field names and types, with brief descriptions, for each database table.

Middle Tier Design

The middle tier consists of a COM+ application known as Contact Manager. This application sits between the client program and the database server. Its function is to provide a high-level way to access the database.

To facilitate communications between the client and server, there is another set of objects called the Contact Types. These objects provide a high-level view of the information in the database. Because these objects are used by both the client and the middle-tier application program, they must reside on both the client computer with the application and the transaction server with the COM+ application.

Client Application Design

The client application is a rather simple design that uses three forms to present the information from the database.

The Main Form

Figure 14.1 shows the main form, which displays information about a single person in the application.

If you know the proper value for `ContactId`, you can enter it and click the Get button to retrieve information about a single contact. You can change any field on the form and click the Commit Changes button to run a transaction that updates the database.

The Search Form

If you don't know which contact you want to retrieve, you can click the Search button to display the Contact Search form, shown in Figure 14.2. This form allows you to search any field in the `Contacts` table based on the specified relational operator and value. This is useful when you know that someone works for a particular organization, for example.

FIGURE 14.2:

The Contact Search form

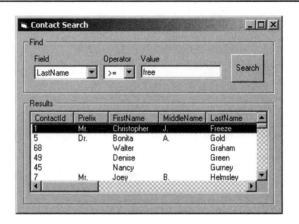

After entering the search request in the Find section of the form, you will see a list of contacts in the Results section of the form. Clicking one of these entries will close the Contact Search form and display the main Contact Manager form with all of the corresponding information.

The Details Form

The third form in the application is started from the Contact Manager form by clicking the Details button. This form provides details about each contact with the customer, as shown in Figure 14.3.

The Date Contacted field has a drop-down list of all of the dates and times the person was contacted. The currently displayed value dictates the information displayed in the Contact Information section of the form. Changing to a different Date Contacted value will refresh the display with the information related to that date and time. Clicking the New Contact button clears the Contact Information section of the form and displays the current date and time in the Date Contacted field.

The follow-up date is displayed in a `DateTimePicker` control. This helps the user to select the appropriate date. (I didn't include a When Hell Freezes Over follow-up date option; users will simply have to use their best guess as to when that event will occur.)

FIGURE 14.3:

The Contact Details form

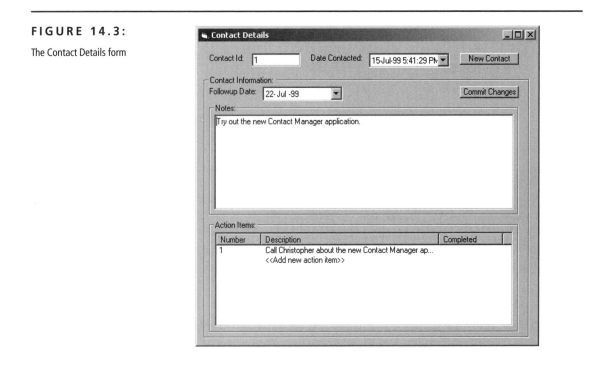

The Notes section of the Contact Details form holds up to 4,096 characters. Users can type in whatever information they want to record.

The Action Items section contains a list of action items requested by the customer. Clicking any of these fields will toggle the Date Completed information. Clicking the last line, <<Add new action item>>, will prompt the user for a one-line task to be added to the end of the Action Items list.

Communicating Using Objects

This application uses a series of objects found in the ContactTypes ActiveX DLL that can be passed back and forth between the client program and the COM+ transaction server. These objects contain an object-oriented view of a subset of the information from the database. This means that you only need to include the appropriate object when using a transaction.

The database for this application represents a hierarchy of information. A single record in the Contacts table may point to multiple records in the ContactInfo table, and a single record in the ContactInfo table may point to many records in the ActionInfo table. To represent this structure in object terms, I use two basic types of objects:

- Single-record objects contain just the fields from a database table. The single record objects are Contact, ContactInfo, and ActionItem.

- Collection objects hold multiple single-record objects. Using Microsoft's convention of denoting a collection of objects by appending an *s* to the end of the single-record objects, I've created the Contacts, ContactInfos, and ActionItems collections.

This means that the three database tables are translated into six different objects.

The Contacts Collection

The Contacts collection, shown in Listing 14.1, is a simple object that is based on the Collection object. It contains five methods: Add, Item, Remove, Count, and NewEnum. These methods are commonly found in any collection.

Listing 14.1   **The Contacts collection**

```
Option Explicit

Private c As New Collection

Public Sub Add(Item As Contact)

c.Add Item, FormatNumber(Item.ContactId, 0)

End Sub
```

```
Public Function Item(Key As Variant) As Contact

Set Item = c.Item(Key)

End Function

Public Sub Remove(Key As Variant)

c.Remove Key

End Sub

Public Function Count() As Long

Count = c.Count

End Function

Public Function NewEnum() As IUnknown

Set NewEnum = c.[_NewEnum]

End Function
```

The idea behind this object is to pass the basic operations onto the collection object for execution. Thus, the Add method merely accepts a Contact object as its parameter and passes it onto the Add method of the internal collection object. This approach is repeated for the Item, Remove, and Count methods.

The NewEnum method is somewhat unusual. In order to use the For Each statement, an object must support the NewEnum method. This method is present in all collections, even though you don't see it. Because it is present in the collection c, we just need to pass along the request to the collection's NewEnum method.

Of course, this isn't all we need to do. We also must set the Procedure ID to –4 and mark the member as hidden using the Procedure Attributes tool, as shown in Figure 14.4. And just to make things confusing, the routine's name is really _NewEnum, not simply NewEnum. This type of name can't be processed by Visual Basic, so you need to surround it with square brackets ([_NewEnum]) to prevent parsing errors. However, the bit of extra work is worth being able to iterate through the object using For Each.

FIGURE 14.4:

Using the Procedure Attributes tool to modify NewEnum

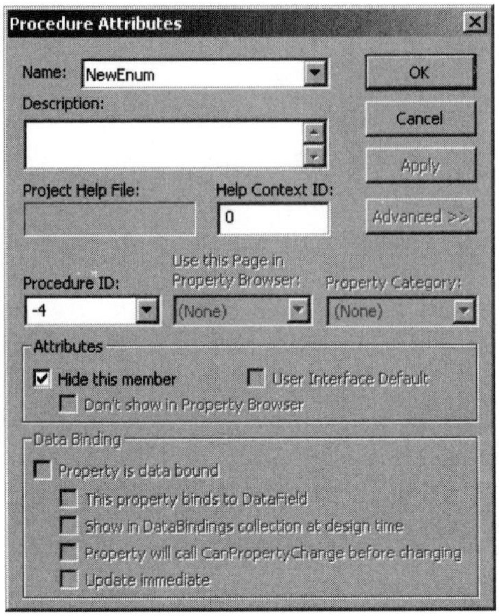

The Contact Object

For the most part, the Contact object is just a list of the fields from the Contacts
database table. Because they are defined as Public, anyone using the object can
read or change their values. Listing 14.2 shows the header from the Contact
object.

> **NOTE** I should have created these properties using Property Let and Property Get
> routines. However, I decided I didn't really need to spend all that time checking
> the data for errors. I chose to assume that the user of this application would never
> enter bad data.

Listing 14.2   The header from the Contact object

```
Public ContactId As Long
Public FirstName As String
Public MiddleName As String
```

```
Public LastName As String
Public Prefix As String
Public Title As String
Public Organization As String
Public Street As String
Public City As String
Public State As String
Public Zip As String
Public Telephone As String
Public FAX As String
Public EMail As String

Public Dirty As Boolean
Public ContactInfos As ContactInfos
```

In addition to the fields in the Contacts database tables, I added two other properties: ContactInfos and Dirty. The ContactInfos property is an object reference to the ContactInfos collection. By using this property, I can reference the set of related records from the ContactInfo table.

The Dirty property will be used later to determine if the contents of this object have been updated. When the object is created, this value will be set to False. If the application updates this value, it must set this property to True in order for the database to be updated.

The ContactInfos Collection

The ContactInfos collection is similar to the Contacts collection. It has the same Add, Item, Remove, Count, and NewEnum methods. However, there are two minor differences in the declarations section, as you can see in Listing 14.3.

Listing 14.3   The header from the ContactInfos collection

```
Public ContactId As Long
Public Dirty As Boolean

Private c As New Collection
```

This collection includes the `Dirty` property (discussed in the previous section) and also a property to hold a `ContactId` value.

This collection is referenced through the `ContactInfo` property in the `Contact` object. Thus, all of the objects in this collection have the same value for `ContactId`.

NOTE   Although we could push the `ContactId` property into each member of the collection, keeping it in the `ContactInfos` collection reduces the storage required for the object. But the most important reason is that it underscores the idea that this object contains information about a single `ContactId`.

The ContactInfo Object

The `ContactInfo` object contains the remaining three fields from the `ContactInfo` database table. Listing 14.4 shows the header for this object.

Listing 14.4   **The header from the ContactInfo object**

```
Public DateContacted As Date
Public FollowupDate As Date
Public Notes As String

Public Dirty As Boolean
Public ActionItems As ActionItems
```

A reference is included to the `ActionItems` collection, which will contain the list of action items that developed from the conversation with the customer. Also, as with the other objects, the `Dirty` property is used to indicate when the information in this object or in the `ActionItems` collection has been changed.

The ActionItems Collection

The `ActionItems` collection, shown in Listing 14.5, contains the set of action items stemming from a meeting from a customer. Since the values of `ContactId` and `DateContacted` are common to all entries in the collection, these values are stored in the collection object, rather than in each individual item in the collection.

Listing 14.5   The header from the ActionItems collection

```
Public ContactId As Long
Public DateContacted As Date

Public Dirty As Boolean
Private c As New Collection
```

The ActionItem Object

The ActionItem object, shown in Listing 14.6, is the lowest level object in this application.

Listing 14.6   The header from the ActionItem object

```
Public ActionItemNumber As Long
Public ActionItem As String
Public DateCompleted As Date

Public Dirty As Boolean
```

As you can see, this object merely contains the fields from the ActionItems database table that were not included in the ActionItems collection. It also contains the Dirty property that indicates when the values in this object were changed.

Programming the Contact Manager Application

The Contact Manager application is a three-tier, client/server-based program:

- The first tier is the Visual Basic program that runs on the client's computer. This program typically manages the user interface though which the user will request and update information.

- The second tier is the COM+ transactions running under the control of the COM+ transaction server. These transactions implement the business logic for the application.

- The third tier is the database server, which contains the data for the application.

Although it is possible to perform processing on each tier, the Contact Manager application has code associated only with the client computer and the COM+ transaction server. These two tiers communicate with each other by using the six objects described in the previous sections.

Getting Information about a Contact

As explained earlier in the chapter, the main form is designed to display and update the information about a single contact. If you know the contact's `ContactId` value, you can enter that into the Contact Id field and click the Get button. This prepares a request on the client, which will be sent to the transaction server for execution. The results will then be returned to the client and displayed on the main form.

Requesting Contact Information from the Server

Clicking the `Get` button triggers the `Command1_Click` event, listed in Listing 14.7.

Listing 14.7   The Command1_Click event in Form1 of Contact client

```
Private Sub Command1_Click()

Dim c As Integer
Dim cm As Object

If IsNumeric(Text1.Text) Then
    c = Screen.MousePointer
    Screen.MousePointer = vbHourglass

    Set cm = CreateObject("ContactMgr.ContactManager")
    Set CurrentContact = cm.GetAContact(CLng(Text1.Text))
    Set cm = Nothing

    Screen.MousePointer = c
```

```
        If CurrentContact Is Nothing Then
            MsgBox "Can't find ContactId = " & Text1.Text

        Else
            Text1.Text = CurrentContact.ContactId
            Text2.Text = CurrentContact.Prefix
            Text12.Text = CurrentContact.FirstName
            Text13.Text = CurrentContact.MiddleName
            Text14.Text = CurrentContact.LastName
            Text3.Text = CurrentContact.Title
            Text4.Text = CurrentContact.Organization
            Text5.Text = CurrentContact.Street
            Text6.Text = CurrentContact.City
            Text7.Text = CurrentContact.State
            Text8.Text = CurrentContact.Zip
            Text9.Text = CurrentContact.Telephone
            Text10.Text = CurrentContact.FAX
            Text11.Text = CurrentContact.EMail

        End If

        Set cm = Nothing

    Else
        MsgBox "Illegal value for ContactId"

    End If

End Sub
```

This routine begins by verifying that the value for ContactId is numeric. While this doesn't guarantee that the value is valid, it does prevent us from trying to assign a nonnumeric value to the ContactId property.

After switching the cursor to the hourglass, we create a new instance of the ContactManager object and use the GetAContact method to retrieve a new value for CurrentContact. Once this method has finished, we no longer need the ContactManager object, so we set it to Nothing. This releases the resources on the COM+ transaction server so that they may be used for other purposes.

After resetting the mouse pointer, we check the value of CurrentContact. If it is set to Nothing, it means that GetAContact couldn't locate the entry in the Contacts table. Otherwise, we display the information from the CurrentContact object in the corresponding text boxes.

Returning Contact Information to the Client

When the client program calls the GetAContact method, it waits until the transaction server processes the request and returns the results. Listing 14.8 shows this method.

Listing 14.8   The GetAContact method in Contact Manager

```
Public Function GetAContact(ContactId As Long) As Contact

Dim c As New Contact
Dim o As ObjectContext
Dim rs As ADODB.Recordset

On Error Resume Next

Set o = GetObjectContext()

Err.Clear
OpenDB
Set rs = New ADODB.Recordset
Set rs.ActiveConnection = db
rs.Source = "Select * From dbo.Contacts " & _
    "Where ContactId = " & FormatNumber(ContactId, 0)
rs.CursorType = adOpenDynamic
rs.LockType = adLockReadOnly
rs.Open

If Err.Number = 0 Then
    rs.MoveFirst
    c.ContactId = rs.Fields("ContactId")
    c.FirstName = rs.Fields("FirstName")
    c.LastName = rs.Fields("LastName")
    c.MiddleName = rs.Fields("MiddleName")
    c.Prefix = rs.Fields("Prefix")
```

```
        c.Title = rs.Fields("Title")
        c.Organization = rs.Fields("Organization")
        c.Street = rs.Fields("Street")
        c.City = rs.Fields("City")
        c.State = rs.Fields("State")
        c.Zip = rs.Fields("Zip")
        c.Telephone = rs.Fields("Telephone")
        c.FAX = rs.Fields("FAX")
        c.EMail = rs.Fields("EMail")
        c.Requested = False
        c.Dirty = False
        Set c.ContactInfos = GetContactInfos(ContactId)

    Else
        Set c = Nothing

    End If

    rs.Close
    Set rs = Nothing
    CloseDB

    Set GetAContact = c
    Set c = Nothing

    Set o = Nothing

    End Function
```

On the server side, the routine begins by declaring a few local variables include one (c) that will hold the value that we'll return from the function. Next, we establish an object context using the `GetObjectContext` function and open a connection to the database by calling the `OpenDB` routine. Then we create a new `Recordset` object with the `Set New` statement. Notice that we qualify the `Recordset` object using the ADODB prefix to clearly indicate that the record is not the usual DAO `Recordset` object. The DAO library is included in a new Visual Basic project by default. Although this qualification isn't strictly necessary, it will prevent problems if you forget to include the ADO library in your program.

We use the connection object we already have to initialize the ActiveConnection property of the Recordset and specify values for the Source, CursorType, and LockType properties. The Select statement is designed to retrieve only the information about the specific contact. Then we can open the Recordset.

Next, we see if we retrieved any records. The expression rs.BOF And rs.EOF is True only when the Recordset is empty; hence, Not (rs.BOF And rs.EOF) means that at least one record was retrieved. Since ContactId is the primary key for the table, a maximum of one record can be retrieved. This means that we have the record we want, and all we need to do is to return the information to the application program. Notice that we call the GetContactInfos routine in this component to get the entire tree of information for the specific contact.

If there isn't a record, we set c to Nothing. This will indicate to the caller that there isn't a contact for the specified value of ContactId. To end the routine, we close the Recordset object and assign the return value to the name of the function. We set the ObjectContext variable o to Nothing at the end of the routine.

Notice that we didn't need to use the SetComplete method or the SetAbort method, because we didn't make any changes to the database.

Connecting to the Database

COM+ maintains a pool of database connections that you can use as you need them, so it is undesirable to keep a connection open longer than necessary. The OpenDB routine, shown in Listing 14.9, serves as a shortcut for opening the database connection (similarly, the CloseDB routine is a shortcut for closing the connection).

Listing 14.9 **The OpenDB routine in Contact Manager**

```
Private Sub OpenDB()

Set db = New ADODB.Connection
db.Provider = "sqloledb"
db.ConnectionString = "Athena"
db.Open , "sa", ""
db.DefaultDatabase = "VBCOM"

End Sub
```

This routine initializes the module-level variable db with a valid connection to the database. This is a relatively straightforward process. We simply initialize the db.Provider property with the OLE DB driver for SQL Server and point to the database server (located on Athena in this example). Then we use the Open method with a user ID of sa and a blank password to establish the connection. As a matter of convenience, we set the default database to VBCOM.

Updating the Contact Information

If you allow users to retrieve information from the database, they probably will want to modify it from time to time. Updating database information is a three-step process that involves detecting the changes, waiting for the user to commit the changes, and then actually changing the database.

Detecting the Changes

Detecting the changes is fairly easy. We simply add code to set the Update property in each of the Change events in the application and save the new value into the appropriate property. Listing 14.10 shows an example of a Change event.

Listing 14.10   The Text2_Change event in Form1 of Contact Client

```
Private Sub Text2_Change()

CurrentContact.Prefix = Text2.Text
CurrentContact.Dirty = True

End Sub
```

Starting the Commit Process

When the user clicks the Commit Changes button, we check to see if the Dirty property is True. This means that the data has changed and the PutAContact method needs to be called to update the database. This button's Click event is shown in Listing 14.11.

Listing 14.11 **The Command5_Click event**

```
Private Sub Command5_Click()

Dim c As Integer
Dim cm As Object

If CurrentContact.Dirty Then
    c = Screen.MousePointer
    Screen.MousePointer = vbHourglass
    Set cm = CreateObject("ContactMgr.ContactManager")
    cm.PutAContact CurrentContact
    Set cm = Nothing
    Screen.MousePointer = c

End If

End Sub
```

Committing the Changes

The PutAContact method is similar to the GetAContact method discussed earlier. Listing 14.12 shows this method.

Listing 14.12 **The PutAContact method in Contact Manager**

```
Public Sub PutAContact(c As Contact)

Dim o As ObjectContext
Dim rs As ADODB.Recordset

On Error Resume Next

If c.Dirty Then
    Set o = GetObjectContext()

    Err.Clear
    OpenDB
```

```
Set rs = New ADODB.Recordset
Set rs.ActiveConnection = db
rs.Source = "Select * From dbo.Contacts " & _
    "Where ContactId = " & FormatNumber(c.ContactId, 0)
rs.CursorType = adOpenDynamic
rs.LockType = adLockOptimistic
rs.Open

If Err.Number = 0 Then
    rs.MoveFirst

    rs.Fields("FirstName") = c.FirstName
    rs.Fields("LastName") = c.LastName
    rs.Fields("MiddleName") = c.MiddleName
    rs.Fields("Prefix") = c.Prefix
    rs.Fields("Title") = c.Title
    rs.Fields("Organization") = c.Organization
    rs.Fields("Street") = c.Street
    rs.Fields("City") = c.City
    rs.Fields("State") = c.State
    rs.Fields("Zip") = c.Zip
    rs.Fields("Telephone") = c.Telephone
    rs.Fields("FAX") = c.FAX
    rs.Fields("EMail") = c.EMail

    Err.Clear
    rs.Update
    If Err.Number <> 0 Then
        rs.Close
        Set rs = Nothing
        o.SetAbort
        Set o = Nothing

    Else
        rs.Close
        Set rs = Nothing
        o.SetComplete
        Set o = Nothing

    End If
```

```
      End If

    End If

    CloseDB

  End Sub
```

We check the `Dirty` property to determine if we need to update this record. If so, we create a `Recordset` object using a `Select` statement that retrieves the record for the specified `ContactId`. If we find the record, we update all of the values associated with the record, except for `ContactId`, which hasn't changed.

After updating the values, we issue the `Update` method to commit the changes to the database. We carefully clear the `Err` object before executing this method and check the results afterward to determine whether we should abort the transaction or mark it as successfully completed. In either case, we close the `Record-set` first and clean up the loose objects before exiting the routine.

Finding a Client

The second major function in this application allows you to search for a particular entry in the `Contacts` table. When the user clicks the Search button on the main form, the Contact Search form is displayed. This form is used to collect information to build the `Where` clause of a `Select` statement and then update the fields in the main form with the new information.

Building the Search Request

After the user has selected the search field in the `Combo1` combo box, chosen the relational operator in the `Combo2` combo box, entered a value in the `Text1` text box, and clicked the Search button, the `Command1_Click` event in the search form will be fired. This event is shown in Listing 14.13.

Listing 14.13   **The Command1_Click event in Form3 of Contact Client**

```
Private Sub Command1_Click()

Dim c As Contact
Dim cm As Object
```

```
Dim cs As Contacts
Dim l As ListItem

Dim m As Integer

m = Screen.MousePointer
Screen.MousePointer = vbHourglass
Set cm = CreateObject("ContactMgr.ContactManager")
Set cs = cm.GetContacts(Combo1.Text & Combo2.Text & _
    "'" & Text1.Text & "'")
Set cm = Nothing

If cs Is Nothing Then
    MsgBox "No entries were found."

Else
    For Each c In cs
        Set l = ListView1.ListItems.Add(, "CID-" & _
            FormatNumber(c.ContactId, 0), c.ContactId)
        l.SubItems(1) = c.Prefix
        l.SubItems(2) = c.FirstName
        l.SubItems(3) = c.MiddleName
        l.SubItems(4) = c.LastName
        l.SubItems(5) = c.Title
        l.SubItems(6) = c.Organization
        l.SubItems(7) = c.Street
        l.SubItems(8) = c.City
        l.SubItems(9) = c.State
        l.SubItems(10) = c.Zip
        l.SubItems(11) = c.Telephone
        l.SubItems(12) = c.FAX
        l.SubItems(13) = c.EMail

    Next c

End If

Screen.MousePointer = m

End Sub
```

We put together the Where clause information and pass it to the GetContacts method, which returns a Contacts object. (We declared the variable cs at the module level as a Contacts object.) If the routine returns Nothing, this means that the selection criteria didn't return any records, and we let the user know that. If we do find some records, we display them in a ListView control using the Report format.

Populating the Contacts Object

The GetContacts method, shown in Listing 14.14, searches the database for the records that meet the criteria specified in RecFilter.

Listing 14.14   **The GetContacts function in Contact Manager**

```
Public Function GetContacts(RecFilter As String) _
    As Contacts

On Error Resume Next

Dim o As ObjectContext
Dim c As Contact
Dim cc As Contacts
Dim i As Long
Dim rs As ADODB.Recordset

Set o = GetObjectContext()

Err.Clear
OpenDB
Set rs = New ADODB.Recordset
Set rs.ActiveConnection = db
rs.Source = "Select * from dbo.Contacts Where " & RecFilter
rs.Open
If Err.Number <> 0 Then
    App.LogEvent "ContactManager(GetContacts): " & _
        "Can't retrieve records (" & _
        RecFilter & ") - " & _
        Err.Description & "-" & _
        Hex(Err.Number)
```

```
            Set cc = Nothing

    Else

            Set cc = New Contacts
            cc.Requested = False
            cc.Dirty = False

            rs.MoveFirst
            Do While Not rs.EOF
                Set c = New Contact
                c.ContactId = rs.Fields("ContactId")
                c.FirstName = rs.Fields("FirstName")
                c.LastName = rs.Fields("LastName")
                c.MiddleName = rs.Fields("MiddleName")
                c.Prefix = rs.Fields("Prefix")
                c.Title = rs.Fields("Title")
                c.Organization = rs.Fields("Organization")
                c.Street = rs.Fields("Street")
                c.City = rs.Fields("City")
                c.State = rs.Fields("State")
                c.Zip = rs.Fields("Zip")
                c.Telephone = rs.Fields("Telephone")
                c.FAX = rs.Fields("FAX")
                c.EMail = rs.Fields("EMail")
                c.Requested = False
                c.Dirty = False
                Set c.ContactInfos = Nothing

                cc.Add c
                rs.MoveNext

        Loop

    End If

    rs.Close
    Set rs = Nothing
    CloseDB

    Set GetContacts = cc
```

```
Set c = Nothing
Set cc = Nothing
Set o = Nothing

End Function
```

This routine begins by getting an object context and then attempts to create a Recordset using RecFilter. Since it is possible that the calling program could have passed a bad value for RecFilter, we check for the error using the Err object and use the App.LogEvent method to write the relevant information into the application log file.

If the query worked, we use the results to populate the Contacts object, even if the Recordset contains no records. We do this by creating a new instance of the Contacts object. Then we loop through each record in the Recordset and create a new Contact object for each record. We use the Add method of the Contacts object to add the Contact object into the collection.

In addition to setting the various properties corresponding to the fields in the Recordset, we also set the Update property to False and set the ContactInfos collection to Nothing. The main reason for not returning all of the details via the ContactInfos property is that we don't use the information, so we don't need to spend the extra overhead to retrieve those unused records.

At the end of the routine, we destroy the objects we're finished with and return the Contacts object as the value of the function.

Returning the Information to the Main Form

The last part of this process is to return the information to the main form. Clicking a row in the ListView control in the search form triggers the ListView1_BeforeLabelEdit event, shown in Listing 14.15.

Listing 14.15   **The ListView1_BeforeLabelEdit event in Form3 of Contact Client**

```
Private Sub ListView1_BeforeLabelEdit(Cancel As Integer)

Set Form1.CurrentContact = _
    cs.Item(ListView1.SelectedItem.Text)
```

```
Form1.Text1.Text = ListView1.SelectedItem.Text
Form1.Text2.Text = ListView1.SelectedItem.SubItems(1)
Form1.Text12.Text = ListView1.SelectedItem.SubItems(2)
Form1.Text13.Text = ListView1.SelectedItem.SubItems(3)
Form1.Text14.Text = ListView1.SelectedItem.SubItems(4)
Form1.Text3.Text = ListView1.SelectedItem.SubItems(5)
Form1.Text4.Text = ListView1.SelectedItem.SubItems(6)
Form1.Text5.Text = ListView1.SelectedItem.SubItems(7)
Form1.Text6.Text = ListView1.SelectedItem.SubItems(8)
Form1.Text7.Text = ListView1.SelectedItem.SubItems(9)
Form1.Text8.Text = ListView1.SelectedItem.SubItems(10)
Form1.Text9.Text = ListView1.SelectedItem.SubItems(11)
Form1.Text10.Text = ListView1.SelectedItem.SubItems(12)
Form1.Text11.Text = ListView1.SelectedItem.SubItems(13)

Unload Me

End Sub
```

This routine changes the `CurrentContact` object in the main form to point to the newly selected contact. Then we copy each of the fields back into the main form and unload this form.

Final Thoughts

As you probably noticed, the example presented in this chapter isn't intended to be a production-quality application. There are many ways to improve it.

The first improvement I would make is to use stored procedures in the database. This would make retrieving information more efficient by just executing a new `Select` statement for each database request.

Then I would put additional information in each table to reflect who updated the record last and when it was updated. I would also switch the Notes field to be a Text field in SQL Server. This would allow a much larger note. You might even consider using the Rich Text control with some additional capabilities to display a more complex set of meeting notes.

Another way to improve the application would be to expand the search facility to allow you to return a list of contacts for a specific follow-up date. This would allow the person using the application to find out who needed to be contacted today. If you implemented the search properly, you could also produce a list of contacts who should have been followed up, but hadn't.

In the Contact Search form, it would be useful to search the database for follow-up information. For instance, you might want to find all of the outstanding action items. It would also be useful to know if all of the action items have been completed before contacting an individual.

Notice that these issues relate to the database design and how the client program works. Because the focus here is on how COM+ components work, I leave these improvements to you.

CHAPTER

FIFTEEN

15

Developing COM+ Transactions for IIS Applications

- IIS Application fundamentals

- Main web page design

- Details web page design

- Contact Manager transactions

When you build a client/server application in Visual Basic, you have a choice of two different approaches. You can choose to build a traditional client/server application, which is what we did in Chapter 14 (technically that is a three-tiered application, but it still requires the users to install software on their computers). The other choice is to build a web browser–based application.

The traditional client/server program has one big drawback: You must install the client on each and every computer that needs the application. For small networks, this isn't too bad; for large networks, it can be a royal headache. And even though you can run the application across the Internet, it really isn't an Internet application.

On the other hand, IIS Applications are true Internet applications. The client side of the application uses a web browser, and the server side of the application is a natural fit into a transaction-processing environment. You don't have the problem of how to distribute the application to the client computers—nearly any computer with a web browser can use the application. The main drawback to IIS Applications is that they are a little harder to program because you need to know both HTML and Visual Basic. But the results are worth it, as you'll see in this chapter.

NOTE   IIS Applications are primarily a high-performance replacement for interpreted programs written in Perl or VBScript. Because IIS Applications are compiled rather than interpreted, you get much better performance. For more information about IIS Applications and other ways to use Visual Basic over the Internet, see the *VB Developer's Guide to ASP and IIS*, by A. Russell Jones (Sybex, 1999).

Moving ContactManager to the Web

In the last chapter, we developed a simple application called ContactManager, a three-tier client/server program that uses COM+ transactions. That application has three main parts:

- The ContactClient program, which provides the user interface

- The ContactManager COM+ application, which implements the database logic

- The `ContactTypes` program, which holds COM objects that are used to pass information back and forth between the client program and the COM+ application

In this chapter, you'll see how easy it is to replace the client/server interface with a web browser–based interface using a Visual Basic IIS Application program. The `ContactManager` and `ContactTypes` projects are basically unchanged from those described in Chapter 14. However, I saved the discussion of some of the methods in those programs for this chapter.

Understanding IIS Applications

The Visual Basic IIS Application project type is a great way to build Internet applications. An IIS Application communicates with Microsoft's Internet Information Server (IIS) by way of the Internet Service API (ISAPI) interface. This is the same technology used by Active Server Pages (ASP). However, unlike Active Server Pages, IIS Applications are compiled for better performance.

How IIS Applications Work

IIS Applications respond to requests from a web browser. Thus, they act much like a function. Based on the input parameters, you return a result. In this case, the input parameters contain information from the URL specified by the user and return a new web page as the result.

To access an IIS Application from the web browser, you must specify a URL, as in the following example:

```
http://Athena/VBCOM/vbcom.asp?wci=detailsform&dc=36348.0000
```

where:

- `Athena` is the name of the web server.
- `VBCOM` is the name of the virtual directory containing the IIS Application.
- `vbcom.asp` is the name of the ASP file used to launch the application.

- `wci=detailsform` indicates the name of the routine to be called in the IIS Application.

- `&dc=36348.0000` represents a parameter that was passed to the `details-form` routine.

In addition to the information specified in the URL, you can also pass information to the routine using form fields on the web page. Each session with the web server will create a new instance of the IIS Application. Thus, it is also possible to keep state information in the module-level variables. If no response is received from the user in a reasonable amount of time, the instance of the application is destroyed, along with any state information.

The IIS Application Object Model

Besides using the same ISAPI interface to the IIS web server, IIS Applications use the same object model as used by Active Server Pages. The two objects used in the sample application are `Request` and `Response`.

The Request Object

The `Request` object has a number of properties, but the most useful are `Query-String` and `Form`.

The `QueryString` property returns the value of the variable from the URL. For example, in the following URL, `QueryString("dc")` will return the string `"36348.0000"`.

```
http://Athena/VBCOM/vbcom.asp?wci=detailsform&dc=36348.0000
```

Form elements work in the same way. With the following HTML statement, `Form("zip")` would return the string `"20705"`, which is the default value or whatever value the user entered into that field.

```
<input type="text" name="Zip" value="20705" size="8">
```

The Response Object

The `Response` object includes various properties and methods. However, the only one we'll use in this application is the `Write` method. The `Write` method is used to send a piece of information back to the client's web browser. All of the output is buffered until the routine is finished, then the entire document is transmitted to the web browser. The following line of code generates the <HTML> tag that marks the beginning of an HTML document.

```
Write "<HTML>"
```

NOTE   The `Write` method doesn't append a carriage return or line feed at the end of each statement. This doesn't bother a web browser, but it does make it difficult to read the HTML source. You can always append a constant `vbCrLf` to the string you pass to the `Write` method to break the character stream into smaller lines.

Programming the Main Web Page

The web application mirrors the client/server application we built in Chapter 14. It includes a main form, a search form, and a details form. Each form looks and works a little differently in the IIS Application than in the client/server application. However, they are similar enough that anyone who has used one should be capable of using the other.

IIS Applications versus Client/Server Applications

You can compare the main web page with the main form we used in the previous chapter. They both perform the same tasks and they look pretty much the same. However, under the surface, they look totally different. This leads directly to an important question: Which one is better? This is a very difficult question to answer.

From a programming standpoint, IIS Applications require that you know HTML as well as Visual Basic. You can use a tool like FrontPage to help you lay out your web pages, but you still need at least a working knowledge of HTML. You want to be able to take advantage of the fact that you can change how the web page looks on the fly. If you don't know anything about HTML, you won't know how to create the HTML on the fly.

Continued on next page

The main advantage of an IIS Applications program is that it allows nearly any client computer to access your application. This will make that Mac user in your office happy. It also means that your application is automatically Internet-enabled, which can be both a blessing and a curse.

A traditional client/server application generally will have better performance because the workload is split between the client and server machines, rather than being done primarily on the server. While you can move some of the processing to the web browser, you start to lose the benefits of a general-purpose Internet application, because not all web browsers support the same scripting languages. From a COM+ perspective, this really doesn't matter. You can have a number of different front-end programs written in as many programming languages as you wish (as long as they support calls to COM+ transactions) without modifications to the back-end transactions themselves.

Starting the Application

When the web server receives a request for this program, a new instance of this program is created, which implies a copy of the module-level variables found in Listing 15.1 will be created.

Listing 15.1   The module definitions

```
Option Explicit
Option Compare Text


Dim CurrentContact As Contact
Dim LastContactDate As Date
Dim LastField As String
Dim LastOperator As String
Dim LastValue As String
```

These variables will be preserved from one call to this instance to the next. Note that this instance of the object will not be used to process requests from any other users, so you can safely use these variables to hold information unique to a single user's session. The instance will automatically be destroyed if the web server hasn't received any requests for a long time.

Next comes the WebClass_Start event, shown in Listing 15.2.

Listing 15.2   **The WebClass_Start event**

```
Private Sub WebClass_Start()

Dim cm As ContactManager

Set cm = New ContactMgr.ContactManager
Set CurrentContact = cm.GetAContact(1)
Set cm = Nothing
WriteMain CurrentContact

End Sub
```

In this event, we create a new instance of the ContactManager object called cm. Next, we get a value into the CurrentContact module-level object variable by using the GetAContact method and destroy cm to free the resources on the transaction server. Finally, we display the main page by calling the WriteMain routine and using the CurrentContact object.

Displaying the Main Web Page

Unlike a Visual Basic form, a web page can't be drawn and automatically included in your Visual Basic application. You need to create the HTML statements and explicitly send them to the web browser. In turn, the web browser will be used to create the web page.

The main web page for this application is very simple as web pages go, as you can see in Figure 15.1.

NOTE   The only difference between a simple web page and a complex web page is the amount of HTML tags needed to add the extra features. Since extra HTML tags don't change how the program works, I decided to leave them out.

The main drawback to using an IIS Application project is that there isn't a graphical design tool to help you design your web pages. You need to explicitly code the HTML tags in your program as a series of calls to Write. Since this can make a rather large subroutine, I like to separate the statements that draw a form from those that process the request. The sole purpose of the WriteMain routine, shown in Listing 15.3, is to display the main web page with the supplied data. The MainForm routine, discussed in the next section, will handle any responses from the buttons on this form.

Listing 15.3   The WriteMain routine

```
Private Sub WriteMain(c As Contact)

With Response
    .Write "<html>"
    .Write "<head>"
    .Write "<title>Contact Manager: Main Form</title>"
    .Write "</head>"
    .Write "<body>"
    .Write "<p><strong><big><big>Contact Manager: "
    .Write "Main Form</big></big></strong></p>"
    .Write "<form align=""left"" action="""
    .Write "VBCOM.ASP?wci=mainform"" name=""mainform"""
    .Write " method=""post"">"
    .Write "<table border=""0"">"
    .Write "<tr>"
    .Write "<td>ContactId:</td>"
    .Write "<td><input type=""text"" name=""ContactId"""
    .Write " size=""6"" value="""
    .Write FormatNumber(c.ContactId, 0) & """>"
    .Write "</td>"
    .Write "</tr>"
    .Write "<tr>"
    .Write "<td>Name:</td>"
    .Write "<td><input type=""text"" name=""Prefix"""
    .Write " size=""4"" value=""" & c.Prefix & """>"
    .Write "<input type=""text"" name=""FirstName"""
    .Write " size=""10"" value=""" & c.FirstName & """>"
    .Write "<input type=""text"" name=""MiddleName"""
    .Write " size=""3"" value=""" & c.MiddleName & """>"
    .Write "<input type=""text"" name=""LastName"""
    .Write " size=""14"" value=""" & c.LastName & """>"
    .Write "</td>"
    .Write "</tr>"
    .Write "<tr>"
    .Write "<td>Title:</td>"
    .Write "<td><input type=""text"" name=""Title"""
    .Write " size=""37"" value=""" & c.Title & """>"
    .Write "</td>"
```

```
.Write "</tr>"
.Write "<tr>"
.Write "<td>Organization:</td>"
.Write "<td><input type=""text"""
.Write " name=""Organization"" size=""37"" value="""
.Write c.Organization & """>"
.Write "</td>"
.Write "</tr>"
.Write "<tr>"
.Write "<td>Address:</td>"
.Write "<td><input type=""text"" name=""Street"""
.Write " size=""37"" value=""" & c.Street & """>"
.Write "</td>"
.Write "</tr>"
.Write "<tr>"
.Write "<td></td>"
.Write "<td><input type=""text"" name=""City"""
.Write " size=""19"" value=""" & c.City & """>"
.Write "<input type=""text"" name=""State"""
.Write " size=""6"" value=""" & c.State & """>"
.Write "<input type=""text"" name=""Zip"""
.Write " size=""8"" value=""" & c.Zip & """>"
.Write "</td>"
.Write "</tr>"
.Write "<tr>"
.Write "<td>Telephone:</td>"
.Write "<td><input type=""text"" name=""Telephone"""
.Write " size=""37"" value=""" & c.Telephone & """>"
.Write "</td>"
.Write "</tr>"
.Write "<tr>"
.Write "<td>FAX:</td>"
.Write "<td><input type=""text"" name=""FAX"""
.Write " size=""37"" value=""" & c.FAX & """>"
.Write "</td>"
.Write "</tr>"
.Write "<tr>"
.Write "<td>EMail:</td>"
.Write "<td><input type=""text"" name=""EMail"""
.Write " size=""37"" value=""" & c.EMail & """>"
```

```
        .Write "</td>"
        .Write "</tr>"
        .Write "</table>"
        .Write "<p>"
        .Write "<input type=""submit"" value=""Get"""
        .Write " name=""get"">"
        .Write "<input type=""submit"" value=""Search"""
        .Write " name=""search"">"
        .Write "<input type=""submit"""
        .Write " value=""Commit Changes"" name=""commit"">"
        .Write "<input type=""submit"" value=""Details"""
        .Write " name=""details"">"
        .Write "<input type=""reset"" value=""Reset"""
        .Write " name=""reset"">"
        .Write "</form>"
        .Write "</body>"
        .Write "</html>"
    End With

End Sub
```

For the most part, this form just contains a number of input fields and submit buttons. The only interesting part is that we use the value attribute in the various input tags to display the contents of the Contact object variable.

Another important part of this web page is found inside the form tag. The action attribute contains the value "VBCOM.ASP?wci=mainform". This value provides the URL that will be used when any of the input submit buttons are clicked. When programming an IIS Application, this information is important because it dictates the name of the routine that will be called. In this case, IIS will call the MainForm_Respond routine to handle the user's request.

| NOTE | There are two ways to write HTML. The first is to manually code each and every tag. This approach is slow because you need to repeatedly test your web page until you get it right. The other way is to use a tool like FrontPage to develop the web page and then copy and paste the statements into your program. When you use such a tool, you don't need to worry about the details of the HTML syntax and can concentrate on the page design. |

Processing the Main Web Page

After displaying the web page, the user can click any of the buttons at the bottom of the web page. Because all of the buttons are included in the same form tag, the `MainForm` event will be triggered no matter which button is pressed. Listing 15.4 shows this event.

Listing 15.4   **The MainForm_Respond event**

```
Private Sub MainForm_Respond()

Dim cs As Contacts
Dim cm As ContactManager

If Len(Request.Form("get")) > 0 Then
    Set CurrentContact = _
        cm.GetAContact(CLng(Request.Form("ContactId")))
    Set cm = Nothing
    WriteMain CurrentContact

ElseIf Len(Request.Form("search")) > 0 Then
    WriteSearch cs

ElseIf Len(Request.Form("commit")) > 0 Then
    CurrentContact.ContactId = Request.Form("ContactId")
    CurrentContact.Prefix = Request.Form("Prefix")
    CurrentContact.FirstName = Request.Form("FirstName")
    CurrentContact.MiddleName = Request.Form("MiddleName")
    CurrentContact.LastName = Request.Form("LastName")
    CurrentContact.Title = Request.Form("Title")
    CurrentContact.Organization = Request.Form("Organization")
    CurrentContact.Street = Request.Form("Street")
    CurrentContact.City = Request.Form("City")
    CurrentContact.State = Request.Form("State")
    CurrentContact.Zip = Request.Form("Zip")
    CurrentContact.Telephone = Request.Form("Telephone")
    CurrentContact.FAX = Request.Form("FAX")
    CurrentContact.EMail = Request.Form("EMail")
```

```
        CurrentContact.Dirty = True
        Set cm = New ContactManager
        cm.PutAContact CurrentContact
        Set cm = Nothing
        WriteMain CurrentContact

    ElseIf Len(Request.Form("details")) > 0 Then
        LastContactDate = 0
        WriteDetails CurrentContact

    End If

    End Sub
```

Since any of the four buttons on the form could have triggered this event, the first thing we need to do is to find out which button was clicked. To do this, we take advantage of the fact that only the button that was clicked will be included in the Request object. By checking if the length of the value of a button is greater than zero, we'll know which button was clicked.

In the case of the Get button, we use the GetAContact method of the Contact-Manager object to retrieve the information about a specific contact. For the Search button, we call the WriteSearch routine to display the search form. For the Details button, we call the WriteDetails routine to show the details form.

The Commit Changes button has the most code, but it merely copies the field values from the Request.Form object to the CurrentContact object. Then it sets the Dirty flag and calls the PutAContact routine. When its finished, we call the WriteMain routine to redisplay the main form.

WARNING   It is very important to respond to every request you receive with some sort of a web page. If you don't return a web page, the user's web browser displays a blank web page, leaving the user without any way to continue working with the application.

Programming the Details Web Page

The details web page, shown in Figure 15.2, contains information about a single contact with a customer. It's started when someone selects a contact using the main or search form and then clicks the Details button.

FIGURE 15.2:

The details web page

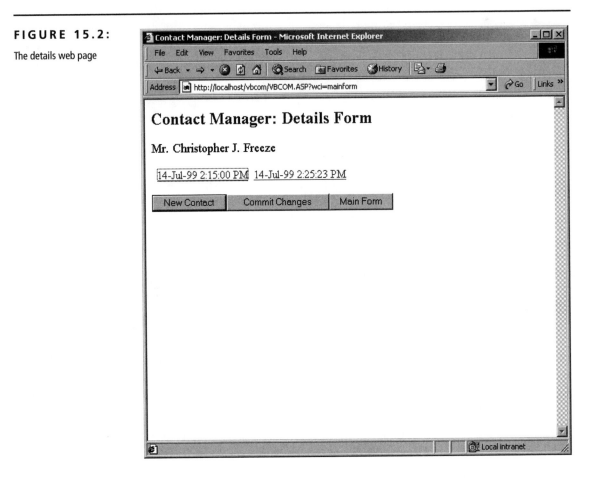

Initially, only the list of contact dates is shown on the page. Clicking one of the dates will display the detailed contact information for that particular date, as shown in Figure 15.3. The fields that you can change are displayed inside input boxes or text areas. The fields that you can't change are displayed as normal text.

Displaying the Details Web Page

The routine to generate the details web page is shown in Listing 15.5. This code is similar in nature to the code that we used to create the main form. However, this routine takes advantage of the fact that we can generate the HTML tags on the fly to display information. For instance, we can display each DateContact value, without using a drop-down box or displaying only a fixed number of values. The ability to change the HTML that is sent to the web browser is one of the biggest reasons to use IIS Applications.

Listing 15.5   **The WriteDetails routine**

```
Private Sub WriteDetails(c As Contact)

Dim ai As ActionItem
Dim ci As ContactInfo
Dim i As Long
Dim k As String

With Response
    .Write "<html>"
    .Write "<head>"
    .Write "<title>Contact Manager: Details Form</title>"
    .Write "</head>"
    .Write "<body>"
    .Write "<p><strong><big><big>Contact Manager: "
    .Write "Details Form</big></big></strong></p>"
    .Write "<form align=""left"" action="""
    .Write "VBCOM.ASP?wci=detailsform"" name=""detailsform"
    .Write """ method=""post"">"
    .Write "<big>" & c.GetFullName & "</big>"
    .Write "<p>"
    For Each ci In c.ContactInfos
        .Write "  "
        .Write "<a href=""VBCOM.ASP?wci=detailsform&dc="
        .Write FormatNumber(ci.DateContacted, 6, , , vbFalse)
        .Write """>"
        .Write FormatDateTime(ci.DateContacted, _
            vbGeneralDate)
        .Write "</a>"
    Next ci

    If LastContactDate > 0 Then
        k = FormatNumber(c.ContactId, 0) & " " & _
            FormatDateTime(LastContactDate, vbGeneralDate)
        Set ci = c.ContactInfos.Item(k)

        .Write "<p><hr><br><strong>Date Contacted:</strong>"
        .Write FormatDateTime(ci.DateContacted, _
            vbGeneralDate)
```

```
            .Write "<p><strong>Followup Date:</strong>"
            .Write "<input type=""text"" size=""20"""
            .Write "name=""followupdate"" value="""
            .Write FormatDateTime(ci.FollowupDate, vbGeneralDate)
            .Write """>"
            .Write "<br>"
            .Write "<input type=""submit"" value=""Change "
            .Write "Followup Date"" name=""changedate"">"
            .Write "<p><strong>Notes:</strong><br>"
            .Write "<textarea rows=""5"" cols=37 name=""notes"">"
            .Write ci.Notes
            .Write "</textarea>"
            .Write "<br>"
            .Write "<input type=""submit"" value=""Change "
            .Write "Notes"" name=""changenotes"">"
            .Write "<p><strong>Action Items:</strong><br>"
            .Write "<table border=""0"">"

    If Not ci.ActionItems Is Nothing Then
        For Each ai In ci.ActionItems
            .Write "<tr>"
            .Write "<td>"
            .Write FormatNumber(ai.ActionItemNumber, 0)
            .Write "</td>"
            .Write "<td>"
            .Write ai.ActionItem
            .Write "</td>"
            .Write "<td>"
            If IsNull(ai.DateCompleted) Or _
                    ai.DateCompleted = 0 Then
                .Write "<a href=""VBCOM.ASP?"
                .Write "WCI=DetailsForm&"
                .Write "ActionItem="
                .Write FormatNumber(ai.ActionItemNumber, 0)
                .Write """>Mark Complete</a>"
            Else
                .Write FormatDateTime(ai.DateCompleted, _
                    vbGeneralDate)
            End If
            .Write "</td>"
```

```
            .Write "</tr>"
        Next ai

    End If

    .Write "<tr>"
    .Write "<td>"
    .Write "</td>"
    .Write "<td>"
    .Write "<input type=""text"" size=""37"" "
    .Write "name=""newactionitem"">"
    .Write "</td>"
    .Write "<td>"
    .Write "<input type=""submit"" "
    .Write "value=""New Item"" name=""newitem"">"
    .Write "</td>"
    .Write "</tr>"
    .Write "</table>"

    .Write "<p><hr>"

End If

    .Write "<p>"
    .Write "<input type=""submit"" "
    .Write "value=""New Contact"" name=""newcontact"">"
    .Write "<input type=""submit"" value=""Commit Changes"""
    .Write " name=""commit"">"
    .Write "<input type=""submit"" value=""Main Form"""
    .Write " name=""mainform"">"
    .Write "</form>"
    .Write "</body>"
    .Write "</html>"
End With

End Sub
```

This routine starts by sending out web page information similar to that found in the WriteMain routine. Then we quickly jump into something new. We use a

For Each loop to generate a hyperlink reference for each value of DateContacted in the ContactInfos collection. This hyperlink reference includes a parameter called dc in the URL and uses the numeric value of the Date value. Notice that we need to display six decimal places so that enough information is included to resolve the time part of the Date value.

NOTE   Date values can be displayed as a Double value. The whole portion represents the number of days since January 1, 1900. The fractional part represents the time of day, with 0 being midnight, 0.5 being noon, and 0.999999 being midnight again.

Once we've output the DateContacted information, we check LastContact-Date to see which date we should display the detailed information for. If Last-ContactDate is zero, then we know the user hasn't selected a date, so we should skip this part of the document. In this case, we display the information directly in the object.

Notice that the user is allowed to change the FollowupDate field and the Notes field, but not the DateContacted field. This is in line with the way the object is created. The DateContacted value is used as the key value to each object in the collection.

We also include a Change button for the FollowupDate and Notes fields. This is a little awkward, but it's easier to implement than a generic update button. (If this were a real application, I would have designed a much more complex form—possibly with local code—to handle updating the information on the form.)

The next part of this form is designed to display the list of action items. We create a table and output each action item as a single row. The fields across the table are ActionItemNumber, ActionItem, and DateCompleted. If the DateCompleted value is zero, this means that the item is still open. So instead of displaying the DateCompleted value, we display a hypertext link. When clicked, the hyperlink assigns the current date and time to this field. On the last row of the table, we display an input text field where the user can enter a new action item value. Another hypertext link adds this field to the list of action items.

At the bottom of the form, three buttons appear, even if none of the information about a single contact is displayed. These buttons are used to trigger the functions associated with their values by the DetailsForm routine, discussed next.

Processing the Details Web Page

The processing required for the details web page is more complex than the main web page, due to the number of different actions on the web page. Like the Main-Form routine, the DetailsForm routine simply looks for each of the different ways that will trigger this event and handles the situation accordingly. Listing 15.6 shows the DetailsForm routine.

Listing 15.6   **The DetailsForm_Respond event**

```
Private Sub DetailsForm_Respond()

Dim ai As ActionItem
Dim ci As ContactInfo
Dim cm As ContactManager
Dim k As String

If Len(Request.Form("newcontact")) > 0 Then
    CurrentContact.ContactInfos.Dirty = True
    LastContactDate = Now
    Set ci = New ContactInfo
    ci.DateContacted = LastContactDate
    ci.Dirty = True
    CurrentContact.ContactInfos.Add ci
    WriteDetails CurrentContact

ElseIf Len(Request.Form("commit")) > 0 Then
    Set cm = New ContactManager
    cm.PutContactInfos CurrentContact.ContactInfos
    Set CurrentContact = _
        cm.GetAContact(CurrentContact.ContactId)
    Set cm = Nothing
    WriteDetails CurrentContact

ElseIf Len(Request.Form("mainform")) > 0 Then
    WriteMain CurrentContact

ElseIf Len(Request.QueryString("dc")) > 0 Then
    LastContactDate = CDbl(Request.QueryString("dc"))
    WriteDetails CurrentContact
```

```
ElseIf Len(Request.QueryString("actionitem")) > 0 Then
    k = FormatNumber(CurrentContact.ContactId, 0) & " " & _
        FormatDateTime(LastContactDate, vbGeneralDate)
    CurrentContact.ContactInfos.Dirty = True
    CurrentContact.ContactInfos.Item(k).Dirty = True
    CurrentContact.ContactInfos.Item(k).ActionItems.Dirty _
        = True
    CurrentContact.ContactInfos.Item(k).ActionItems. _
        Item(Request.QueryString("actionitem")).Dirty = True
    CurrentContact.ContactInfos.Item(k).ActionItems.Item _
        (Request.QueryString("actionitem")).DateCompleted _
        = Now
    WriteDetails CurrentContact

ElseIf Len(Request.Form("changenotes")) > 0 Then
    k = FormatNumber(CurrentContact.ContactId, 0) & " " _
        & FormatDateTime(LastContactDate, vbGeneralDate)
    CurrentContact.ContactInfos.Dirty = True
    CurrentContact.ContactInfos.Item(k).Dirty = True
    CurrentContact.ContactInfos.Item(k).Notes = _
        Request.Form("notes")
    WriteDetails CurrentContact

ElseIf Len(Request.Form("changedate")) > 0 Then
    If IsDate(Request.Form("followupdate")) Then
        k = FormatNumber(CurrentContact.ContactId, 0) & _
            " " & FormatDateTime(LastContactDate, _
            vbGeneralDate)
        CurrentContact.ContactInfos.Dirty = True
        CurrentContact.ContactInfos.Item(k).Dirty = True
        CurrentContact.ContactInfos.Item(k).FollowupDate = _
            CDate(Request.Form("followupdate"))
        WriteDetails CurrentContact
    End If

ElseIf Len(Request.Form("newitem")) > 0 Then
    k = FormatNumber(CurrentContact.ContactId, 0) & " " _
        & FormatDateTime(LastContactDate, vbGeneralDate)
    Set ai = New ActionItem
    ai.ActionItem = Request.Form("newactionitem")
    ai.ActionItemNumber = _
        CurrentContact.ContactInfos.Item(k).ActionItems.Count _
        + 1
```

```
ai.DateCompleted = 0
ai.Dirty = True
CurrentContact.ContactInfos.Dirty = True
CurrentContact.ContactInfos.Item(k).Dirty = True
CurrentContact.ContactInfos.Item(k).ActionItems.Dirty _
    = True
CurrentContact.ContactInfos.Item(k).ActionItems.Add ai
WriteDetails CurrentContact

End If

End Sub
```

The first situation we handle is when the user clicks the New Contact button. In this case, we set LastContactDate to Now. This does two things:

- It gives us a date and time value that we can use later when we create the object.

- It automatically forces the WriteDetails routine to display the information about the newly created object in the collection.

Next, we flag the ContactInfos object as being updated. Then we can create a new instance of the ContactInfo object, set the DateContacted property to Last-ContactDate, and mark the object as being updated. Finally, I add the object to the ContactInfos collection and call the WriteDetails routine to redisplay the web page with the newly added contact.

The logic to handle committing the data to the database is fairly simple. We use the PutContactInfos method to update the database and then call the Write-Details routine to refresh the web page.

When the user clicks the Main Form button, all we need to do is call the Write-Main routine. This displays the information on the main form using the values from the CurrentContact object.

Changing the ContactInfo object displayed is triggered when this routine encounters the dc parameter in the query string. We take the value of this parameter, assign it to the LastContactDate variable, and redisplay the form by calling WriteDetails.

Marking an action item as complete merely involves setting the `actionitem` parameter in the query string, marking all of the related information as updated, and setting the `DateCompleted` property to `Now`. The only tricky part is that we create the key value to locate the `ContactInfo` object by combining the `ContactId` from the `CurrentContact` object with the `LastContactDate` variable. Then we can use the value associated with the `actionitem` parameter to determine the key of the actual action item to be updated.

The logic for `changenotes` and `changedates` is nearly identical. We flag the `ContactInfos` collection and the specific `ContactInfo` object as being updated and then assign the new value to the appropriate field. The only difference between the two routines is that we check to make sure the date is valid before we assign it to the field.

Adding a new `ActionItem` is relatively complex due to the number of places that we need to mark as updated. If you ignore those parts, all we need to do is to create the new `ActionItem` object, assign its properties the new values specified by the user, and add it to the `ActionItems` collection.

Using the Contact Manager Transactions

So far, all I've talked about in this chapter is how the IIS Application program works. Now it's time to look at the transactions.

If you read Chapter 14 and looked at the Contact Manager application developed in that chapter, these transactions will look familiar. That's because both programs use the same transactions. This demonstrates that by moving the business logic away from the user interface, you can more easily adapt your application to multiple environments.

NOTE   Both the client/server and IIS Application programs have three forms: Main, Search, and Details. In Chapter 14, I discussed only the Main and Search forms. Here, I discuss only the Main and Details forms. When you download the full programs from the book's web page, you can compare all three forms to better understand their similarities and differences.

Probably the most complicated thing in the ContactManager object is the set of routines required to update the ContactInfos collection. The entire process requires four distinct routines, one for each of the collections (ContactInfos and ActionItems) and one for each of the objects in each collection (ContactInfo and ActionItem). Each of these routines will be called as necessary to update the object associated with them. This means that one error in any of these routines is sufficient to abort the entire transaction.

The PutContactInfos Method

The PutContactInfos method iterates through the ContactInfos collection and calls the PutAContactInfo method for each of the ContactInfo objects. Listing 15.7 shows this method.

Listing 15.7   **The PutContactInfos method**

```
Public Sub PutContactInfos(c As ContactInfos)

Dim ci As ContactInfo
Dim o As ObjectContext
Dim rs As ADODB.Recordset

On Error Resume Next

Set o = GetObjectContext()

For Each ci In c
    PutAContactInfo c.ContactId, ci

Next ci


Set o = Nothing

End Sub
```

Notice that we don't bother to update the ContactId member of this object, because we don't permit anyone to change this value once the object has been created.

The PutAContactInfo Method

The PutAContactInfo method, shown in Listing 15.8, is a bit more complex than the PutContactInfos method, because it needs to perform database operations.

Listing 15.8   **The PutAContactInfo method**

```
Public Sub PutAContactInfo(ContactId As Long, _
   ci As ContactInfo)

Dim o As ObjectContext
Dim rs As ADODB.Recordset

On Error Resume Next

Set o = GetObjectContext()

If ci.Dirty Then
   Err.Clear
   OpenDB
   Set rs = New ADODB.Recordset
   Set rs.ActiveConnection = db
   rs.Source = "Select * from dbo.ContactInfo " & _
      "Where ContactId = " & _
      FormatNumber(ContactId, 0) & _
      " and DateContacted = '" & _
      FormatDateTime(ci.DateContacted, vbGeneralDate) & "'"

   rs.CursorType = adOpenDynamic
   rs.LockType = adLockOptimistic
   rs.Open

   If rs.BOF And rs.EOF Then
      rs.AddNew
      rs.Fields("ContactId") = ContactId
      rs.Fields("DateContacted") = ci.DateContacted
      rs.Fields("FollowupDate") = ci.FollowupDate
      rs.Fields("Notes") = ci.Notes
      rs.Update
      If Err.Number <> 0 Then
         rs.Close
         Set rs = Nothing
         CloseDB
```

```
      o.SetAbort
      Set o = Nothing
      Exit Sub

    End If

  Else
    rs.MoveFirst
    rs.Fields("FollowupDate") = ci.FollowupDate
    rs.Fields("Notes") = ci.Notes
    rs.Update
    If Err.Number <> 0 Then
      rs.Close
      Set rs = Nothing
      CloseDB
      o.SetAbort
      Set o = Nothing
      Exit Sub

    End If

  End If

  PutActionItems ContactId, ci.ActionItems

End If

CloseDB
o.SetComplete
Set o = Nothing

End Sub
```

The first step in this routine is to determine if the object actually needs to be updated by looking at the Dirty property. If the object hasn't been updated, we exit the routine without doing any database calls.

If we decide we need to update the database, we build a Select statement using ContactId and the DateContacted values to find the appropriate record. If the Beginning of Recordset (BOF) and End of Recordset (EOF) flags are both True, we know the record doesn't exist in the database, so we need to add it. We use the Recordset.Add method to create a new, blank record in the table and then assign values from the object to each of the fields in the record. Using the Update method saves the newly created record into the database. If there is any error caused by the Update method, we abort the transaction and exit the routine.

If the record does exist in the database, we use the MoveFirst method to make the record current and then assign the new values into the fields we can update. (We don't allow the DateContacted value or the ContactId fields to be updated after they've been created.) Then we use the Update method to save the updated record into the database. If there are any errors in this process, we use the Set-Abort method to kill the update process.

If the update process worked, then we update the information in the Action-Items collection by calling the PutActionItems method. Finally, we can exit the routine by closing the Recordset and calling the SetComplete method.

The PutActionItems Method

Much like the PutContactInfos method merely calls the PutAContactInfo method for each of the ContactInfo objects in the collection, the PutActionItems method does the same thing with the ActionItem object and the PutAnActionItem method. This method is shown in Listing 15.9.

Listing 15.9   The PutActionItems method

```
Public Sub PutActionItems(ContactId, a As ActionItems)

Dim ai As ActionItem
Dim o As ObjectContext

On Error Resume Next

Set o = GetObjectContext()

For Each ai In a
    PutAnActionItem ContactId, a.DateContacted, ai

Next ai

Set o = Nothing

End Sub
```

The PutAnActionItem Method

The PutAnActionItem method, shown in Listing 15.10, is similar to the PutA-ContactInfo method, because it has a similar purpose. The PutAnActionItem is designed to update a single object from the ActionItems collection.

Listing 15.10 **The PutAnActionItem method**

```
Public Sub PutAnActionItem(ContactId, _
    DateContacted As Date, ai As ActionItem)

Dim o As ObjectContext
Dim rs As ADODB.Recordset

On Error Resume Next

Set o = GetObjectContext()

If ai.Dirty Then
    Err.Clear
    OpenDB
    Set rs = New ADODB.Recordset
    Set rs.ActiveConnection = db
    rs.Source = "Select * from dbo.ActionItems " & _
        "Where ContactId = " & _
        FormatNumber(ContactId, 0) & _
        " and DateContacted = '" & _
        FormatDateTime(DateContacted, vbGeneralDate) & _
        "' and ActionItemNumber = " & _
        FormatNumber(ai.ActionItemNumber, 0)

    rs.CursorType = adOpenDynamic
    rs.LockType = adLockOptimistic
    rs.Open

    If rs.BOF And rs.EOF Then
        rs.AddNew
        rs.Fields("ContactId") = ContactId
        rs.Fields("DateContacted") = DateContacted
        rs.Fields("ActionItemNumber") = ai.ActionItemNumber
        rs.Fields("ActionItem") = ai.ActionItem
        rs.Fields("DateCompleted") = ai.DateCompleted
```

```
        rs.Update
        If Err.Number <> 0 Then
            rs.Close
            Set rs = Nothing
            o.SetAbort
            Set o = Nothing
            CloseDB
            Exit Sub

        End If

    Else
        rs.MoveFirst
        rs.Fields("ActionItem") = ai.ActionItem
        rs.Fields("DateCompleted") = ai.DateCompleted
        rs.Update
        If Err.Number <> 0 Then
            rs.Close
            Set rs = Nothing
            o.SetAbort
            Set o = Nothing
            CloseDB
            Exit Sub

        End If

    End If

End If

CloseDB
o.SetComplete
Set o = Nothing

End Sub
```

The routine begins by checking the Dirty flag and then building a Select statement to retrieve the specific action item record.

When we open the Recordset object, we decide if we need to update the existing record or add a new record and then perform the appropriate activity using the values from the object. As in the previous routines, we don't permit the `ContactId`, `DateContacted`, and `ActionItemNumber` values to be changed once the object has been created.

If we encounter any errors with the updates, we abort this particular method, which also will abort the entire transaction and all of the updates. Otherwise, we close the `Recordset` and call the `SetComplete` method.

Final Thoughts

As with the client/server application presented in Chapter 14, this IIS Application program could use some improvements to make it a production-quality application.

The first change I would make would be to automatically set the `Dirty` flag for each of the objects. I ran into this problem while I was testing the application and had forgotten to set one of the `Dirty` properties when I changed a value. The best fix would be to include a `Property Let` routine for each property in an object. This routine would automatically set the `Dirty` property as necessary. In fact, it could even record whether the change was an addition or an update, which would simplify some of the code in the `Put` object routines.

As I mentioned earlier, there really should be only one button to make the changes locally and one button to commit the changes to the database. With a little careful planning, this shouldn't be hard to do. However, it might mean that the web application would function quite differently from the client/server application, which wasn't acceptable for this particular application.

Another issue I dodged in this version of the application was security. I assumed that users needed to log on to the Internet server, and once their security authenticated, they had full run of the application. This process works only for Internet Explorer, but that isn't even the whole problem. Although COM+ transactions have fairly good security, the username the transactions see is the username associated with the web server, not the original user. A mechanism needs to be included with this application to map an application user onto a security role and then build some more detailed security into the COM+ transactions. With some careful thought and planning, you would still have transactions that could be used by both traditional client/server programs and IIS Application programs.

CHAPTER SIXTEEN

Developing COM+ Transactions for MSMQ

- A local copy of the data for the client

- Update request packages

- Request and response queues

- Persistent collections

For the final project in this book, I decided to be a little creative and build the classic program for message queues—an application for the laptop computer that doesn't have a full-time connection to the corporate network. This program is based on the work we've already done in Chapters 14 and 15. Because most of the details should be familiar by now, I'm going to focus on the issues that relate to making this program different from the previous versions.

Application Design

In this chapter, we're going to build the third and final version of the Contact Manager application. For this version, we want to reuse the same set of business logic from the previous chapters. Thus, we don't need to make any changes to the ContactManager COM+ application.

Also, since the focus of this chapter is on how to replace the synchronous connection with the COM+ transaction server with an asynchronous one, we should reuse as much as possible of the existing code from the ContactClient program. This makes the job of building the user interface program much easier.

Design Issues

You might think that this application lends itself to being implemented with queued components, but that approach won't work. We need to establish a two-way communications link. One way generates requests that are queued up to send to the server, and the other way returns results to the client. Both ways must use queues, because we can't assume that the client computer has a permanent connection to the COM+ transaction server. Queued components allow only one-way transmissions.

Since we aren't going to use queued components to handle the queuing, we need another method to listen for requests, execute them, and return the results. This will require a custom program on the server side that performs the same functions as the queued components listener and player.

Another issue that must be addressed is that all of the objects that pass through a message queue must be persistent. Unless you take specific steps to make an object persistent in Visual Basic, it isn't. Fortunately, Visual Basic makes it relatively painless by providing the `PropertyBag` object and the `ReadProperties`, `WriteProperties`, and `InitProperties` events.

Design Concept

In order to make this program work, we need to make changes in both the `ContactClient` program and the `ContactTypes` program, plus introduce a new program called `ContactQueue`. The `ContactManager` program remains unchanged.

In `ContactClient`, we need to add code that will place a request into a message queue and pull the response out of a different message queue. This change has a ripple effect. The `ContactTypes` object needs a new object to contain the request. This object needs to contain everything necessary to use the `GetAContact` and `PutAContact` routines in `ContactManager`. Also, we need to ensure that the objects that pass through the message queue are persistent.

Finally, we need to build a program called `ContactQueue`. This program runs on a computer that has a full-time connection to the COM+ transaction server. This program can be on the same machine as the server or on a different machine, as long as the full-time connection is maintained. It will listen to the requests coming from the `ContactClient` program, then execute the appropriate method to satisfy the request and return the results to the client program.

Programming the Contact Client

As explained in the previous section, the `ContactClient` program is built on the program we created in Chapter 14. However, there are many subtle and not-so-subtle differences between the two programs. The biggest difference is that we can't call the transactions directly. We need to build a message that we can send to the queue dispatcher, which will execute the transaction and send the results back to the client program, via another queue.

Keeping Local Information

One problem with this scenario is that we need to keep a local copy of the data; otherwise, the client computer wouldn't have access to any data. There are a number of different ways to accomplish this. Perhaps the ultimate way is to create an exact copy of the database on the local computer and use some of the sophisticated database tools to keep the copies in sync. However, this approach is probably overkill for many applications.

Another option is to use a scaled-down database to cache a subset of the data. If I were developing a production-quality application, I would probably use this approach. I like having a database to store information because of the tools I can use to retrieve information. However, this approach is more complicated to implement because it requires one set of database logic to access the database on the server and a second set of database logic to access the information locally.

The approach we will take here is to modify the ContactManager objects we created in Chapter 14 so that they hold information on multiple people rather than just one person. Then all we need to do is to save the information locally when we're finished with the program, and load it back the next time we run the program.

Because the CurrentContact object holds information about a single contact, we need to add a new public variable in Form1, which we'll call ContactBuffer, to hold a Contacts collection. Then we just need to adjust the CurrentContact object to point to the specific object in the collection the user wants to view.

Saving the Data Locally

We could have unpacked the object and saved it into a disk file, but instead, we create a new message queue to hold the ContactBuffer object. Then we call the PutLocalInfo routine from the Form_Unload event, shown in Listing 16.1.

Listing 16.1   The PutLocalInfo routine in ContactClient

```
Sub PutLocalInfo()

Dim li As MSMQQueueInfo
Dim lq As MSMQQueue
Dim m As MSMQMessage

Set m = New MSMQMessage
m.Body = ContactBuffer
```

```
Set li = New MSMQQueueInfo
li.PathName = "Athena\Private$\ContactLocal"
Set lq = li.Open(MQ_SEND_ACCESS, MQ_DENY_NONE)
m.Send lq

lq.Close

End Sub
```

This routine begins by creating a new MSMQMessage object and saving a copy of the object into the Body of the message. (Notice that we didn't use the Set statement, because we want a copy of the object, not just a new pointer to the object.) Then we open the queue called Athena\Private$\ContactLocal, which we'll use to hold the data. Next, we use the Send method to send the message, then close the message queue. This leaves the data in the queue, ready to retrieve the next time we run the program.

Restoring the Data

Retrieving the information from the message queue when the program is started is a little more complicated. This is because we need to handle the situation where there isn't any data to retrieve. The GetLocalInfo routine, shown in Listing 16.2, is called from the Form_Load event.

Listing 16.2   **The GetLocalInfo routine in ContactClient**

```
Sub GetLocalInfo()

Dim li As MSMQQueueInfo
Dim lq As MSMQQueue
Dim m As MSMQMessage

Set li = New MSMQQueueInfo
li.PathName = "Athena\Private$\ContactLocal"

Set lq = li.Open(MQ_RECEIVE_ACCESS, MQ_DENY_NONE)

Set m = lq.Receive(, , , 100)
```

```
    If Not m Is Nothing Then
        Set ContactBuffer = m.Body

    Else
        Set ContactBuffer = New Contacts

    End If

    lq.Close

End Sub
```

This routine begins by opening the ContactLocal queue and using the Receive method to get the first message in the queue. We allow only 100 milliseconds to receive the message, because either the message is already in the queue or there isn't one to retrieve.

If the message is present, then we set ContactBuffer to the contents of the message's Body. If it isn't, then we create an empty copy of the Contacts collection. In either case, we close the queue and return to the Form_Load event.

Requesting Data

With a local copy of the data, retrieving data takes a few more steps. We need to check to see if the data is available locally. If it isn't, we generate a request for the data. We also need to track any data we've already requested to prevent sending duplicate requests to the transaction server.

Handling the Get Request

The Command1_Click event, shown in Listing 16.3, has been modified to handle the new requirements for processing data.

Listing 16.3   The Command1_Click event in ContactClient

```
Private Sub Command1_Click()

On Error Resume Next
```

```
Dim r As New Request

If IsNumeric(Text1.Text) Then
    Err.Clear
    Set CurrentContact = ContactBuffer.Item(Text1.Text)
    If Err.Number > 0 Then
        RequestAContact Text1.Text

    ElseIf CurrentContact.Requested Then
        MsgBox "Information has been requested, " & _
            "but not yet received."

    Else
        Text1.Text = CurrentContact.ContactId
        Text2.Text = CurrentContact.Prefix
        Text12.Text = CurrentContact.FirstName
        Text13.Text = CurrentContact.MiddleName
        Text14.Text = CurrentContact.LastName
        Text3.Text = CurrentContact.Title
        Text4.Text = CurrentContact.Organization
        Text5.Text = CurrentContact.Street
        Text6.Text = CurrentContact.City
        Text7.Text = CurrentContact.State
        Text8.Text = CurrentContact.Zip
        Text9.Text = CurrentContact.Telephone
        Text10.Text = CurrentContact.FAX
        Text11.Text = CurrentContact.EMail

    End If

Else
    MsgBox "Illegal value for ContactId"

End If

End Sub
```

This routine begins by verifying that there is a numeric value for ContactId in the Text1 text box. Then we attempt to retrieve the information from the Contact-Buffer object. If the object is found, then we update the CurrentContact variable to point to the new `Contact` object. This means that all of the existing code that uses the `CurrentContact` object to identify the current contact's information will continue to work without needing any changes.

If the contact isn't present in the collection, we get an error condition. This means that we need to retrieve the data from the remote server, which we do by calling the `RequestAContact` routine (discussed in the next section). This routine also creates a `Contact` object in `ContactBuffer` and flags it as being retrieved.

Just because a `Contact` object exists with the proper value of `ContactId` doesn't mean that it has valid data. If the `Requested` property is `True`, the data has been requested from the server, but it hasn't arrived yet. We display a message to that effect and leave the current display unchanged. If the data does exist, we simply copy the various fields from the object into the appropriate text boxes on the form.

Building a Request

The `RequestAContact` routine is used to build a `Request` object with sufficient information to send to the server for processing and to build a place to hold the response from the request. Listing 16.4 shows this routine.

Listing 16.4   **The RequestAContact routine in ContactClient**

```
Public Sub RequestAContact(ci As String)

Dim c As New Contact
Dim r As New Request

c.ContactId = ci
c.Requested = True
ContactBuffer.Add c

r.ContactId = CLng(Text1.Text)
r.Request = CMGetAContact

SendRequest r

End Sub
```

This routine creates a new instance of the Contact object with the specified value for ContactId, flags the object as Requested, and then adds it to the ContactBuffer collection. In the new Request object, we indicate that we want to get a specific contact's information and specify the ContactId that we want to retrieve. Then we call the SendRequest routine to put the request into the appropriate message queue.

Sending the Request

The SendRequest routine, shown in Listing 16.5, takes a Request object and sends it to the ContactManager queue for processing.

Listing 16.5	The SendRequest routine in ContactClient

```
Private Sub SendRequest(r As Request)

Dim ri As MSMQQueueInfo
Dim rq As MSMQQueue
Dim rm As MSMQMessage

Set rm = New MSMQMessage
Set rm.ResponseQueueInfo = RespQueue.QueueInfo
rm.Body = r

Set ri = New MSMQQueueInfo
ri.PathName = "Athena\Private$\ContactManager"
Set rq = ri.Open(MQ_SEND_ACCESS, MQ_DENY_NONE)
rm.Send rq

rq.Close

Set r = Nothing
Set ri = Nothing
Set rm = Nothing
Set rq = Nothing

End Sub
```

This is basically the same logic used in the `PutLocalInfo` routine (shown earlier in Listing 16.1). However, here we specify the response queue where the remote system should return any results.

Receiving Data

One problem with building an application like this one is that you never know when you're going to receive data from the remote server. There are two ways to handle this situation:

- You can periodically check the response queue to see if there are any incoming messages.

- You can use the `MSMQEvent` object to create an event that will be fired whenever a message arrives in the queue.

In most cases, firing an event is the easiest approach, because it operates independently from the rest of the program.

Preparing to Receive Data

To receive messages as they are added to the message queue requires a few module-level declarations, as shown below.

```
Dim WithEvents RespEvent As MSMQEvent
Dim RespInfo As MSMQQueueInfo
Dim RespQueue As MSMQQueue
```

Then the `Form_Load` event, shown in Listing 16.6, can open the message queue and set up the events associated with the `RespEvent` object.

Listing 16.6   **The Form_Load event in ContactClient**

```
Private Sub Form_Load()

GetLocalInfo

Set RespInfo = New MSMQQueueInfo
RespInfo.PathName = "Athena\Private$\ContactClient"
```

```
Set RespQueue = RespInfo.Open(MQ_RECEIVE_ACCESS, _
    MQ_DENY_NONE)
Set RespEvent = New MSMQEvent
RespQueue.EnableNotification RespEvent, , 90000

End Sub
```

Notice that we call the GetLocalInfo routine before opening the response queue. This ensures that we have all of our local data in place before we can receive any messages. Without this call, we might receive a response and not have the associated data structures ready to receive the information.

We set the timeout on the RespEvent object to 90000 milliseconds (90 seconds). If a message is received before the 90-second interval elapses, the RespEvent_Arrived event is fired, and we can retrieve the message. If no messages are received after the 90-second interval, the RespEvent_ArrivedError event is fired. In either case, it is important to use the EnableNotification method to reset the RespEvent events; otherwise, no more messages will be received.

Receiving a Message

Receiving a message is fairly straightforward, as you can see in Listing 16.7.

Listing 16.7   **The RespEvent_Arrived event in ContactClient**

```
Private Sub RespEvent_Arrived(ByVal Queue As Object, _
    ByVal Cursor As Long)

Dim c As Contact
Dim cs As Contacts
Dim m As MSMQMessage

Set m = Queue.Receive(, , , 1000)
If Not (m Is Nothing) Then
    If m.Label = "GetAContact" Then
        Set c = m.Body
        ContactBuffer.Remove FormatNumber(c.ContactId, 0)
        ContactBuffer.Add c

        Set c = Nothing
```

```
    ElseIf m.Label = "GetContacts" Then
        Set cs = m.Body
        Set ContactBuffer = cs
        Set cs = Nothing

    End If

  End If

  RespQueue.EnableNotification RespEvent, , 90000

  End Sub
```

This routine uses the `Receive` method against the message queue passed to the event to retrieve the new message. Then we select the action to take based on the `Label` property of the message. This value is set by the code on the server, as part of the steps needed to process a message.

When we retrieve a single contact (`m.Label = "GetAContact"`), we merely remove the old `Contact` object and replace it with the `Contact` object this is included in the message's `Body` property. This approach is simpler than trying to update each individual property of the `Contact` object. It also will automatically handle any new properties that may be added to the `Contact` object over time.

Updating Data

We update data in basically the same way as in the nonqueued version of the program (discussed in Chapter 14). However, instead of triggering the transaction to update the database, we merely package a request to send the update to the server, like this:

```
RequestPutAContact CurrentContact
```

In this case, we mark the `Contact` object as `Requested`, so that we know a request has been sent to the server to update the database. Then we add the new contact information to the object, set the `Request` property to `CMPutAContact`, and call the `SendRequest` routine to send it onto the server. Listing 16.8 shows the `RequestPutAContact` routine.

Listing 16.8   **The RequestPutAContact routine in ContactClient**

```
Public Sub RequestPutAContact(c As Contact)

Dim r As New Request

c.Requested = True

Set r.Contact = c
r.Request = CMPutAContact

SendRequest r

End Sub
```

Programming the ContactQueue Manager

The ContactQueue manager program receives the requests sent from the Contact-Client program and passes them on to the appropriate method in ContactManager for execution. If there is a response, the ContactQueue manager will package the results into a message and return it using the specified response queue.

Processing a Request

The ReqEvent_Arrived event is used to receive a message sent from the ContactClient application and execute it. This event is shown in Listing 16.9. The message contains a Request object, which in turn contains information about what action should be performed (the Request property) and any information needed to perform the request.

Listing 16.9   **The ReqEvent_Arrived event in ContactQueue**

```
Private Sub ReqEvent_Arrived(ByVal Queue As Object, _
    ByVal Cursor As Long)
```

```vb
Dim c As Object
Dim m As MSMQMessage
Dim o As ObjectContext
Dim r As Request
Dim cm As ContactManager

Set o = GetObjectContext()
Set cm = New ContactManager

Set m = Queue.Receive(, , True, 1000)
If Not (m Is Nothing) Then
   Set r = m.Body
   Text1.Text = Text1.Text & FormatNumber(r.Request, 0) & _
      " @ " & FormatDateTime(Now) & vbCrLf

   If r.Request = CMGetAContact Then
      Set c = cm.GetAContact(r.ContactId)
      SendResponse c, m, "GetAContact"

   ElseIf r.Request = CMGetActionItems Then
      Set c = cm.GetActionItems(r.ContactId, _
         r.DateContacted)
      SendResponse c, m, "GetActionItems"

   ElseIf r.Request = CMGetContactInfos Then
      Set c = cm.GetContactInfos(r.ContactId)
      SendResponse c, m, "GetContactInfos"

   ElseIf r.Request = CMGetContacts Then
      Set c = cm.GetContacts(r.RecFilter)
      SendResponse c, m, "GetContacts"

   ElseIf r.Request = CMPutAContact Then
      cm.PutAContact r.Contact

   ElseIf r.Request = CMPutContactInfos Then
      cm.PutContactInfos r.ContactInfos

End If

End If
```

```
Set m = Nothing
Set c = Nothing
Set r = Nothing
Set cm = Nothing

Req.EnableNotification ReqEvent, , 90000

Set o = Nothing

End Sub
```

The routine begins by receiving the message from the queue. Then it maps the body of the message to the Request object called r. This isn't necessary, but using this approach makes it easier to access the various properties of the Response object. Then we append the request type and current date and time to the Text1 text box on the form. We do this to verify that the message was properly received.

Next, we use the Request property to determine the type of request and call the appropriate ContactManager transaction to perform the request. If the transaction returns a value, we save the value into a local variable and call the SendResponse routine to return the response to the client.

Returning a Response

Returning a response to the client involves a little more work than merely sending a message. The SendResponse routine is shown in Listing 16.10.

Listing 16.10   **The SendResponse routine in ContactQueue**

```
Private Sub SendResponse(c As Object, m As MSMQMessage, _
    l As String)

Dim rm As MSMQMessage
Dim rq As MSMQQueue

Set rq = m.ResponseQueueInfo.Open(MQ_SEND_ACCESS, _
    MQ_DENY_NONE)

Set rm = New MSMQMessage
rm.Label = l
```

```
rm.Body = c
Set rm.ResponseQueueInfo = m.DestinationQueueInfo
rm.CorrelationId = m.Id

rm.Send rq
rq.Close

Set rm = Nothing
Set rq = Nothing

End Sub
```

This routine uses the original message sent by the client to open the message queue where the response will be sent. It uses the `ResponseQueueInfo` property to get to the `MSMQueueInfo` object and its `Open` method to return an `MSMQQueue` object.

Then we build a new message object whose body contains the response information (c) and set the `Label` property to the text description of the response. This is the same value we use in the `RespEvent_Arrived` event to determine how to process the contents of the message. We also set the `ResponseQueueInfo` property in the new message and the `CorrelationId` property using the information from the old message. Finally, we send the response message, close the queue, and destroy the temporary objects.

Programming ContactTypes

The `ContactTypes` program is basically the same set of objects I've introduced in the previous chapters. However, I've now included a new object called `Request`, which is used to package information to send from the `ContactClient` program to the `ContactQueue` program. The information from this object is used to pass the request to the `ContactManager`.

Using the Request Object

The `Request` object is designed to hold the information needed by the `ClientQueue` program to perform a transaction on behalf of the `ClientContact` program.

All of this information is passed via a series of Public properties, as shown in Listing 16.11.

Listing 16.11   **The Public properties of the Request object**

```
Public Enum CMRequestType
    CMUnknown = 0
    CMGetAContact = 1
    CMGetContacts = 2
    CMGetContactInfos = 3
    CMGetActionItems = 4
    CMPutAContact = 5
    CMPutContactInfos = 6

End Enum

Public Request As CMRequestType
Public ContactId As Long
Public DateContacted As Date
Public RecFilter As String
Public Contact As Contact
Public ContactInfos As ContactInfos
```

The CMRequestType enumerated type contains the functions available in the ContactQueue program. The value CMUnknown is included in the type in case someone passes an uninitialized object to the ContactQueue program. Thus, a value of zero will not cause the program to perform any undesirable actions.

The rest of the properties in this object are designed to hold information that will be passed to the various transactions that ContactQueue will perform. You only set the properties needed to perform the requested function.

Making the ActionItems Object Persistent

One of the problems with using message queues to send an instance of an object is that you must make your object persistent. Otherwise, the object may lose its contents when you send the object through a message queue. Some Visual Basic objects by nature are persistent; others are not. The Collections object is a good example of an object that you would expect to be persistent, but it isn't. Without explicit code to make it persistent, all of the objects stored in the collection will be lost. Let's review the ActionItems object to see what we need to do.

The ActionItems object contains four simple variables that make up its properties, as shown in Listing 16.12.

Listing 16.12   The properties of the ActionItems object

```
Public ContactId As Long
Public DateContacted As Date
Public Requested As Boolean
Public Dirty As Boolean

Public c As New Collection
```

Two of the properties—ContactId and DateContacted—contain data. The other two—Requested and Dirty—contain the status of the object. The remaining property is c, which is a collection object that is used to hold a set of ActionItem objects.

Initializing the Properties

The Class_InitProperties event, shown in Listing 16.13, allows us to define initial values for each of the properties in the object.

Listing 16.13   The Class_InitProperties event in ActionItems

```
Private Sub Class_InitProperties()

ContactId = -1
DateContacted = 0
Requested = False
Dirty = False
Set c = Nothing

End Sub
```

This routine isn't strictly required, but it is a good idea to make sure that the default values are set properly. These default values will be used again in the

Class_ReadProperties and Class_WriteProperties events, as you will see in the following listings.

Saving the Properties

The Class_WriteProperties event, shown in Listing 16.14, is used to save the properties of an object before it's destroyed. The values are saved into a special object called the PropertyBag. In Chapter 6, I mentioned how you can use the PropertyBag object to save the properties associated with an ActiveX control at design time. In the current example, the properties will be saved into a persistent storage area that will be transmitted as part of the MSMQMessage object.

Listing 16.14   The Class_WriteProperties event in ActionItems

```
Private Sub Class_WriteProperties(PropBag As PropertyBag)

Dim pb As PropertyBag
Dim i As Long
Dim z As Variant

PropBag.WriteProperty "ContactId", ContactId, -1
PropBag.WriteProperty "DateContacted", DateContacted, 0
PropBag.WriteProperty "Requested", Requested, False
PropBag.WriteProperty "Dirty", Dirty, False

Set pb = New PropertyBag

For i = 1 To c.Count
    pb.WriteProperty "c" & FormatNumber(i, 0), c.Item(i)

Next i

pb.WriteProperty "c0", c.Count, 0

z = pb.Contents

PropBag.WriteProperty "z", z

End Sub
```

Saving the values for the four simple properties involves using the WriteProperty method of the PropBag object that was passed to the event. All we need to do is specify the name of the property, the current value of the property, and the default value. If the current value is different from the default value, the current value is saved in the PropBag object.

However, saving the c object is a much different story. The Visual Basic Collection object is not persistent, which means that you can't save its value into a PropertyBag. Only a string of binary zeros will be saved. This won't generate an error, but when you try to access the object again, you'll find nothing there.

To work around this problem, we store each of the ActionItem objects in the collection in a separate PropertyBag object called pb and then store pb into PropBag. We create a new instance of the PropertyBag object and then use a For loop to access each item in the collection by its index. We assign each object a name that is created by appending the index number to the letter c. Thus, the first object is known by the property name c1, the second c2, and so forth.

Once we've loaded all of the individual objects, we add another property called c0, which contains the total number of objects in the collection. (Remember that the first item in a collection always has an index value of one.) We'll use this value when we restore the collection.

But this doesn't totally solve my problem. Like the Collection object, the PropertyBag object isn't persistent. However, the PropertyBag object has a property called Contents, which returns the contents of the PropertyBag object as a Byte array. Since a Byte array is really just a simple variable like an Integer or String, we can save it into the PropBag PropertyBag without losing its value.

Restoring the Properties

The Class_ReadProperties event in the ActionItems object is used to restore the properties from the PropBag created by the Class_WriteProperties event. This event is shown in Listing 16.15. As you would expect, we use the ReadProperty method to restore the value of the four simple properties to their previous values, but the Collection object needs a bit more work.

Listing 16.15   **The Class_ReadProperties event in ActionItems**

```
Private Sub Class_ReadProperties(PropBag As PropertyBag)

Dim pb As New PropertyBag
Dim i As Long
Dim x As ActionItem
Dim m As Long
Dim z As Variant

ContactId = PropBag.ReadProperty("ContactId", -1)
DateContacted = PropBag.ReadProperty("DateContacted", 0)
Requested = PropBag.ReadProperty("Requested", False)
Dirty = PropBag.ReadProperty("Dirty", False)

z = PropBag.ReadProperty("z")

pb.Contents = z

Set c = New Collection

m = CLng(pb.ReadProperty("c0", 0))

For i = 1 To m
   Set x = pb.ReadProperty("c" & FormatNumber(i, 0))
   Add x
Next i

Set pb = Nothing

End Sub
```

We start unpacking the collection by creating a new PropertyBag object and setting its Contents property to the Byte array value we saved in Class_Write-Properties event. Then we get the number of items in the collection from the c0 property and use a For loop to visit the rest of the items in the PropertyBag. Then we use the Add routine to add the ActionItem object to the collection again.

Final Thoughts

One problem with using a message queue to store data when the program isn't executing is that you're limited to storing a maximum of 4MB in a single message. This might prove to be a big problem in some applications that need to hold more data. One simple fix would be to store each of the Contact objects in the collection as a separate message. Although this technique means that you can store a lot more information, you also need to be concerned about the amount of main memory you're using. There are two main problems with this. First, using a lot of memory can have a negative impact on performance, especially on machines with a limited amount of memory. Second, keeping everything in memory means that you can easily lose everything if the program or system crashes. This is especially true on a laptop when the user unsuccessfully tries to use the application with the last few seconds of battery life. Losing power means losing data.

A different problem I had with this program relates to managing collections of objects. Having to code the NewEnum routine to be able to use the For Each statement to iterate through the collection is bad enough, but needing to add some trick code to make the collection persistent is really bad.

With 20-20 hindsight, I should have built my own collection object that supported persistence and the For Each statement. The method I used is very inefficient, because I create and destroy several copies of the objects in the collection each time the object is created or destroyed. This extra overhead isn't significant for small collections, but it will be very noticeable for larger collections or for larger objects.

APPENDIX

A

Glossary

ACID   Stands for *atomic, consistent, isolation,* and *durable,* which describe the major characteristics of a *transaction.*

Active Directory   A component of Windows 2000 that allows you to find information about various resources located across a network.

ActiveX   A set of technologies that allows you to build and use *objects* created using the *Component Object Model* (COM) and *Distributed Component Object Model* (DCOM).

ActiveX controls   Compiled software components developed with *ActiveX* technology and run on client computers. They present a graphical interface that can be included on a Visual Basic form.

ActiveX Data Objects (ADO)   An object-oriented way to access databases such as Microsoft SQL Server, Access, and Oracle. This technology replaces older technologies such as Data Access Objects (DAO) and Remote Data Objects (RDO). This is a high-level implementation of *OLE DB,* just like DAO is a high-level implementation of *ODBC.*

ActiveX DLL   A COM component residing in a DLL file that is loaded into the main program's address space at runtime. It is also known as an *in-process object.*

ActiveX EXE   A COM component residing in an EXE file that is loaded into a separate *address space.*

address space   The range of addresses that can be accessed by a program in virtual memory. Address space includes memory that can be used by an application and memory reserved for use by the operating system.

ADO   See *ActiveX Data Objects.*

administration queue   A *queue* that is used to hold system-generated acknowledgment messages, which indicate whether or not an *application message* reached its destination.

apartment model threading   A method that ensures that objects created in Visual Basic can be used by *multithreaded applications.* As each object is created, it is assigned to a single thread. All calls from code on different threads will need to be *marshaled* to access the object.

API   See *Application Programming Interface.*

application   A collection of programs and *databases* that solve a problem.

application message   A message generated by an application and sent using *COM+ queued components.* This is different from a *system message,* which is generated by the COM+ queued components to store copies of application messages after they are processed.

Application Programming Interface (API)   A well-defined set of rules and calling conventions that describe how a programmer can invoke the services of another application or the operating system.

application queue   A public or private *queue* that is used to send and receive application-specific messages.

application server   A computer dedicated to running the *business rules* of an organization. These rules are often implemented using *transactions* running under control of a *transaction server*.

asynchronous processing   The type of processing that occurs when a program calls another program or component to perform a task and both programs continue to operate independently. See also *synchronous processing*.

atomic   Part of the *ACID* definition of *transaction*. It refers to the concept that either all of the processing in the transaction must complete successfully or none of it completes. It ensures that there is no such thing as a partially completed transaction.

authentication   The process of verifying a user's identity.

authorization   The rights granted to a particular user to perform certain functions or access specific data.

binary large object   A *database* field containing a binary value such as an image, sound bite, or other large binary value.

binding   The process of locating an object and associating with your program. See also *early binding* and *late binding*.

blob   See *binary large object*.

browser   A program that is designed to translate *HTML* tags into a visible document.

business logic   The set of rules used to operate a business. The rules describe what an application program is supposed to do in a given situation. For example, a business rule might require a program to place an order for an item in inventory when its quantity on hand falls below a certain level.

business rule   A set of instructions that implement a business procedure. For example, the steps to place an order for a book would be considered a business rule.

by reference   A type of parameter passing in which the address of a variable is passed to a routine. This allows the routine to directly change the variable. See also *by value*.

by value   A type of parameter passing in which a copy of the variable is passed to the routine. If the routine changes the value of this parameter, the original variable remains unchanged. See also *by reference*.

cache   A buffer in memory where database information is kept to reduce the number of physical I/O operations by changing them into logical I/O operations.

class module   A template from which an object is created. This template allows you to define properties, methods, and events, which can be used by other parts of your application. A COM component is built from one or more *class modules* in an *ActiveX DLL* or *ActiveX EXE*.

client/server   A programming technique where a client program makes requests of a server program. In the case of SQL Server, the client program running on the user's computer generates requests for information or supplies commands to the *database server*, which processes them and returns the results to the calling application.

CLSID   The class identifier for an object. All objects are assigned a CLSID, which is used as a key in the Windows Registry to locate the object's code. A CLSID value is stored as a *GUID*, so that it will always be unique.

COM   See *Component Object Model*.

COM+   The next version of COM that includes many new services, some of which were previously independent of COM. These services include the *Microsoft Transaction Server*, *In-Memory Database*, and *queued components*.

COM+ application   The primary unit of management by the *Component Services* tool. It consists of a single DLL or EXE file that contains a set of one or more COM components.

COM+ queued components   An easy way to incorporate *message queues* with COM+ components. This feature allows you to issue a method or access a property in an asynchronous fashion.

COM+ Transaction Server   A function that manages the execution of *transactions* under Windows 2000 Server.

compile time   Refers to activities performed and events that occur while compiling a program.

component   An object that contains a set of properties, methods, and events. It is implemented in Visual Basic as a *class module* and represents a type that can be associated with a variable.

Component Object Model (COM)   A technology used to create and access *objects* from a Windows program. See also *COM+*.

Component Services   A utility included with Windows 2000 that is used to manage the COM+ *transactions* installed on the system.

concurrency   Occurs when multiple users share a resource; often requires locks to ensure that the sharing is done in an orderly fashion.

consistent   Part of the *ACID* definition of a *transaction*. It ensures that the work done by a transaction leaves the application in a consistent state.

constituent controls   The set of controls that are included in an *ActiveX* UserControl object.

container   A *control* that can contain other controls.

control   An *object* that can be placed on a Visual Basic form or report to provide a specific function or to interact with the user. Some examples of controls are text boxes where the user can enter and edit text strings, labels that display test values, and buttons that can be pushed by the user.

cookie   A set of data that is maintained by a user's *browser* and is available for processing by web server–based *applications*.

data-bound controls   A way of linking a *control* in a Visual Basic program to a column in a *recordset*. Whenever the value in the column changes, it will automatically be displayed in the control. Changing the value in the control will change the value in the *database*.

data consumer   Receives data from a *data source* in the ADO object model.

data control   A Visual Basic *control* that links other controls on a form to a *database*. This control supports scrolling through a *recordset* one record at a time and displaying the contents of the recordset on the linked controls. You can also use the data control to insert new records, update existing records, or delete existing records.

data source   The source of data in the ADO model. It provides data to *data consumers* for processing.

database   A collection of tables, indexes, and other *database objects* that are used by one or more *applications* stored inside a *database server*.

database object   A table, column, index, trigger, view, constraint, rule, stored procedure, or key in a *database*.

database server   A special program that manages the collection of *databases*.

DCE   See *Distributed Computing Environment*.

DCOM   See *Distributed Component Object Model*.

DCOM Configuration utility (DCOM-CNFG)   A utility program available in Windows 98/95 and Windows 2000/NT that is used to maintain the additional information necessary to find COM components in a distributed environment.

dead-letter queue   A *system queue* used to hold *application messages* that can't be delivered.

delegation   The impersonation of clients over a network.

design time   Refers to activities performed and events that occur while writing a program.

Distributed Component Object Model (DCOM)   A superset of the Component Object Model (COM) that allows the distribution of objects over local area and wide area networks.

Distributed Computing Environment (DCE)   The Open Software Foundation standards for distributed application services. These services include a distributed file system, a distributed security system, and *remote procedure calls*.

DLL   See *dynamic link library*.

durable   Part of the *ACID* definition of a *transaction*. It ensures that once a transaction has been completed, the operating system can always recover the work done by the transaction after a system failure.

dynamic link library (DLL) A file containing compiled code that can be shared by multiple programs at *runtime*.

early binding Occurs when Visual Basic is able to determine the type of object you wish to access at development time. To implement early binding, you must declare your variable as a specific object type, such as `Recordset` rather than `Object`. Early binding makes your program more efficient because less work is needed at runtime to determine the object's type.

endpoints Represent each end of a TCP/IP connection. A specific TCP port number characterizes each endpoint.

event An external subroutine called by an *object* when a specific situation is encountered. This allows the program using the object to supply additional information to the object or take a specific action based on information supplied by the object.

EXE See *executable file*.

executable file (EXE) Contains a compiled version of a program that can be loaded into memory and executed.

external transaction A *transaction* that includes units of work from more than one *resource manager*.

friend property A *property* that appears to be part of the public interface to a COM object, but can be accessed only by the other routines in the same project. Thus, you can define a friend property in one *class module* and access it in another class module, just as if you had declared it to be public. Friend properties can be used only in *ActiveX EXEs*, *ActiveX DLLs*, or *ActiveX controls*.

globally unique identifier (GUID) A 128-bit (16-byte) value that is generated by an algorithm that guarantees that the value will be unique. The algorithm that generates this value can be used at the rate of one new *GUID* per second for several centuries and never duplicate a value on your local computer nor any other computer.

GUID See *globally unique identifier*.

HTML See *Hypertext Markup Language*.

HTTP See *Hypertext Transport Protocol*.

HTTP user agent A unique string that identifies the name and version of a web browser. From this value, you can deduce the web browser's capabilities.

Hypertext Markup Language (HTML) A simple language used to create a hypertext document consisting of tags to define formatting options and hypertext links.

Hypertext Transport Protocol (HTTP) A stateless object-oriented protocol used by web clients and servers to communicate.

IID See *interface identifier*.

IIS See *Internet Information Server*.

IMDB See *In-Memory Database*.

impersonation   The ability to perform a task using the security permissions of one user, while executing under the security permissions of another.

In-Memory Database (IMDB)   A highly specialized *database* system that is optimized to retrieve information very quickly by keeping everything in memory. Note that this database is not based on SQL, although it can be accessed via ADO.

in-process object   A COM object that is loaded into the same address space as the calling program. It is implemented in Visual Basic as an *ActiveX control* or an *ActiveX DLL*.

instance   An object that has been allocated memory to hold information based on a template found in an *ActiveX DLL*, *ActiveX control*, or *ActiveX EXE*.

interactive user   Refers to the username associated with the keyboard and display on a Windows computer. While there is always an interactive user on a Windows 98/95 machine, there may not always be an interactive user on a Windows 2000/NT machine. This is especially true of Windows 2000/NT Server systems.

interface   A way to access the services supplied by an *object*. A COM-based object can contain zero or more *properties*, zero or more *methods,* and zero or more *events*. Standard interfaces are those defined by Microsoft. All COM objects are expected to implement IUnknown. IDispatch is required when you want to support *late binding*.

interface identifier (IID)   The *GUID* that uniquely identifies an *interface*.

internal transaction   A transaction where the *COM+ queued components* features supplies the only resource manager.

Internet Information Server (IIS)   Microsoft's high-performance web server that runs on a *Windows NT Server* system.

Internet Server Application Programming Interface (ISAPI)   A programming *interface* that permits a programmer direct access to facilities inside Microsoft *Internet Information Server*.

intrinsic controls   *Controls* available in Visual Basic that are included with the runtime library. They are usually limited to performing relatively simple functions.

ISAPI   See *Internet Server Application Programming Interface*.

isolation   Part of the *ACID* definition of a *transaction*. It provides the viewpoint that each transaction operates independently of other transactions.

journal queue   A *system queue* that is used to hold messages that have been processed and removed from a *transactional queue*.

late binding   Occurs when Visual Basic is unable to determine the type of object you wish to access at development time. This happens when you declare your object variable as a general type, such as Object or Variant. Late binding slows your program at runtime because Visual Basic must determine the object's type each time it is accessed.

license key   A way to prevent someone from redistributing an ActiveX control you develop without your permission. The license key must be present either in the Windows Registry of the computer using the control or in the program using the control. Only controls whose license key is in the Registry can be used in the Visual Basic development environment.

load balancing   The act of assigning new work or shifting existing work to the least busy server in a defined group of computers. This helps to improve network performance by ensuring that all of the servers in the group of computers are equally busy.

MAPI   See *Messaging Application Programming Interface*.

marshaling   The technique of sending interface method calls to an object on a different thread in the same address space or in a different address space.

Messaging Application Programming Interface (MAPI)   An interface developed by Microsoft to provide functions that developers can use to create mail-enabled applications.

message   Information that is generated by an application or by the system and stored in a *message queue*.

message queue   An application-generated queue that contains application-generated messages. Also used to refer to *Microsoft Message Queues*.

method   A way to access a subroutine or function to perform a specific task within an *object*.

Microsoft Message Queues (MSMQ)   A feature that allows you to send asynchronous messages from one application program to another.

Microsoft Transaction Server (MTS)   A server that manages distributed application *objects*. This has been replaced by the *COM+ Transaction Server*.

module-level variable   A variable defined at the start of a module. This variable can be accessed by any routine in the module, even if it is declared private. If it is declared public, it may be referenced by code outside the module. A *public variable* in a *class module* is treated as an object's property.

multiprocessor   A computer system with more than one CPU that is under Window's direct control. This allows two or more *threads* to be running at the same time.

multithreaded   A process that can have one or more active *threads* running at the same time.

MTS   See *Microsoft Transaction Server*.

***n*-tier application**   Indicates the number of computers where processing is performed as part of an application. A stand-alone computer is one-tier, and client/server computing is two-tier. DCOM and COM+ allow you to perform three-tier processing, by adding another computer in between the client and server computers.

nontransactional message   A *message* generated by an application that is not part of a *transaction*.

nontransactional queue A *queue* that is used to receive *nontransactional messages*.

object A software component that contains one or more *interfaces* that can be used to request information or perform functions.

Object Browser A function of the Visual Basic IDE that allows you to see the definitions of the properties, methods, and events available to your program.

object code A collection of machine instructions and data that is loaded into memory for execution.

object pooling A facility in COM+ that allows you to create a set of object instances that can be shared by the *transactions* running in the COM+ Transaction Server.

ObjectContext The object used to track the status of a transaction under COM+. It is created at the beginning of a *transaction*. At the end of the transaction, you can mark the transaction as successfully completed or abort all of the activities associated with the transaction.

OCX file A file that contains one or more *ActiveX controls*. It is similar in structure to an *Active DLL* file, but it must include extra *interfaces* that provide the graphical interface.

ODBC See *Open Database Connectivity*.

OLE DB A high-performance database-access method developed by Microsoft to be language and database-system independent.

The *ActiveX Data Objects* model uses this access method to provide an object-oriented way to access a database.

Open Database Connectivity (ODBC) Microsoft's *API* that permits Windows programs to access different database systems. ODBC has been superseded by *OLE DB*.

out-of-process object A COM object that is loaded into its own address space. It is implemented as a Visual Basic *ActiveX EXE* file.

pathname The fully qualified name of a queue. It is stored using the format *machinename\queuename*, where *machinename* is the name of the computer containing the queue, and *queuename* is the name of the queue.

persistence The ability to save the information inside an object before it is destroyed and restore it after it was recreated. An example of persistence is when Visual Basic saves the property values associated with an *ActiveX control* from one development session to the next.

Personal Web Server (PWS) A lightweight web server designed for use with *Windows 98/95* and *Windows 2000/NT Workstation*.

private message An message that has been encrypted before being sent to a *queue*.

private queue A *message queue* that is registered only on the local machine. This queue is not published in the *Active Directory*, making it harder to find.

private variable A variable whose scope is limited to the routine or module in which it was declared. If the variable is declared inside a routine, it may not be accessed from outside the routine. If it was declared as a *module-level variable*, it cannot be accessed from outside the module.

process The collection of an *address space*, *threads*, and other information that is associated with the running of a single program.

property A way to access a data attribute stored inside an *object*. A property may be read/write, read-only, or write-only.

property bag An object associated with a Visual Basic *class module* that is used to provide persistent storage. Before the object is destroyed, you are allowed to save information into the property bag. When the object is created, you can restore this information.

property page A COM object that allows a user to access the properties associated with an *ActiveX control* at design time.

protocol A set of rules that define how two or more computers communicate with each other.

public queue A *queue* registered in the *Active Directory*, which makes it easy to find.

public variable A variable that can be accessed from any module in your application program. If it is included as part of a COM object, it becomes a *property* available for any routine to read or write.

PWS See *Personal Web Server*.

queue An object to hold messages between applications. Implemented by the *COM+ queued components*.

queue name The name of a *queue*. It may contain up to 124 characters, except for backslash (\), semicolon (;), and dollar sign ($).

RDBMS See *relational database management system*.

Recordset An object in *ADO* that holds the collection of rows that resulted from a database query.

Registry The area in Windows that holds configuration information about the operating system and application programs.

relational database A *database* that appears to the user as a simple collection of tables, where each table consists of a series of columns or fields across the top and a series of rows or records down the side. The underlying data structures used to hold the data are invisible to the user.

relational database management system (RDBMS) A collection of *relational databases* on a single *database server*.

remote procedure call A technique used to allow a program on one computer to call a subroutine on another computer that is attached over a network.

report queue A *queue* used to track the progress of messages as they move to the destination queue.

response message   An application-generated message that is returned to a *response queue* specified by the sending application.

response queue   A *queue* used to receive a *response message* from the application that received a message.

RPC   See *remote procedure call*.

runtime   When the program is being executed, as opposed to *design time* (when the program is being written) or *compile time* (when the program is being compiled).

single threaded   A block of code that can be executed by only one thread at a time. This typically includes such functions where global data is in the process of being updated, such as a global counter or complex database update that affects global data.

source file   Contains the programming language statements that a compiler will translate into an *executable file*, which can be loaded into memory and run.

SQL   See *Structured Query Language*.

Structured Query Language (SQL)   A language originally developed by IBM in the 1970s that has become the standard language for accessing *databases*.

synchronous processing   The type of processing that occurs when a program calls another program or component to perform a task and the calling program is blocked from performing any other work until the program it called completes. See also *asynchronous processing*.

system queue   A *queue* created by the *COM+ queued components* feature that is required to operate the queued components.

thread   An execution path through the same *instance* of a program.

threading model   Describes how your application will use threads in an address space. A *single-threaded* application can take advantage of only one execution path through the program. A *multithreaded* application can have more than one execution path active at the same time.

transaction   A logical unit of work that consists of one or more changes to the *database*. Either all of the steps in a transaction are completed or none of them are completed. The classic example of a transaction is transferring money from one account to another, where the funds are subtracted from the source account and then added to the destination account. If only half of the transaction is completed, the database will be in error. In COM+, every transaction must meet the *ACID* test.

transaction log   A file containing a list of changes made to the *database*. This information can be used to undo changes made to the database or it can be combined with a backup file to recover *transactions* made after the backup was made.

transaction server   A piece of operating system software that manages the execution of *transactions*. See also *COM+ transaction server*.

transactional message   A message sent as part of a *transaction*.

transactional queue   A *queue* that is used to hold *transactional messages*.

Unicode   A way to store international characters in a 16-bit character. This makes it easier for processing multilingual data.

Visual Basic Extensions (VBX)   The predecessors to ActiveX controls. They are supported only in the 16-bit version of Visual Basic that existed prior to Visual Basic version 5.

Windows 98/95   An operating system designed to support interactive processing.

Windows 2000 Professional Edition
An operating system designed to support interactive processing, typically used by power users.

Windows 2000 Server   An operating system designed to support various servers such as a *database server* or a web server. This is the successor to *Windows NT Server*. It includes standard features such as the *COM+ Transaction Server*, the *COM+ queued components*, and the *Active Directory*.

Windows NT Server   An operating system designed to support various servers, such as a *database server* or a web server.

Windows NT Workstation   An operating system designed to support interactive processing, typically used by power users.

INDEX

Note to the Reader: Throughout this index **boldfaced** page numbers indicate primary discussions of a topic. *Italicized* page numbers indicate illustrations.

B

C

D

F

M

Z

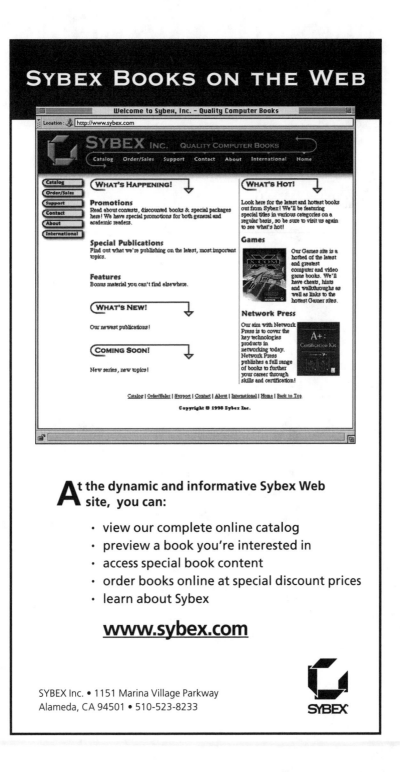

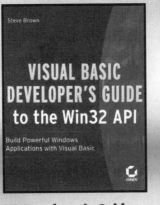

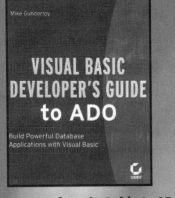